WILLIAM BYRD

William Byrd

BY

EDMUND H. FELLOWES

SECOND EDITION

LONDON
OXFORD UNIVERSITY PRESS
NEW YORK   TORONTO

Oxford University Press, Ely House, London W.1

GLASGOW NEW YORK TORONTO MELBOURNE WELLINGTON
CAPE TOWN SALISBURY IBADAN NAIROBI LUSAKA ADDIS ABABA
BOMBAY CALCUTTA MADRAS KARACHI LAHORE DACCA
KUALA LUMPUR HONG KONG TOKYO

First Edition - 1936
Second Edition - 1948
Reprinted 1953, 1963 *and* 1967

Printed in Great Britain

PREFACE

IN 1923 the three-hundredth anniversary of the death of
William Byrd was celebrated. This greatly stimulated
interest in his work, and much of his music was heard
during that year which had lain in complete oblivion for
nearly three centuries.

Since then the study and practice of sixteenth-century
music, both sacred and secular, has been so far-reaching
that, by common consent, Byrd has come to be regarded
as being in the front rank of the world's composers; and
it is difficult to realize that in 1923 many people, even in
musical circles, were asking the bald question, 'Who was
Byrd?'

There was little to which the inquirer might turn for
enlightenment in 1923, although the valuable work of
Barclay Squire and Godfrey Arkwright must not be for-
gotten. What was known of Byrd's personal history at
that time was mainly the result of the researches of Squire
and E. H. L. Reeve. Squire's work is recorded in his
articles in *Grove's Dictionary of Music and Musicians* and in
the *Dictionary of National Biography*; and Byrd's association with Stondon was dealt with by Canon Reeve in his
History of the Parish of Stondon Massey. Arkwright's researches are recorded in the Preface to vols. vi–ix of his
Old English Edition, in which he published Byrd's *Songs
of sundrie natures*.

In addition to these sources of information mention may
be made of the chapter on Byrd in the present author's
English Madrigal Composers, the Prefaces to vol. ii of the
Carnegie edition of *Tudor Church Music* and vols. xiv–xvi
of *The English Madrigal School*, all of which were published
before 1923.

The general demand at that date for some kind of book
about Byrd was met by the present author, whose *William
Byrd: A Short Account of his Life and Work* was published
a few days before the actual anniversary of the composer's
death. In the Preface the author made it clear that this
was no more than a brief summary, put together as a

matter of emergency to meet a special need at very short notice. He entertained a hope that at some future date he might be in a position to deal more fully with the subject.

In 1928, when a second edition of this little book was demanded, there was still much research work to be accomplished, and it seemed wise to leave the text practically untouched.

Meanwhile the author has been able to extend his knowledge of Byrd's work to far greater lengths. He has now scored with his own hand the whole of the known vocal works, as well as the compositions for strings, leaving only the keyboard works, most of which have been made available in print, while all the unpublished pieces have been transcribed by Mr. Stephen D. Tuttle, of Malden, Massachusetts, who has generously placed his work at the author's disposal.

With the whole of the composer's work now in his hands he feels justified in attempting a critical study that may replace the 'stop-gap' produced by him on the occasion of the Byrd tercentenary.

As regards biographical details the author has gone over the whole ground again, examining all the former sources of information in the original documents. He has been able to correct certain errors, and he has been fortunate in adding many fresh details as the result of his personal researches. He purposely dealt lightly with this side of the subject in his short book, having then little to add to the statements of Squire and Reeve.

The author desires to repeat his grateful acknowledgements to those whose help he received in writing his former book, for this has naturally formed the basis of the present work. He would particularly mention the list of Byrd's keyboard works, compiled in 1923 as a result of Mr. Gerald Cooper's scholarly researches. This list has now been entirely recast and revised with the very valuable help of Mr. Tuttle. The author's most cordial thanks are due to Mr. Tuttle, as well as to Mr. Cooper.

The author is hoping that a complete edition of Byrd's vocal works, which he has prepared in practical form for performance, will soon be published. It is his intention that this should be followed by a volume of the chamber music for strings, which is also ready for the press. Mr. Stephen Tuttle proposes shortly to publish the whole of Byrd's keyboard works, which he has edited in a most scholarly manner. It seems, therefore, that at long last the works of this great English composer will be made available, as they ought to be, in complete form both for performance and study.

E. H. F.

THE CLOISTERS,
   WINDSOR CASTLE,
      25 *February* 1936.

PREFACE TO THE SECOND EDITION

THE issue of a second edition provides a welcome opportunity for revising a few statements as well as correcting some typographical errors almost unavoidable in a first edition. Since the first edition was published the author has collected and scored the whole of Byrd's keyboard music and has thus acquired a knowledge of this branch of the subject which has led to the re-writing of the greater part of Chapter XIV. Mr. Stephen Tuttle's proposal to publish the whole of Byrd's keyboard works has not been found possible to carry out, but he has made an important contribution to musical scholarship by the issue of his critical edition of all the keyboard works of Byrd not previously printed. This edition was published by the Lyrebird Press in Paris just before the fall of France in 1940.

The author's edition of the collected vocal works of Byrd, planned in sixteen volumes with an additional volume to include the chamber works for strings, has been interrupted by the conditions brought about by the war. The first three volumes appeared in 1937 and nine were published before the war broke out in 1939. These nine volumes include the whole of the vocal works set to Latin words. The remaining volumes, including the instrumental volume, are in the hands of the publishers and will be issued as soon as it becomes possible.

The publication of the collected keyboard works is still under consideration. It is much to be hoped this may be found possible, and that thus the entire compositions of this great composer, both vocal and instrumental, may become available in practical form for performance.

E. H. F.

THE CLOISTERS,
WINDSOR CASTLE,
1947.

CONTENTS

LIST OF ILLUSTRATIONS

CHAPTER I

PERSONAL HISTORY, 1543–93

THE only source of information as to the date of
Byrd's birth is the statement in his Will that he
was then in his eightieth year. The Will was executed on
15 November 1622.[1] The phrase suggests that his seventy-
ninth birthday was comparatively recent rather than that
his eightieth was imminent. It may therefore be inferred
with some certainty that he was born in the year 1543.

As regards his parentage and birthplace our knowledge
is less definite. It is remarkable that in the official pedigree
of the Byrd family, recorded some years after his death by
the Heralds in the Visitation of Essex,[2] no mention whatever is made of William Byrd's parents. It is possible that
Thomas Byrd, a member of the Chapel Royal in the reigns
of Edward VI and Mary, was his father. This suggestion
has no positive evidence to support it. Yet it fits in with
Anthony a Wood's statement[3] that Byrd was 'bred up under
Tallis', who had already been organist of the Chapel for
several years at the date of Byrd's birth.

It is more likely that Byrd was one of the Children of
the Chapel than that he was a chorister at St. Paul's Cathedral. The conjecture that he was at St. Paul's is no longer
accepted; it was founded solely on the belief that his name
occurred in a petition of the St. Paul's choristers, made in
the year 1554, for the recognition of certain rights which
they claimed. Among the boys' names were those of John
and Simon Byrd, but not that of William.[4]

An alternative conjecture is that he was a native of
Lincolnshire. The surname was far from uncommon in the
county at this period. Henry Byrde, formerly Mayor of
Newcastle, was buried in Lincoln Cathedral, but he died
thirty years before the composer was born. There were

[1] P.C.C. Swan 106.   [2] Harl. Soc. xiii. 366.
[3] Wood, Bodleian MS. 19 D (4) 106.
[4] Queen's Remembrancer, Mem. Rolls 1 & 2 Phil. & Mary, 232, 238,
262b.

families of the name of Byrd living at Spalding, Epworth, Moulton, Pinchbeck, and other Lincolnshire villages, and the probability that William Byrd sprung from one of these families agrees with the earliest fact of his life as to which there is any definite certainty: namely, that he became organist of Lincoln Cathedral early in the year 1563. Moreover, this does not rule out the probability that he spent part of his boyhood in London or Greenwich as a pupil of Tallis.

There seems no reason to question the truth of Wood's statement. Ferdinand Richardson wrote a lengthy set of Latin Elegiacs which was printed, with other prefatory matter, in the Set of *Cantiones Sacrae* that Tallis and Byrd produced in 1575. Richardson was seeking to show that the glory of the continental composers was surpassed by these two Englishmen; and the following four lines occur in the poem:

> Cuius cum cuperent tristem finire querelam,
> Tallisius magno dignus honore senex
> Et Birdus, tantum natus decorare magistrum,
> Promittunt posthac non fore ut ante fuit.

It has been held that the word *magistrum*, as used here, means that Tallis was Byrd's master; yet it may also mean no more than that Tallis was a composer of masterly standing.

We may pass, then, from Byrd's childhood and the regions of conjecture to his early manhood and details of greater certainty. He was appointed organist of Lincoln Cathedral[1] on 27 February 1562/3, when scarcely twenty years of age. Five years later, on 14 September 1568, he was married at St. Margaret's-in-the-Close, Lincoln, to Juliana Birley. A few months after this, on 22 February 1569/70, he was sworn a gentleman of the Chapel Royal[2] in succession to Robert Parsons, a composer of considerable note who met with a tragic death, drowned in the River Trent at Newark. But this appointment did not immediately involve the resignation of his post at Lincoln.

[1] Lincoln Cathedral Chapter Acts.
[2] E. F. Rimbault, *The Old Cheque Book of the Chapel Royal*, p. 2

It was not an uncommon experience for a provincial organist to retain his position in such circumstances; for example, Thomas Tomkins, one of Byrd's pupils, continued as organist of Worcester Cathedral many years after becoming a member of the Chapel Royal. Byrd remained at Lincoln till the end of 1572. Meanwhile his two eldest children were born: Christopher was baptized at St. Margaret's on 18 November 1569 and Elizabeth on 20 January 1571/2.[1]

On 7 December 1572 Thomas Butler was appointed organist and master of the choristers by the Dean and Chapter of Lincoln on the nomination and commendation of Byrd.[2] It seems to have been at this date that Byrd left Lincoln to share with Tallis the duties of organist of the Chapel Royal.

We next hear of him in connexion with a property in Essex. It must not be inferred that he definitely contemplated living on this property in the immediate future, for his tenure was dependent upon the life of the then tenant. And as the subject of leases will find frequent mention in these pages, it may be well to state that they were commonly purchased and held as a form of investment and as a source of income, rather than with the idea of the holder of the lease residing on the property.

About the year 1573 or 1574 'the Earl of Oxenford made a lease for 31 years of the manor of Battylshall in the County of Essex to W. Byrde one of the gent. of her Maties Chapple to take place at the deathe of Aubrey veare[3] Esquier or at the deathe of his Lawful wyfe'.[4]

This Earl of Oxford was Edward, 17th Earl, the poet; and Aubrey Vere was his uncle. Battylshall, or Battails Hall, was situated in the parish of Stapleford-Abbot and belonged in early days to the Batayle family. It came to the Veres through the marriage of Elizabeth, daughter and sole heiress of Sir John Howard, to John, 12th Earl of Oxford. When John, the 16th Earl, was attainted, Battails Hall was one of several manors settled on Aubrey de Vere,

---

[1] Registers of St. Margaret's-in-the-Close.
[2] Lincoln Cathedral Chapter Acts.
[3] Squire (Grove's *Dictionary, sub* Byrd) misread *veare* as *Ware*, and Howes copied the error. In Anthony Luther's statement the name is spelt *veere*.
[4] P.R.O., *Domestic State Papers, Eliz.*, clvii. 26.

his brother. The 17th Earl recovered the estates[1] which had been forfeited to the Crown when the 16th Earl was attainted. If the Earl had died before Aubrey Vere or his wife, the lease would have been void.

The value of Byrd's lease in these circumstances was somewhat speculative. Meanwhile one William Lewyn,[2] if we may accept the truth of the pleadings on Byrd's behalf,[3] set himself to get the lease by fraudulent means.

'Being in greate favor and creditt about the sayd Earle,' Lewyn spread rumours that 'ther was a former lease for xxi yeares made of the sayd manor by the sayd Earle'; his purpose was to depreciate the value of Byrd's lease in the minds of possible purchasers, and thus eventually 'to obtayne it himself for a tryffell'.

A year or so later Lewyn approached Byrd with the object of buying his interest in the lease, affirming still 'that ther was a former lease therof and that he cared not for that, but for the ten yeares that the lease made to Byrd had, more than the other supposed leases'.

After many meetings Byrd and Lewyn met one Saturday morning and agreed 'what money shuld be payde and what conditions should passe betwene them, and that all should be put in Wryghtynge agaynst the afternoone of that day at wch time they both appoynted to meet to make up ther sayd communication of the bargayne'. Byrd kept the appointment, but Lewyn did not; 'Wheruppon ther was nothyng more done.'

About six years later Aubrey Vere died, his wife having predeceased him; 'Wherby the sayd lease granted to W Byrd is in present possession being well worth 100 marks a year. . . .' 'Now D Lewen seing the benefyt therof and repentyng that he went not forward wth the bargayne when he myght, hath devysed to get it by a lease parroll uppon the private talke that was betwene the sayd W Byrd and hym vj yeares synce.'

Accordingly Lewyn decided to take the case to the Courts; but finding that he could not be a witness in his

[1] Morant's *History of Essex*, ii. 293.

[2] Called William Lewyn throughout Luther's pleading but D. Lewen throughout Byrd's.

[3] P.R.O., *Domestic State Papers, Eliz.*, clvii. 26.

own case, he 'enfeoffed his brother[1] Anthony Luther with
the thing, affirming that W Byrd made him an absolute
grant Parroll thereof for his sayd brother'.

Lewyn then seems to have resorted to perjury.

He deposed flatlye that W Byrd made an Assignment to him for his
brother Anthony Luther and that the same was not reffered to
wryghtyng, and yet affyrmed he uppon his othe also that he wylled
his man to draw the wryghtynge and the wryghtynge weare drawen,
so that he must neds make a false othe ether in the fyrst parte or in
the second.

How unlykelye is it W. Byrd shuld make an absolute grant to one
whome he never sawe nor delyvered his lease nor receyved any
monye. And how unlykelye is it that D. Lewen would accepte of
a grant by speache wth out wryghtynge of an assignment of a lease
that was so uncertayne when it shuld take place. And to what end
was ther appoyntment to meete in the afternoone if the bargayne
was fullye dispached in the forenoon. How so ever this practyse may
be lawfull it is not expedient for that by the lyke devyse any subjecte
of this realme may be (by the othe of one man) foresworne out of all
that he hathe.

As it happened, this was Byrd's actual experience. Luther's
case was set out in a separate document[2] of considerable
length, headed 'Proofes on behalf of Anthony Luther gent.
in the cause depending in the King's Bench betwene him
and Willm̄ Birde gent'.

When the case was heard in 1582 (the year assigned
tentatively to these documents in the Public Record Office)
Lewyn stated that he had promised Byrd that 'if there
were no sound lease as was then doubted and that this lease
had happened to commence tymely and beneficially' for
Luther, Byrd should receive further recompense, the amount
of which was to be left to Lewyn's conscience. Byrd, not
unreasonably, set small value upon Lewyn's 'conscience',
and preferred to take his chance in the Courts. But here
again Lewyn got the better of him by packing the Jury.
'A frendlye Jurye was empaneled being ye neyghbors
kynsfolke and frends of Luther and Lewen, and xvj of
them appered uppon the fyrst sum̄ons and gave ther ver-

---

[1] Probably brother-in-law.
[2] P.R.O., *Domestic State Papers, Eliz.*, clvii. 25.

dicte agaynst Wm Byrd. Wheruppon he and all his is lyke
to be undone.'

Lewyn's final comment was to the effect that Byrd lost
a good chance when he refused his offer of further recompense, which, he said, 'was much lyked by the judges'; and
that Byrd, having 'proceeded to tryall and having the ver-
dett geven against him, nowe slandereth the adverse party
witnesses and Jurye'. Byrd certainly seems to have been the
victim of a grave injustice. A letter from the Earl of Northumberland to Lord Burghley, written at the time of this
dispute, may have reference to it. The writer evidently
believed in the justice of Byrd's cause and desired to enlist
Burghley's support for him. Dated 28 February 1579, the
letter reads:[1]

My dere good lorde I am ernestly required to be a suiter to your
l. for this berer m^r berde that your lp. wyll have hime in remembrance
wth your faver towardes hime seing he cane not inioye that whyche
was his firste sutte and granted unto him. I ame the more impor-
tunat to your l. for that he is my frend and cheffly that he is scolle
master to my daughter in his artte the mane is honeste and one whome
I knowe your lp. may Comande.

It has not hitherto been noticed that Stapleford-Abbot is
only five or six miles from Stondon Massey, where Byrd subsequently lived. Both villages are in the hundred of Ongar.
The family of Luther was of some standing in the
county. William Luther, who died in 1566, had leases for
various properties in Stapleford-Abbot, including Battails
Hall. His son, John Luther, died in 1611. Perhaps Anthony
was a younger son of William. Anthony and his brother
Richard resided for nearly forty years at the manor of
Milles's (known later as Myles's)[2] in the parish of Kelvedon
Hatch, next to Stondon. It was this Anthony who at a later
date acted as mediator between Byrd and Lolly at Stondon,
and he was mentioned in Byrd's Will.

Byrd may have had some special reason for his persistent
endeavour to be connected with this part of Essex, even
though in each instance it involved him in lawsuits. But
what this reason may have been none can guess.

---

[1] B.M., Lansdowne MS. 29, no. 38.
[2] Burke's *Commoners*, iv. 9.

THOMAS TALLIS AND WILLIAM BYRD

By some error in the original plate the portrait of Tallis has been reversed.
There is no reason to think he was left-handed, and the music in his hand
seems to run backwards

Reproduced by permission of the Trustees of the British Museum

Byrd's work at the Chapel Royal at this period brought him into close association with Tallis, and the intimate partnership of these two, even though Tallis was Byrd's senior by nearly forty years, has nothing to resemble it in English musical history. The statement that Byrd was Tallis's pupil may be accepted, and it may readily be imagined that it was through the influence of Tallis that his former pupil should have been brought from Lincoln to share with him the duties of organist at the Chapel Royal when he himself was beginning to feel old. Another personal tie between the two had been created when Tallis became godfather to Byrd's second son, who was called Thomas after him.[1] The two were partners in a printing licence granted to them by the Crown. Jointly they petitioned the Queen for further benefits; they also collaborated in producing a set of *Cantiones Sacrae*.

It was in 1575 that the licence was granted which gave them what was practically a printing monopoly. The full text was as follows:[2]

Elizabeth by the grace of God, Quene of Englande Fraunce and Ireland

To all printers bokesellers and other officers ministers and subjects greeting. Knowe ye, that we for the especiall affection and good wil that we haue and beare vnto the science of Musicke and for the aduancement thereof, by our letters patent dated the xxij of January, in the xvij yere of our raigne have graunted ful priueledge and licence vnto our wel-beloued seruaunts Thomas Tallis and William Birde two of the Gentlemen of our Chappell, and to the ouerlyuer of them, and to the assignees of them and ouer the suruiuer of them for xxj yeares next ensuing, to imprint any and so many as they will of set songe or songes in partes, either in English, Latine, Frenche, Italian or other tongues that may serue for musicke either in Churche or chamber, or otherwise to be either plaid or soonge, And that they may rule and cause to be ruled by impression any paper to serue for printing or pricking of any song or songes, and may sell and vtter any printed bokes or papers of any song or songes, or any bookes or quieres of such ruled paper imprinted. Also we straightly by the same forbid all printers bookesellers subjects and

---

[1] Tallis's Will, P.C.C., 52 Brudenell.
[2] P.R.O., Rot. Pat. 17 Elizabeth, pars. 7, m. 2.

strangers, other then is aforesaid to doe any the premisses, or to bring
or cause to be brought out of any forren Realmes into any our domin-
ions any song or songes made and printed in any forren countrie, to
sell or put to sale, vppon paine of our high displeasure, And the
offender in any of the premisses for euery time to forfet to vs our
heires and successors fortie shillinges, and to the said Thomas Tallis
and William Birde or to their assignes and to the assignes of the
suruiuer of them, all and eurie the said bokes papers song or songes,
We haue also by the same willed and commanded our printers maisters
and wardens of the misterie of Stacioners, to assist the said Thomas
Tallis and William Birde and their assignes for the dewe executing of
the premisses.

This Licence passed to Byrd on the death of Tallis. At
the end of the twenty-one years it was granted to Thomas
Morley, and later to Thomas East. Many of the English
Madrigal part-books were printed under it and there are
extant examples of manuscripts written on the paper ruled
'to serue for pricking any song'. To mention but one
example: a single part-book in the Tenbury Library[1] is
bound in the original vellum and stamped with the initials
T.E. This book has also the initials W.B. written in ink on
the top margins of the pages, possibly indicating that it
belonged to Byrd.

In the same year Tallis and Byrd published the set of
Cantiones Sacrae which will be more fully discussed in a
subsequent chapter. The printer was Thomas Vautrollier.
It is probable that he was acting under the new licence, as
an epitome of it was printed at the end of each part-book.
The work was dedicated to Queen Elizabeth, no doubt as
a graceful acknowledgement of the benefit she had con-
ferred on them. The dedication, which is in Latin, is
couched in terms of liberal flattery of the Queen's musical
accomplishments, saying how she excelled *vel vocis elegan-
tia vel digitorum agilitate*.[2]

This monopoly was one among many of the same kind
that were resented by the printing trade. A statement of
their grievances 'susteined by reson of priuilidges granted
to privatt persons . . . which will be the overthrowe of the
Printers and Stacioners within this Cittie being in nomber

---

[1] Tenbury MS. 389.
[2] 'both in the charm of her voice and in the dexterity of her fingers'.

175,' was drawn up in 1582.[1] Among those who signed it was Thomas East, who in later years actually held the music monopoly.

The list of licensees included John Daye, well known for his publication of *Certaine Notes* in 1560, who in 1553 obtained a licence to print '*A B C* and *Cathechismes*'; Thomas Vautrollier 'a stranger', who 'hath the sole printinge of other *latten bookes* as *the Newe Testament*'; and 'one Byrde a Singing man hathe a licence for printinge of all *Musicke bookes* and by that meanes he claimeth the printing of *ruled paper*'.

In a letter to Lord Burghley, dated 23 October 1582,[2] T. Norton, summing up the complaints, stated that 'Bird and Tallys have musike bookes with note which the complainantes confesse they wold not print nor be furnished to print though there were no priuilege. They have also ruled paper for musike.'

Later in the year Christopher Barker issued a Report on the subject of the printing patents.[3] Referring to that of 'Master Birde and Master Tallis of her Maiesties Chappell', he said: 'In this patent are included all musicke bookes whatsoever and the printing of all ruled paper, for the pricking of any songes to the lute, virginalls or other instrumentes: The paper is somewhat beneficiall, as for the musicke bookes, I would not provide necessarie furniture to have them. This patent is executed by Henry Binneman also.' As to this disparagement of the value of the 'musicke bookes' it is interesting to recall that only one had been printed under the licence at this date. In spite of all these representations none of the special privileges was modified. But the complainants were right in saying that the music licence was not a source of profit. Consequently, Tallis and Byrd had no hesitation in informing the Queen of this fact, and in 1577 they presented the following petition:[4]

To the quenes most excellent Matie

Most humblie beseache yor Matie yor poore serṽnts Thomas

[1] B.M., Lansdowne MS. 48, fo. 180–1.
[2] Arber's *Transcript of the Stationers' Registers*, ii. 775
[3] Ibid. i. 144.
[4] Hatfield House MSS., C.P. 160, 134.

Tallis and William Birde gent of yor highnes chappell. That whereas
the said Thomas Tallys is now verie aged and hath served yor Matie
and yor Royall ancestors these fortie yeres, and hadd as yet never
anie manner of preferment (except onely one lease w^h yor Matie
late deare syster quene Marie gave him, which lease being now the
best pte of his lyvinge is wthin one yere of expiracõn and the reason
thereof by yor Matie graunted on unto another: And also for that
the saide William Birde beinge called to yor highnes s^ervice from the
cathedrall churche of Lincolne where he was well setled is now
through his greate charge of wief and children come into debt &
greate necessitie, by reason that by his dailie attendaunce in yor
Matie saide service he is letted from reapinge such cõmodytte by
teachinge as heretofore he did & still might have done to the greate
releyff of him self and his poore famylie: And further yor Matie of
yor princely goodnes entendinge the benefitt of us your said poore
s^erv^ents did geve unto us about ii^o years past a lycense for the printinge of musicke. So it is most gracyous sovereigne that the same hath
fallen oute to oure greate losse and hinderaunce to the value of
two hundred markes at the least. It might therefore please yor Matie
of yor moste aboundant goodnes for the bettar releavings of our
poore estates To graunt unto us wthoute Fyne a lease in revcõn for
the terme of xxj^{te} yeres of the yerely rent of xxx^{li} to the ten^ente use.
So shall we most dutifullie praie unto almightie god for the prosperous
preservacõn of yor Matie longe to Reigne over us.

The petition was endorsed:

At Grenewiche xxvii Junii 1577
It then pleased her Matie to signify her pleasure that thies peticoners
in cõsideracon of their good service don to her highnes shold have
(w^tout fine) a lease for xxj^{te} yeres of lande in possession on Rev̂sion
not exceding the yerely rent of xxx^{li} they abyding suche order as
shold be taken by the L. Thres. or Sr Walter Mildmay Knight for
the behoof of the ten^ants in possession

(signed) Thomas Selford.

The lease granted to Byrd on this occasion was almost
certainly that which some thirty years later became the
subject of a lawsuit in which he was involved.[1] It was a
lease of the Manor of Longley in the county of Gloucester,
and it was granted by the Queen 'out of her princely
bounty' to William Byrd, his wife Juliana, and their son
Thomas Byrd, 'to gratifie the service of the said William
Byrd'. This grant was dated 1 March 21 Elizabeth.

[1] P.R.O., Chancery Proceedings, *Byrd v. Jackson*, C. 2, Jas. 1, B. 16/78.

GREENWICH PALACE AT THE END OF THE SIXTEENTH CENTURY

From a contemporary painting on panel attributed to Joris Hoefnagel

Reproduced by permission of the Trustees of the National Maritime Museum, Greenwich

Byrd was thirty-four years old at this time, and he was evidently having a hard struggle for existence. His daily attendance at Greenwich was exacting and took most of his time. He had lost his pupils, and the Battails Hall lawsuit must have been worrying as well as costly.

The Queen's grant would therefore have been very welcome; and it was perhaps this pecuniary aid that enabled him at this date to take up his new abode at Harlington, a village in West Middlesex lying a short distance away from the London and Bath road on the north side. He is first heard of at Harlington in 1577, at which date his wife's name appears in the list of recusants living in the village.[1] There is some reason to think that Byrd's house was situated near the open space by the pond in this village. His Chapel Royal duties, whether at Greenwich or Whitehall, when he was not actually in residence with the Court, must have involved frequent journeys on horseback; he would probably have avoided the perils of Hounslow Heath in choosing his route to London, and may have preferred to go through Hanwell, Ealing, Acton, and Kensington.

The latest record of Byrd's residence at Harlington is that of 7 April 1592, when a true bill was found against him for being a recusant, for the period from 31 August 1591 to 31 March following. This was the last of a long series of entries in the Sessions Rolls of the county of Middlesex[2] dealing with him or members of his family as recusants—i.e. 'for not going to Church, Chapel, or any usual place of common prayer'. Mrs. Byrd's name was invariably given as Juliana in these records. It is significant that she was not cited after the year 1586, and that the Mrs. Byrd who was constantly charged with recusancy at Stondon had the name of Ellen. It would seem therefore that Juliana died shortly after 1586 and that Ellen was Byrd's second wife.

Byrd may not have left Harlington immediately after the spring of 1592. Another year elapsed before he came to Stondon and it seems likely that he remained at his old home during this interval.

In the previous year Byrd had been much occupied with

[1] P.R.O., *Domestic State Papers, Eliz.*, cxviii. 73.
[2] Middlesex Sessional Rolls (G.D.R.), 7 April, 34 Eliz.

another lawsuit. His adversaries in this suit were Basil
Fettiplace and William Boxe. Basil Fettiplace, or Bessels,
as he was more properly called, was at this time High
Sheriff of Berkshire. The subject of dispute was the validity
of a lease of two mills and a farm, called Horspane or Horse-
path, in the parish of Marcham, co. Berks.

The case was a complicated one, and voluminous documents concerning it survive in three bundles kept among
the records of the Court of Requests, at the Public Record
Office.[1] These contain a mass of legal details including a
number of sworn depositions by the witnesses on both
sides.

In 1546 Henry VIII had granted the manor of Marcham in fee to William Boxe, an alderman of the City of
London. He also granted him a messuage and 100 acres
of land in Marcham, called Horspath.[2] William Boxe and
his son William granted a lease in reversion of the farm
called Horspath to George Garrett and Elizabeth his wife.
The elder Boxe entailed all the lands on his son and then
died. Meanwhile the younger Boxe had previously granted
a separate lease to George and Elizabeth Garrett for 49
years in reversion of one Hawkins, who then had an estate
in being for a term of 12 or 13 years if the Garretts 'should
happen to live so long'. The Garretts assigned their term
of years to William Byrd and executed a deed to that effect
in April 1589, which deed Byrd was subsequently prepared
to produce at the trial.

Meanwhile the younger Boxe sold all his property to
Sir Henry Unton, and in 1589 Unton resold it to Basil
Fettiplace.

In due course the Garretts died, and Byrd asserted his
claim. This was disputed by Fettiplace and Boxe, who
claimed that the Garretts had surrendered and conveyed
their interest in the estate to William Boxe the elder and
William his son.

Byrd accordingly petitioned Queen Elizabeth in support of his claim on 15 October 1590. The Queen in reply
issued an injunction under the privy seal, dated 26 October
1590, ordering that sworn depositions should be made by

[1] P.R.O., Court of Requests, Proceedings, 164/18, 178/48, 180 14.
[2] *Victoria County Hist. Berks.* iv. 357.

witnesses and that the case should be brought before the Court of Requests at the coming feast of St. Martin.

The first trial was abortive owing to a small technical error in Byrd's Bill of Complaint.

The Queen issued a second injunction under the privy seal, dated 20 May 1591, 'at our mannor of Grenewiche', sending to the Masters of the Court of Requests 'certen articles and Interrogatories to be mynystred to the witnesses' on behalf of William Birde Complainant against Basill Fetiplace and Willm Boxe defendants. The case was to be tried at the law sittings of 'the hollye Trinitie comming'.

Byrd's bad luck at the former trial had excited the sympathy of a powerful friend of his in Admiral Lord Howard of Effingham, who addressed a letter 'To my very lovinge Frends M^r D Aubrey Mr Herbert and other the Masters of hir Maties Requests'[1] as follows:

I commend me right hartely unto you: Where I have hertofore writen to yo^u touchinge a cause in suite dependinge before yo^u betwene Willm̃ Byrde one of hir Ma^ts servaunts Compl^t: against Basill Fetiplace defend^t. W^ch matter being once hard before yo^u: by reason of the wante of some two words that were left forthe of the compl^ts Bill, The said Byrde was dryven to comence his suit agayne to his no small charge & hinderaunce. And now being adv̂tized that the same cause (after many delayes and other procrastinacons) is shortly appointed to be hard, I am (on the behalfe of the saide Byrde) ernestly to desier you (the rather for my sake) to afforde & shew him such lawfull favour as wth equity and good consciens yo^u may: And what frindship it shall please yo^u to shew him, I shall as thankfully accepte of, as if it were done unto my selfe And wilbe redy to pleasure yo^u or eith^r of yo^u with the like: At the Courte this x^th of June 1591
yor very lovinge frend
Howard

The letter is endorsed 'My L. Admirall in the cause betwene Byrd & phetiplace'.

On 12 June, two days after the date of this letter, the case came on.[2] The Masters ruled that the

cause seemed more aptly to be tryed by the ordinary course of the comon lawes then in this Court. Therefore it is now . . . ordered that the same matter be out of this said Court cleerely dismissed and

---

[1] P.R.O., *Domestic State Papers, Eliz.*, Addenda, xxxii. 17.
[2] P.R.O., Court of Requests, Orders and Decrees, 16, fo. 936.

the said defendants licensed at their libertie to depart sine die. And
it is further ordered that if the said Complainant do heareafter
com̃ence any accon at the com̃on lawe for or touching the pmisses
that then the defendants shall thereunto make answere without delay.

Whether Byrd took further action after this unsatisfactory ruling has not been discovered. It looks as if he had
right on his side. Moreover, William Boxe the younger
had a bad reputation, though Fettiplace came into the case
solely as a result of his purchase. Boxe was involved in
another case[1] about a property in this same district, which
the owner, 'as was alledged', had been 'led to alienate by
the sinister practising of William Boxe'.

It was in September 1591, while Byrd was still at Harlington, that the famous *My Ladye Nevells Booke*, consisting
of forty-two representative examples of Byrd's keyboard
works, was completed by John Baldwin of Windsor. Certain members of the Nevill family at this period were connected with Uxbridge, only a few miles away from Harlington, while Windsor was also not far distant. As these facts
suggest that Byrd, Baldwin, and the Nevills were at this
time closely associated within these narrow geographical
limits, the question as to who 'the ladye Nevell' was may
suitably be discussed here.

In the family records of the Nevills at Eridge Castle it
is stated definitely that 'the ladye Nevell' was Frances,
who married, as his first wife, Henry, 6th Lord Bergavenny.
She was daughter of Thomas, Earl of Rutland. This lady had
considerable literary gifts. She was mentioned by Walpole
amongst his *Royal and Noble Authors*, and some poems by
her were printed in Bentley's *Monument of Matrons*, 1583.
As she died in 1576 it is manifestly impossible to identify
her with 'the ladye Nevell' for whom Baldwin wrote the
manuscript in 1591. It was no doubt because of her literary
gifts that this lady's name came to be associated with the
manuscript without reference to dates. This careless conjecture developed into tradition and came to be accepted
as truth. In course of time it found its way, without further
investigation, into the family records, whence it has been

[1] P.R.O., Chancery Proceedings (Series 2), bundle 6, no. 9.

copied into standard books of reference, such as Drum-mond's *Noble British Families*.[1]

Another inaccuracy concerning the history of the manu-script has escaped notice and been unchallenged. The book very quickly passed out of the hands of the Nevills. On its restoration in 1668 the following statement was pasted into it and signed 'H. Bergavenny':

This Book was presented to Queene Elizabeth by my Lord Edward Abergavenny called the Deafe, the queene ordered one Sr or Mr North one of her servants to keepe it, who left it to his son who gave it Mr Haughton Attorny of Clifford's Inn & he last somer 1668 gave it to me; this mr. North as I remember mr haughton saide was uncle to the last Ld North.

As Edward 'the Deafe' died in 1589 he cannot have been the donor of the book to the queen. It is likely that the statement is otherwise accurate, but that Edward's son and namesake was the donor.

Who, then, was 'the ladye Nevell'? The problem has to be approached *de novo*, because the claim of Frances seems never to have been questioned until the present author noticed the discrepancy in the dates. Only two names seem possible: Mary, daughter of Frances; and Rachel, daughter of John Lennard of Knole, co. Kent, wife of Sir Edward Nevill, the son of Sir Edward 'the Deafe'. It was this younger Sir Edward who in 1604 established his claim to the barony of Bergavenny against that of his cousin Mary, whereas his father could never have been styled properly 'my Lord Edward Abergavenny'.

Mary was born about 1554 and married in 1575 Sir Thomas Fane of Bodsil. Although she presented her claim to the barony as soon as her father died in 1586/7, she would still have been known as Lady Fane in 1591. There seems to be only one small piece of evidence to support the suggestion that she was 'the ladye Nevell' of the Vir-ginal book. In her portrait at Eridge, painted in 1606, she is represented holding a book which resembles the famous book. But this cannot be the book, because Queen Eliza-beth, to whom the book undoubtedly passed, had been dead three years. The fact that she had a gifted mother

[1] Vol. ii, pt. viii, p. 19.

who for generations was wrongly supposed to be 'the ladye', lends no support whatever to the claim for Mary Fane.

On the other hand there is good reason for the theory that Rachel, wife of Sir Edward Nevill, the younger, and subsequently Lord Bergavenny, was the lady in question. The mention of Edward 'the Deafe' in the memorandum of 1668 is in itself significant, even though it is erroneous. It points to an early tradition connecting the book with that branch of the family; for it is most improbable that either Edward the Deafe, or his son Edward, would have had possession of it if it had belonged to their distant cousin Lady Fane. The confusion between the father and son in the memorandum is a small matter. This evidence alone points directly to Rachel,[1] Lady Nevill.

But there are other indications which lead in the same direction. Byrd was living at Harlington. Members of this branch of the Nevill family were closely associated with Uxbridge, only a few miles from Harlington. Edward 'the Deafe' married, as his second wife, Grisold, daughter of Thomas Hughes of Uxbridge, and at Uxbridge he died in 1588/9. Incidentally, Grisold married again within a year, a fact that rules out the possibility of her being the owner of the manuscript. Byrd and these Nevills would have known each other, and the friendship would have extended to the younger Edward and his wife Rachel. The friendship must have existed, otherwise why was this book of Byrd's music so elaborately executed and presented to any member of the Nevill family, whoever she was?

Windsor too was close at hand; Byrd could have ridden over from Harlington to supervise and correct Baldwin's work from time to time, perhaps reporting progress at Uxbridge, for it is possible that Baldwin was commissioned by Sir Edward Nevill to make the manuscript.

The identity of 'the ladye Nevell' may never be established with complete certainty, but strong probability points to Rachel, wife of Sir Edward, as the original owner of this lovely book.

During Byrd's last few years at Harlington he was busily

---

[1] It is tempting to conjecture that Byrd's daughter Rachel was her god-daughter.

occupied with the publication of his own compositions. Tallis had died in 1585 and Byrd had become the sole proprietor of the printing licence. His output between 1588 and 1591 was very remarkable. *Psalmes Sonets & songs* was published in 1588. In the following year *Songs of sundrie natures* appeared and also the first book of *Cantiones Sacrae*. These were followed in 1591 by the second book of *Cantiones Sacrae*. It must not be supposed that the works contained in these books were composed within the limits of those dates; they represent the accumulation of many years. Several of the compositions included in the printed books are to be found in manuscripts of earlier date.

It seems likely that in the latter years of his life at Harlington Byrd became more prosperous. It is noteworthy that 1588 was the year in which the Spanish Armada was defeated, and perhaps the prosperity which came to the whole country at that date with the new sense of security, also affected the fortunes of Byrd and brought him fresh opportunities.

CHAPTER II

PERSONAL HISTORY, 1593–1623

THE move from Harlington to Stondon marks a very definite epoch in the life of Byrd. He was fifty years old at the time. He had thirty years of life still in front of him, and it was exactly thirty years since his professional life began at Lincoln Cathedral. Four out of seven of his important musical publications had been issued, in addition to the set which he produced jointly with Tallis, and three were yet to follow, though not for many years after he had gone to live at Stondon; for it was not until 1605 that the first book of *Gradualia* was published.

The gap between 1591[1] and 1605 is at first sight a little difficult to account for. But it is easy to attach too much importance to what has been termed by some 'a period of silence'. It must be repeated that these 'Sets' of compositions represented the accumulation of many years, and the works included in them cannot be even approximately dated by the year of publication. It must also be remembered that Byrd wrote a very large number of compositions which survive in manuscript and were not printed in his day. These include practically all that he wrote for the English rites of the Church, a very much larger and more important contribution than it was formerly thought to be. Added to these are a large number of solo-songs, a formidable list of keyboard works, and a good number of chamber works for strings. The date of composition of each of the three Masses is unknown and might belong to this period. Admittedly Byrd published nothing between 1591 and 1605, as far as is known; but there could have been no 'period of silence', if that expression is intended to suggest that he gave up composition during those years. On the contrary, when we consider his immense output it is difficult to imagine how he found time, together with his Chapel Royal duties, his teaching, and the preoccupation of many lawsuits, to write so much as he did, and it becomes impossible to allow for

---

[1] Squire in Grove's *Dictionary* is in error in dating this period from 1588.

the briefest periods of 'silence', even in his long life. It might equally well have been suggested on similar grounds that the years 1575 to 1588 represent a 'period of silence'.

Byrd came to the village of Stondon Massey, situated in the hundred of Ongar in Essex, in 1593. The house occupied by him was known as Stondon Place. There is a residence on the same site still called Stondon Place, but nothing of the old building now remains. Any part of it that might have survived was destroyed by fire at a comparatively recent date. The title-deeds perished in the fire. For the full story of Byrd's connexion with Stondon Place, and the lawsuits in which he was involved before finally securing his claim to it, it is necessary to go back to an earlier date. William Shelley, who owned it in the right of his wife in 1580, was in that year committed to the Fleet prison for being concerned in a Jesuit plot. Three years later, having regained his freedom, he took part with the Earl of Northumberland and Charles Paget in a much more serious affair. The direct purpose of this was to put Mary Queen of Scots on the throne. This plot also failed. Northumberland was executed. Shelley was confined in the Tower and tried for his life on the charge that he 'had imagined and compassed the deposition and death of Queen Elizabeth and the subversion of the established religion and government of the country.'[1] He was discreet enough to plead guilty and so escaped with his life, but his very extensive property was sequestrated to the Crown, and Stondon Place shared the fate of the rest of his estates.

Meanwhile two brothers, Lawrence and William Hollingsworth, had acquired in 1582 a lease of Stondon Place from Shelley for a term of twenty-one years. After Shelley's attainder they paid rent to the Crown during her Majesty's pleasure.

In March 1589 the Hollingsworths proceeded to divide the property, each taking a moiety. Lawrence leased his share to Dyonice, or Dennis, Lolly, reserving to himself the piece called Malepardus, containing about ten or twelve acres, 'together with the parlour, a bed-room, half the hop-ground, and the right of using the pond'. He then died and bequeathed his moiety to his nephew, John Hollingsworth,

[1] Howell's *State Trials*, 27 Eliz.

who seems to have been in Holy Orders and curate to the
the then rector of Stondon.[1] Subsequently John sold his
share back to his uncle William, who thus became sole
tenant under the Crown.

William then mortgaged his lease to William Chambers;
and in 1593 he and Chambers assigned to William Byrd
the whole property of Stondon Place, consisting of about
200 acres, and all their interest in it, for a sum of £300.

Dennis Lolly continued to occupy rooms in the house,
and he paid rent to Byrd until Lady Day 1595. He then
refused to pay any more, claiming that Byrd had invaded
his rights under Hollingsworth's lease and had taken from
him 'certain houses and roomes' to which that lease entitled
him. Byrd sued him successfully in the Court of Chancery,[2]
and the Hollingsworth lease was declared void at law. Then
Anthony Luther, who lived in the neighbouring parish of
Kelvedon Hatch, intervened, and Byrd consented to allow
Lolly to continue his residence till the end of his lease in
1597. Lolly served as churchwarden of Stondon in 1596.
The mention of Anthony Luther recalls Byrd's lawsuit
about Battails Hall nearly twenty years earlier.

On 15 July 1595 Byrd strengthened his position by
securing a Crown lease of Stondon Place for the lives of
his son Christopher and his daughters Elizabeth and Rachel,
successively. There are two records[3] [4] of this lease at the
Public Record Office. The property was described as 'part
of her Majesty's inheritance, parcel of the possessions of
William Shelley, attainted and convicted of high treason'.
At the same time he had a grant from the Crown of the
Malepardus coppice adjoining the Stondon Place estate.

Byrd might then have considered himself firmly established; and for the next two years all went well. On 15
April 1597 William Shelley died without issue; his widow
thereupon set up a plea that Stondon Place was part of
her marriage jointure, and that as such it had been wrongly
sequestrated and should be restored to her.

This Mrs. Shelley was the daughter and sole heiress of

---

[1] Reeve's *History of Stondon Massey*, p. 32.
[2] P.R.O., Chancery Proceedings, *Byrd* v. *Lolly*, C. 2, Eliz. B. 6/56.
[3] P.R.O., Augmentation Office, Enrolment of leases, 37–8 Eliz. 228, 116.
[4] P.R.O., Particulars of Leases, Essex Rolls, no. 3, Eliz.

John Lynden.[1] She married William Shelley as his second wife. Shelley had married firstly Margaret, daughter of Thomas Wriothesley, Earl of Southampton. As Shelley died without issue his heir was his nephew John, eldest son of his brother John.[2] As stated in the injunction of King James I, to be quoted presently, Mrs. Shelley petitioned Queen Elizabeth for the restoration of the whole of the property which she had inherited from her father. Stondon Place was a comparatively small portion of her inheritance. It can cause no surprise that the Queen rejected her petition, seeing that Shelley had been found guilty of a plot against her life.

When King James came to the throne, the Earl of Effingham and others acting with him approached the King to treat for the lands formerly belonging to William Shelley. The King wrote[3] on 4 May 1603 to the Lord Treasurer saying he was pleased to have granted them, 'but that we are informed that in equity we ought rather to regard the offer made by the heire of the said Shelley for redemption of the said lands'. John Shelley's financial offer was clearly a better one than Lord Effingham's, and the King was astute enough to see that it 'would be beneficial to us and ought to affoord us wherwithal to content the Lord Effingham and make a good some besides to our owne Cofers'. William Shelley's estates must have been very extensive, judging from the fact that his nephew paid no less than £11,000 to redeem them; and out of this sum King James gave Lord Effingham £1,000 for compensation.

The King then issued Letters Patent, dated 5 September 1603,[4] by which he restored to Mrs. Shelley

all and singular the landes of inheritance which she hath or had by descent from her said late father and which were seised into the hand of the said late Queene by force of the Attaynder . . . and we do so much as in us lieth grant unto the said Jane Shelley . . . all the rents revenues and profitts thereof ever since the decease of the said

---

[1] P.R.O., Patent Rolls, Jas. 1, C. 66/1618, 23.

[2] Squire was in error in stating that Shelley's heir was his son, and Howes copied this error.

[3] P.R.O., *Domestic State Papers, Jas. I*, viii. 52.

[4] P.R.O., Patent Rolls, Jas. 1, C. 66/1618, 23.

William Shelley . . . and we restore the said Jane Shelley the possession of the premises and doe absolutely remove us and our hands of
and from the possession thereof and restore to the said Jane Shelley
to have and to hold . . . without any accompte or other thing to be
done.

The effect of this upon Byrd's position as a leaseholder
was simply to substitute Mrs. Shelley for the Crown. His
lease still held good so long as the terms were complied
with. But Mrs. Shelley then made a fatal mistake. As the
King's subsequent injunction[1] shows, she presumed to try
to evict Byrd. There is some reference in the margin of
this injunction to her having 'disobeyed to the vexation of
her tenants', among whom was 'William Byrd one of the
gentelmen of o^r Chappell'.

In the result Mrs. Shelley incurred the strong displeasure of the King and forfeited his support. He issued
the following injunction, dated 24 January 1603/4.[2]

When of late uppon yor humble suit we freely delyvered to you
under o^r greate seal yor joynt^r lands being o^r inheritance wch ye late
Q. o^r deare sister refused to do and dispensed wth yor othe wch the
law in y^t Case required being now informed y^t you used o^r said
grant contrary to o^r meaning to the undoing of o^r servant Wyllm̃
Byrd gent of the Chapple who having taken leases of y^o farme and
woods of stondon place in ye County of Essex (now parcell of yor
joynt^r) from the said late Q. for three of his chyldrens lyves payd
fynes and bestowed great Charges of y^r houses and Barnes.[3] . . .
when he entred, deserved well of you and you accepted of his rent
ever synce ye death of y^r husband. Yet not wthstandyng synce the
sayd grant you go about to thrust hym out of his possession to his
present undoing (havyng no other house but y^t) and to ye great
danger of his chyldrens future estate after his decease for staying of
wch yor hard Course nether yor owne concience nor o^r benignity
towards you nor the Decree of o^r exchequer chamber yet in force
nor ye letters of ye ll^{ds} of o^r pryvye Counsayle nor ye travayle of y^e
lo: Peeter auctorized from them to mediate ye sayd cause nor any
reasonable composition offered you by o^r sayd servant to hold his
possession wth yor good favor can any whyt move you being a woman
of great lyvery and no charges and having many better houses then

[1] P.R.O., *Domestic State Papers, Jas. I*, Addenda, xxxvi. 5.
[2] Ibid.
[3] Certain words, occurring where the manuscript has formerly been folded,
are undecipherable.

his to use at yor plesure grownding yor Rigor agaynst o^r sayd servant
Uppon ye strength of o^r sayd grant to you whereof we greatlye mer-
vayle y^t in thos lands wch so latelye you receyved from us and wch are
o^r inheritance you offer so hard measure to o^r servant contrarye to all
gratitude & discretion and convenience Wheruppon (assuryng o^r
selves y^t ye premisses are true) we do hereby requyre you to permit and
suffer o^r sayd servant and his chyldren pattentees of ye late Q.
duryng yor tyme quietlye to enjoy ther possession of ye said farme and
woods accordyng to ther sayd grants & paying you ther rent and using
them selves as good tenants ought to do redely, also y^t you geve them
no just cause hereafter of any new complaynt to us or our Cownsayle
touching y^t cause.

Four years elapsed; and then in 1608 Mrs. Shelley
appealed for support to Lord Salisbury, as Lord High
Treasurer of England, in the following terms:[1]

Your Sup^t having in all dutifull respectfulnes received your Lo^{ps}:
pleasure by her Solicitor touching Birds contynuing in her house at
Stondon (who no doubt by his clamo^r hath gone about to incense your
Lo^P: against her as he hath done some other great parsonages suggesting
unto theire hono^s that your Sup^t intended to take away his living
without any just Cause or title thereunto).

Nowe, for that it may appeare unto your hono^r howe injuriouslie
the said Bird hathe delt with your Supp^t for theis Twelve yeares
space, and what smal or no favour he deserveth of your Sup^t, she
humblie prayeth your Lo^P: would vouchsafe the reading of the
Annexed. And for that your Sup^t being aged Threescore and Tenne
years hath no other house or place of habitation neare the Citty of
London wherein to rest her selfe in this her period of life, save onely
ye said place of Stondon.

Shee most humblie prayeth That with the good likeing of yor
hono^r, shee may quicklie have and enjoye the same, not doubting but
that your Lo^P: in your grave wisdome will putt difference betwene the
Landlord and Tenaunte, to the end it may Appeare unto your hono^r
with what submissivenes & duetye shee entertayneth your Lo^{ps} mocon.

M^{res} Shelleys grievaunces against William Byrde.[2]

1. That Bird being in quiet possession of Stondon place began a suit
against your Sup^t in the Excheq^r Chamber Tenne Yeares since,
& the same pursued ever sithence in his wiefs & Childrens names,
praying thereby that the Court would order her to ratifie his
Lease, which he had from her late Matie for Three Lives.

2. Not prevailing herein, he thereuppon stirred upp all the late Queenes Patentees wth helde any p^t of her joyneture lands, & did combyme himself with them to mainteyne severall suits against her for the same, wch contynued about eight yeares, & procured her Rents to be sequestered, and hath caused her to expend at least 1000^{li} in defence of her title.

3. Sr Thomas Fludd Mr Churchyard and the rest of the Queenes Patentees uppon notice of his highnes L<del>r</del>es patents graunted unto your Sup^t for enjoying of her lands, did surcease their suits, and all submitted them selves, saving the said Bird and one Petiver, who being encouraged by the said Bird, did along tyme contynue obstinate untill of late he likewise submitted himself. For which the said Bird did give him vile and bitter words for doing the same.

4. He hath likewise practized to disgrace her with divers her honorable frends, & others of great quallitie pswading them that she was a woman of no good conscience, and that she went aboute to put him out of his Living without any just cause or title thereunto.

5. And being told by your Sup^{ts} Counsell in her presence, that he had no right to the said Living, hee both then and at other tymes before her said, that yf he could not hould it by right, he would holde it by might, which Course he hath pursued ever since.

6. The said Bird hath cutt downe great store of tymber Trees worth one hundreth marks growing in the grounds belonging to the said place, hath felled all the underwoods worth 100^{li} & made therein greate spoile, & greater would have made, had not the ho^{ble} Court of Excheq^r taken order to the contrary.

7. The lands in question are yearely worth 100^{li} for the which he hath onely paid 40 marks p Ann for syx yeares or thereabouts. But since the said L<del>r</del>es Patents, which beare the date of the Fyft day of September in the First yeare of his highnes Raigne,[1] he hath paid nothing at all; howbeit by the said L<del>r</del>es Patents she was to receave the meane profytt thereof ever since the death of her husband who died about xij yeares since.

8. That for wante of this house, your Sup^t was inforced in this last plague to remove from Towne to Towne, from whence being driven by Reason of the plague, there, shee was at the last constrayned to lye at a Tennts house of hers, neare Colchester farre unfitting for her to her great disgrace and to the great hurt of your Sup^t, being unable in respect of her age to travaile upp and Downe the Countrey.

All wch notwithstanding in her bounden duety to yor hono^r, and

[1] See p. 21.

with a Reverend respect to yor Lo^{ps} motion; shee will be content to Release all her charges & also the moyetie of tharrerays[1] aforesaide, although with exceeding Clamo^r, he hath justly moved her to Afford him no favour.

Lord Salisbury was not disposed to take much interest in this petition. He passed it on to the Court, having endorsed it thus:[2]

27 October 1608
This matter hath bene depending in Court and therefore lett her represent unto the Barons that which hath here delivered unto me, who are better acquainted with the whole proceedings than I am and will take some leysure to heare her complaint for I have none
(signed) R Salisbury.

Mrs. Shelley was certainly overstating her grievances, especially in the final clause, for she was a very large land-owner in her own right.

On Byrd's behalf it was said that he had spent a lot of money in improving the property; for example, he had 'altered some barne dores, erected chimneys, made partitions, and at a cost of £150 brought water into the house in pipes of lead'.[3]

The dispute was by no means settled yet. On 26 January 1609/10, Lord Salisbury, with the consent of both parties, was invited to mediate.[4] Accordingly he ordered that William, Christopher, Rachel, and Anne Byrde should remain in possession until the following feast of St. Michael and then vacate Stondon Place. Anne's name is found nowhere else, and it is probable that it was inserted in this document in error for that of Elizabeth, whose name, and not that of Anne, appears in the original lease of 15 July 1595.[5]

When the time came, Byrd and his family remained obdurate and the plaintiff sought to have them 'punished by the Court for their contempt therein'.[6] They claimed,

---

[1] ? the arrears.
[2] P.R.O., *Domestic State Papers, Jas. I*, xxxvii. 36.
[3] *The Essex Review*, Oct. 1923, article on Byrd by E. H. L. Reeve.
[4] P.R.O., Exchequer Decrees, 7 Jas. 1, series ii, vol. vii, fo. 294.
[5] See p. 20.
[6] P.R.O., Exchequer Decrees, 7 Jas. 1, series ii, vol. vii, fo. 328.

however, that they had 'a grant sufficient in law by lease
of the said plaintiff (since the making of the above named
decree) to hold and enjoy the same until Michaelmas next
coming'. It was therefore ordered that the plaintiff and
defendants be dismissed and referred to the Common Law,
'there to commence any action or actions advised by
Counsel for recovery of the premisses to the plaintiff and
for the punishment or clearing of the defendants'.

There was no further litigation, for Mrs. Shelley died.
This may have been a stroke of good fortune for Byrd, for
it does not appear that his case was a strong one. Shortly
afterwards he bought the Stondon property outright from
John Shelley, William Shelley's nephew and heir, who was
created a baronet in the following year, 1611. Byrd's purchase was made in the names of John and Thomas Petre,
and he settled the property on himself.[1]

Comment has been made upon the fact that Byrd as a
Papist should have been 'granted a Crown lease of a property sequestrated from a Catholic recusant'. But it must
be remembered that Shelley had been found guilty on no
less a charge than plotting against the life and throne of
Queen Elizabeth, whereas the worst charge brought against
Byrd was that of refusing to attend the Reformed services
in his parish church, and moreover he was a loyal servant
of the Queen in the Chapel Royal. But in point of fact
Byrd was not granted this lease. He bought it for £300
from William Hollingsworth.

Byrd was engaged in another lawsuit in connexion with
his Stondon property. This case had its origin about the
year 1550, when Osborne Foster, who was at that time in
occupation of Stondon Place, bought a small property
called Malepardus Farm. Malepardus seems to have been
long associated with Stondon Place. It lies a short distance
down a lane which at that time led from the high road in
Stondon village to Kelvedon Hatch, passing between Malepardus wood and certain glebe lands, known as 'Parson's
bushes', to the property then owned by the Wright family at
Kelvedon Hall. It was little more than a grass track and was
described as being 'so fowle' as to be practically useless.
Foster, having bought the wood, closed up the track by

[1] P.R.O., Chancery Proceedings, 10 Oct. 1635.

planting a hedge across it to secure himself from tres-passers.[1]

Lawrence Hollingsworth, who has already been men-tioned as a tenant of Malepardus after Foster's time, kept the track blocked up. Byrd, as we have seen, succeeded to the tenancy in 1595. Some years later the rector of Stondon, John Nobbs by name, brought an action against Byrd for 'stopping upp the way against the King's liege people'. In the defence of his case Byrd had the support of John Wright of Kelvedon Hall.[2] The trial took place at Brentwood in 1604, and judgement was given against Nobbs on the evidence that during fifty years or more no one had challenged the position.[3]

Details have already been given of as many as five law-suits in which Byrd was concerned, namely, *Byrd* v. *Luther*, *Byrd* v. *Fettiplace and Boxe*, *Byrd* v. *Lolly*, *Shelley* v. *Byrd*, and *Nobbs* v. *Byrd*. There is yet another case to record: that of *Byrd* v. *Jackson and others*. This came before the Court of Chancery in 1608. It concerned a lease of the Manor of Longley in the county of Gloucester, granted by the Crown to Byrd, Juliana his wife, and Thomas their son, as far back as 1 March 1578/9. The documents relating to this suit, now in the Public Record Office, are of great length and are partly undecipherable.[4]

Byrd was entitled to take up this lease on the death of a widow named Elizabeth Spicer, the tenant in possession. In his answer to the sworn depositions of the defendants, Robert Jackson, John a Wintle and Joan his wife, Byrd stated that he

entered into the said tenement and the lands appertaining thereto ab^t the 26 day of March in the one and twentieth year of the raign of the late Q. and did lett the same for a yearly rent unto William Mill and Thomas Watkyns who did occupy the same until 12 Dec. following uppon which day they weare by force and violence ex-pulsed and dispossessed by the said Robert Jackson. The said W^m

---

[1] Reeve, *History of Stondon Massey*, p. 126.
[2] Kelvedon in the Ongar hundred must not be confused with Kelvedon in the Witham hundred in the same county.
[3] P.R.O., Exchequer Depositions by Commission, 2 Jas. 1.
[4] P.R.O., Chancery Proceedings, C. 2, Jas. 1, B. 16 78.

Byrd was in quiet possession by virtue of his lease long time before the same was granted by coppy of Court Roll to the said Robert Jackson, and that the said lease of the petitioners, while they were in quiet possession of the s^d tenements and Farm, was worth to be sould the somme of 200^li. And that the said Robert Jackson John a Wintle and Joane his wife have taken and received all the profitts . . . ever since the said unlawful entry. . . . The preamble of the lease granted to Jackson, dated 23 year of the late Q., was untruly set down . . . and Robert Jackson and Auditor Neale did procure to be set down an allowance of 42^li unto Wm Byrd to surrender his lease uppon the particular of Willm Abbotts lease of the parsonage of Hartland in com Devon without the privitie or consent of Wm Byrd and that the said Jackson or Neale or one of them received the 42^li. The records of the lease are imbezzled and not to be found in the pipe office where they originally were nor yet among the Records of the Court of Augmentation.

Jackson and Neale

procured Christopher Smith the Clerk of the Pype to make a petition in the name of Wm Byrd without his consent or knowledge . . . to have his fine of £18. 11. 6. which he paid for his fine of his lease of Longley to be allowed him upon the fine of the lease of the parsonage of Walsall in com Stafford granted to George Clarkeson whereas Byrd never knew or saw the said Clarkeson or had any dealing with him nor ever spake unto Christopher Smith for any such purpose or ever received £18. 11. 6.

Another document, filed with this one, and addressed to Lord Ellesmere as Lord Chancellor of England, is dated 13 April 1608; the final answer of Jackson is dated 9 June 1608. The result of this suit has not been ascertained.

We may hope that the closing years of Byrd's long life were passed in comparative peace, even though there are hints of trouble of some kind within his own family circle. These years were certainly spent at Stondon, and we may infer from the records of the Chapel Royal, as contained in the Cheque Book, that although he retained his position until the day of his death he was virtually in retirement.

Byrd was present at the funeral of Queen Elizabeth,[1] the Coronation of James I,[2] and the funeral of Queen

---

[1] Lord Chamberlain's Accounts, vol. 554.
[2] Ibid., vol. 556.

Anne, the wife of James I, in 1618.[1] On this latter occasion he was no longer organist, that office being held jointly by Edmund Hooper and Orlando Gibbons.

At the time of his death, as we learn from his will, Byrd had apartments with furniture of his own in the house of Lord Worcester, in the Strand. It is probable that he served in some capacity in the earl's household, perhaps as Master of the Music. No reference to Byrd has been found among the papers now belonging to the Somerset family.

Byrd died on 4 July 1623. His death was recorded in two separate lists in the Cheque Book. In the first of these he was described as 'a Father of Musick'. In his will[2] he expressed a wish to be buried at Stondon, where his wife already lay, and he hoped that he might die at his home. There is no reason to think that he died elsewhere, or to doubt that he was buried in his wife's grave in Stondon churchyard. The Parish Registers of this date do not survive. It would seem that Byrd's second wife, Ellen, died shortly after 1605, the last year in which she is mentioned as a recusant.

A monumental tablet was placed on the south wall of the church on the occasion of the tercentenary celebrations in 1923.

Byrd's pedigree and coat of arms[3] were recorded at the Heralds' Visitation of Essex in 1634, as set out below. The details are very meagre, and in this form they would have been supplied by Thomas Byrd the younger, who signed the pedigree and who, perhaps, had little interest in giving fuller particulars. We know, for example, that all three of Byrd's daughters married twice and it need not be inferred that he himself was not married twice on the lack of evidence derived from this pedigree.[4]

The coat of arms sanctioned by the Heralds is recorded as *ex sigillo*; but the tinctures may be supplied from the only known examples of this coat in connexion with the name of Byrd. They are added here in brackets.

---

[1] *The Old Cheque book of the Chapel Royal*, E. F. Rimbault, p. 126.
[2] P.C.C., Swan 106, and see Appendix.
[3] Harl. Soc. xiii. 366.
[4] For fuller pedigree see Appendix.

Arms: [*Vert*], three stags' heads cabossed [*or*], a canton ermine.

William Byrde of Standen ═ Juliana da. of M.
Place in com. Essex gent │ Birley of Lincolnshire
musician to Q. Elizabeth │

Christopher Bird of Standen Place	= Catherin da. of Thomas Moore of Bamborough in com. York	Thomas Bird of Drury Lane in com. Midd.	Elizabeth ux. i. John Jackson ux. 2. Burdett	Rachel ux. Edward Biggs

Thomas Bird
of Standen Place
1634

Mary
ux. Thomas
Falconbridge

No portrait of Byrd is known except one by G. Van der Gucht, which was engraved *circa* 1729 on the same plate with a portrait of Tallis; this was designed for a history of music by Niccolò Francesco Haym, which was never published. The plate is signed 'N. Haym delin. G. Vandergucht fecit'. Haym was a musician, collector, and writer, and it may fairly be assumed that a man of his culture was dealing with authentic portraits of the two composers.

Byrd, as shown in the pedigree, had five children, for, as already stated, the mention of Anne in a certain legal document is, without doubt, an error for Elizabeth.

Christopher was born at Lincoln in 1569; he married before 1595 when his wife was cited with him as a recusant,[1] and died before 1615, in which year his wife Catherine was described as a widow.[2] It is curious that those who have assumed that the omission of Christopher's name from his father's will implied that he was the subject of his father's displeasure, did not consider the obvious possibility of his having predeceased his father. It is unlikely that he is to be identified with a Christopher Byrd mentioned in a letter among the Salisbury Papers, dated August 1599.[3] This man is described there as 'a servant of my Lord's . . .

[1] Chelmsford Diocesan Registry, Essex Archidiaconal Records, vol. 36, fo. 124.
[2] Ibid., vol. 51, fo. 150*b*.
[3] *Hist. MSS. Commission, Salisbury Papers*, pt. ix, p. 340.

STONDON CHURCH

a gun-maker, a man both very religious and very well acquainted with ordnance matters, having been a long time trained up in the Tower'. This is inconsistent with the fact that Byrd's son Christopher spent most of his time at Stondon at this date. Catherine, Christopher's widow, lived at Stondon Place after the composer's death, in accordance with the terms of his will. There had been some disagreement between her and her father-in-law, as we gather from his will. This affair, however, had been settled 'by an awarde latlye made beetweene Catheren Byrde my daughter in law & mee bee [sc. by] a very good Frend to hus both wch award wee both give our cristian pmisse to pforme but havinge beene letted & hyndred theirein by the undutifull obstinancie of one whome I am unwilling to name'. This passage has been misread and misunderstood.[1] It simply means that 'a very good friend' both to Byrd and Catherine arbitrated between them, but that a third party, described as undutiful and obstinate, tried to stir up trouble.

To this day the 'undutiful one' remains unknown, in accordance with Byrd's intention. It was not Christopher, his eldest son, for he had died several years earlier. It may have been his daughter Elizabeth, who, though living at the time, is unnamed in the will.

By the terms of the will Catherine was made responsible for paying annuities to Thomas and Rachel, her late husband's brother and sister. In 1635, no payment whatever having been made since the composer's death, Thomas and Rachel brought an action against her successfully in the Court of Chancery. It is from the account of this lawsuit that we learn various details about Byrd's purchase of Stondon Place in 1610. The last mention of Catherine is in 1637, when her name occurs in a list of parishioners of Stondon called upon to contribute towards a ship demanded by King Charles I from the county of Essex.[2]

Christopher and Catherine had a son, Thomas, living at Stondon in 1634; nothing further is known of him.

Thomas, the composer's second son, was born *circa* 1576.

---

[1] See Squire, Grove's *Dictionary*, *sub* Byrd, and Howes, *William Byrd*, p. 219, note.

[2] *The Essex Review*, Oct. 1923, article on Byrd by E. H. L. Reeve.

Tallis was his godfather,[1] and he followed his father's profession. According to Dr. Boyce[2] he was appointed to act
as deputy to Dr. John Bull in his various musical offices,
including the Gresham professorship, when Bull's health
had given way. In the Visitation pedigree he was described
as 'of Drury Lane'.

After the death of the widow, Catherine, Stondon Place
was occupied for some years by John Leigh, who died in
1650. Leigh's grave in Stondon Church is marked by a
stone slab. The Farm (by which was probably meant Malepardus) was let by the Byrds to Thomas Warwick. Warwick
sublet it to Francis Petre, a nephew of John and Thomas
Petre,[3] in whose names Byrd had bought Stondon Place in
1610. In 1651 Francis Petre was noted a delinquent and
all his goods were confiscated. The chief sufferer as a result
of this was Thomas Byrd, who had been entitled to an
annuity of £20 secured on the property by a decree in
Chancery in 1635.[4] At the age of seventy-five he was thus
deprived of his only means of subsistence. His case was
brought before the Committee for Compounding with De-
linquents who awarded him the annuity with arrears.[5]
Shortly after this the Stondon property was sold by the
Byrds for a good price to Prosper Nicholas.

Elizabeth Byrd married firstly John Jackson, who died
before 1604, in which year Elizabeth Jackson was described as a widow,[6] and secondly, —— Burdett. Rachel
married firstly John Hooke, of Stanford Rivers, a neighbouring village where she and her husband were living in
1604 (Rachel's name is wrongly given as Catherine in this
list of recusants),[6] and secondly in 1634 Edward Biggs. By
her first husband she had two children: William, and Catherine who married Michael Walton. Mary, Byrd's youngest
daughter, married firstly Henry Hawksworth, by whom she
had four sons, William, Henry, George, and John. She
married secondly Thomas Falconbridge. Her first husband

[1] Will of Thomas Tallis, P.C.C. 52 Brudenell.
[2] Boyce's *Cathedral Music*, vol. iii, Preface.
[3] Harl. Soc. xiii. 469.
[4] P.R.O., Chancery Proceedings, 10 Oct. 1635.
[5] Reeve's *History of Stondon Massey*, p. 42.
[6] Chelmsford, Archidiaconal Records,E. 27, fo. 137.

no doubt belonged to the old Yorkshire family of Hawksworth although his name does not appear in the pedigree
printed by Foster.[1] In 1604 the Archdeacon's Registers[2]
described her as *puella*, implying that she was not then of
age. It is likely that she was the child of his second wife.

Byrd was far from being an uncommon name in the sixteenth century, but it remains here to consider the possibility
of identifying the composer with two other William Byrds,
seeing that the question has been raised in each instance.

Firstly, can the composer possibly be identified with
'William Byrd alias Borne' who figures so constantly in the
diaries of Henslowe and Alleyn? This 'Byrd alias Borne'
became connected with the 'Admiral's' Company of actors
at the Rose Theatre. Henslowe's first reference to him is
dated 10 August 1597, when 'W^m borne came & ofered
him sealfe to come and playe wth my lord Admeralles men
at my howse called by the name of the Rosse'. After this
Henslowe mentioned him frequently and continued to refer
to him as 'Borne' until 23 October 1598, when he made an
entry concerning a loan 'unto Wm Birde ales borne'. But as
early as April that year the man, whoever he was, had set
aside the *alias* and signed himself William Birde. On 26
November 1600 Henslowe made a loan 'unto Mrs Birde
alles Borne'.

This Birde became a shareholder in the Admiral's Company; and on 20 December 1601, 'Birde alias Borne' was
paid for a play, on the subject of Judas, which he wrote in
conjunction with Rowley. In the following year 'Byrde &
Samwell Rowley' were paid £4 for their additions to *Doctor
Faustus*. During this period 'Byrd alias Borne' became the
close friend of Edward Alleyn, in whose diary there are
frequent references to him, the last one being on 23 February 1621.

In support of the suggestion it has been pointed out that
Byrd the composer may have found it convenient on religious grounds to disguise his identity, even if under a rather
thin veil. Then again, Lord Worcester, his patron, was
patron also of the other theatrical Company that played
under Henslowe's management. It has also been thought

[1] Foster's *Yorkshire Pedigrees*.
[2] Chelmsford, Archidiaconal Records, E. 27, fo. 137.

significant that 'Borne' usually played old men's parts. Byrd
alias Borne disappeared from the Admiral's Company in
1603.

The theory is not wholly impossible, but it cannot easily
be accepted. The present writer would unhesitatingly reject
it. In the first place, in spite of the fact that most members
of the Chapel Royal at that date had experience of the stage,
it seems entirely inconsistent, from what we know of the
composer's somewhat austere musical outlook and character, to imagine him playing light comedy. Nor does this
idea fit in with his life and position as the owner of Stondon
Place. Moreover 1597 is the date of William Shelley's death,
when Byrd was first faced with the claims of Mrs. Shelley;
and these must have occupied all his spare time. And in
spite of costly litigation, there is nothing to suggest that the
composer and his wife ever stood in need of loans from
Henslowe.

But a comparison of the signatures seems to determine
the matter beyond all doubt. It is impossible to believe that
the hand that signed the composer's will and the holograph
letter now in the Public Record Office is the same that can
be seen in the diaries at Dulwich.

The second question concerns the appointment by Dr.
Bell, the Vice-Chancellor of Cambridge University, of a
musician named William Byrd to be 'Lord of the Tappes'
at Sturbridge Fair.[1] A document dated 7 September 1583
states that 'time out of minde it hath been a custome and
always used within this fair that some musitian whome they
have usually called Lord of the Tappes should . . . after
sunset and likewise before the sunne rising by sound of
some instrument give notice to shut and open the shops
. . . many of the worshipful citizens of London and other
places have commended unto us William Byrde being a
musitian and now servant and wayht of the University'.

In the opinion of the writer it is impossible to identify
this man with the composer, unless the whole affair took
the form of some elaborate insult or clumsy joke, which
William Byrd, the composer, would have treated with the
contempt that it deserved. It is strange that the Vice-

[1] Cooper's *Annals of Cambridge*, v. 314.

Chancellor should have been associated with such a frivolous concern. It must be supposed that among the City
Waits at Cambridge there was a man named William Byrd,
although why he should have been known to citizens of
London is a question not easily answered. But the Cambridge Waits were musicians of some standing; for example,
William Gibbons, father of Orlando, was a member. The
duties of this 'Lord of the Tappes' were of a menial character, not calling for a skilled musician; he was expected to
be something of a buffoon at the fair.

CHAPTER III

BYRD'S ASSOCIATION WITH THE CATHOLICS

IN his will Byrd expressed a pious wish that he might 'live and die a true and perfect member of God's holy Catholic Church'. And there can be no doubt that throughout his life he adhered to the older traditions of the Church as opposed to the Reformation.

It may therefore seem surprising that from early manhood until the day of his death he held positions uninterruptedly in the service of the Reformed Anglican Church. It may be asked why his services were retained, and why he was content, in a sense, to be serving two masters.

Too much can easily be made of both these points. On the one hand, recusants and Catholics in general were treated with much variety of leniency or severity. Many recusants enjoyed complete immunity on payment of a small fine; but if once they were found guilty of taking part in some dangerous plot they might become liable to imprisonment or death. Much also depended upon the personal animosities or friendships of minor officials in dealing with local cases, and undoubtedly many recusants were harshly treated and heavily fined.

The case of Edward, 4th Earl of Worcester, who incidentally was one of Byrd's special patrons, provides an interesting example of how an openly professing Catholic could nevertheless enjoy complete freedom, and even hold high office and enjoy the personal esteem of Queen Elizabeth and James I. The Queen remarked of him that he succeeded in combining what had seemed to her two irreconcilable things, namely, being 'a stiff papist and a good subject'.[1]

Similarly, Byrd, being the greatest musician of his day, must needs be retained in the service of her Majesty in the Chapel Royal, even if he too were 'a stiff papist', but no

[1] Lloyd's *State Worthies*, 1670, p. 582.

doubt she made the same reservation in his case as when she permitted Sebastian Westcote to retain the Mastership of St. Paul's choristers;[1] she valued Westcote's services and liked him,[2] but he must not involve himself in any popish activities. Byrd may have sailed dangerously close to the wind sometimes in his dealings with the Jesuits and others, but he was never actively associated, as far as we know, with any serious plot. The authorities thought it wise to keep a constant eye upon him, but he does not seem to have been seriously molested.

And, on the other hand, it would be unreasonable to accuse Byrd of duplicity. We may admit that he was an earnest Catholic, but he was no bigot; and we may judge from the beauty and sincerity of his music written for the Reformed Church that the musical Services with which his duties associated him were by no means devoid of spiritual significance to him. Why then need he sacrifice such a position, seeing that his livelihood largely depended on it?

Of Byrd's early religious training we know nothing at all; and while he was organist of Lincoln there is no record to show whether he and his wife were cited as recusants. Their troubles on these lines began at Harlington.

The earliest mention of Byrd yet found in this connexion is in 'The Certificate of the Revrend Father in god John (Aylmer) Bishopp of London made to the Quene her Maiestyes most honorable pryvye Counsayle of the names of all such as refuse to come to their pishe churches wth in the dioces of London according to a letter from their honours to his L. in that behalfe directed.'[3]

This is dated November 1577; and under the heading of Harlington parish it reads: 'The wife of William Bird one of the gent of her Maties chappell.' Curiously enough the name of 'Sebastian Westcott' is also on this 'certificate'. He was described as of 'St. Gregories by Powles', and as 'maister of the children of Paules church, valewed at one hundred poundes in gooddes'.

There were probably many similar charges of recusancy

---

[1] Arkwright, *Mus. Assoc. Proceedings*, April 1914.
[2] 'ita charus Elizabethae fuit.'
[3] P.R.O., *Domestic State Papers*, cxviii. 73.

against Mrs. Byrd between that date and 28 June 1581, when it is recorded in the Middlesex Sessional (Gaol Delivery) Rolls[1] that 'Juliana Birde wife of William Byrde Gentleman and John Reason yoman of Harlington, co. Midd.', were cited as recusants as from 20 May to 28 June of that year. Between that date and January 1586/7, when Juliana Byrd's name appears for the last time in these Rolls, she was summoned as a recusant twelve times.

Byrd himself did not actually figure in these lists as a recusant until 20 August 1585. He was cited again, together with his wife, on 7 October 1586, and also in the following January for periods covering together 30 June 1586 to 1 January. Byrd's name appears alone, and for the last time at Harlington, on 7 April 1592, for the period dating from 31 August 1591 to 31 March following. The name of John Reason, sometimes varied as Rayson and Raysonne, appears almost every time in conjunction with that of Juliana Byrd. In the entry of 20 August 1585 he was described as Byrd's servant. Reason's name occurs in these Rolls for the last time on 3 January 1591/2, and apparently under a more serious charge. Recognizances on that occasion were taken before Sir Owen Hopton in the sum of twenty pounds for his appearance at the next Session of the Peace to be held in Middlesex, 'then and there to answer unto suche thinges as shalbe objected against hym touchinge his Recusancye in absentinge and absteyninge hym self from devyne service used in the Church of England'. The name of John Reason is found in the list of the recusants of St. Margaret's, Westminster, 1599.[2] This was probably the same man. Jane Shelley of St. Martin-in-the-fields, who also appears in that document, was Byrd's adversary in his lawsuits concerning the lease of Stondon Place.

There are other references to Byrd's sympathies with the Catholics at this period of his life. About 1581 a list was drawn up of 'The places were certaine recusantes remove in and about the city of London or are to be com by uppon warninge'.[3] It includes 'Wyllm̃ Byrde of the Chap-

---

[1] *Middlesex County Records*, ed. J. C. Jeaffreson, vol. i, p. 123, &c.
[2] Middlesex Sessional Rolls.
[3] P.R.O., *Domestic State Papers, Eliz.*, cli. 11.

pell At his house in the parish of Harlington in com.
Midd.'

About the same date there is a document[1] labelled 'Suche
as are relievers of papistes and conveyers of money and
other things unto them beyondes the Seas'. It includes
'The names of c̃tain parsons who be great frends and
ayderes of those beyond the seas'. Among these, under
the heading of London, is 'Mr Byrde at Mr Listers his
house on against S^t dunstans or at the Ld Padgettes house
Draighton'. Against this entry, and in another hand, in
which several similar notes are added to this document, is
written: 'The messenger is to tell him things wch he will
well lyke.' There is no clue to the meaning of this note.

Among those then living beyond the seas was one
Michael Tempest, who had been attainted for taking part
in the Northern Catholic Rebellion in 1570. He had
escaped to France, leaving his wife Dorothy and five children in England with little means of support. Byrd inter-
ested himself on her behalf, as is shown by an incident
brought to light in a holograph letter to be seen in the
Record Office, bearing the date 17 October 1581.[2]

Queen Elizabeth had granted an annuity of £20 to be
paid quarterly to Mrs. Tempest, and at this date the payment seems to have been in arrears. William Petre, who,
as we know from other sources, was a personal friend of
Byrd's, was an official of the Court of Exchequer, and Byrd
wrote the following letter which tells the story in full:

To ye worshipfull and my verye good frend Mr Petre on of y^e
officers of her Maties Excheuquer at Westminster. dd

Mr Peter. Meetyng you latelye in aldersgat streete at s^r John
Petres howse. I Moved you for the payment of the Annuitye dew
unto M^ris Dorothe Tempest at Michaellmas last past for ye quarter
before passed. And then you promised me y^t aboute a fortnight
after yf I came unto you I shuld receyve yt for her bringynge a
Certificat yf she is Alyve so yt is s^r y^t my attendance heere at the
Courte is so Requisite as I Can not have as yet any spare tyme to
Come to London for the Receipt of the same. But this is most hartelye
to desyre you to accepte of the Certificat under my hand as you
have verye frendlye done heeretofore And to deliver unto ye partye

[1] Ibid. cxlvii. 137.
[2] P.R.O., Exchequer Rolls, E. 407, 72.

y[t] shall Bring the same unto you (w[ch] I thynke wilbe the gentilwooman her selfe) Suche Monye as is now dew And you shall ever Comande me in any thing wherin I may plesure you or any frend of yo[rs] while I lyve. And thus wth my verye hartye Comendations I Comit you to god. fro the Courte this xvij[th] of octobre. 1581.

yo[r] Assured poore frend to Comande
Willm̃ Byrde

The certificate,[1] also in Byrd's autograph, reads thus:

To all Christian people to whom this Certificat shall Come or to whom yt may appertayne. wheras it hathe plessed the Q. Ma[tie] of her great Clemencye and Goodnes to geve unto Dorothe Tempest wyfe unto Michaell Tempest Late attaynted An Annuitye of xx[li] A yeare—for the Releavyng of her and her fyve Childerne havyng no other thyng left to Releeve and Mayntayne her and her fyve Childerne wth all But onlye y[e] sayde anuitye w[ch] is to be payd quar-terlys As by her Ma[ties] grant under her privye sceale. More at large dothe and may appeere. Thes are to sertifye you y[t] the sayde Dorothe Tempest is Alyve and in Good healthe at the Makyng heereof. The xvij[th] of october Anno Regni Elizabethae Reginae xxiii[mo] 1581

Willm̃ Byrde

Byrd's friendly action in this matter was of course no secret affair, for it concerned a grant from the Crown itself. Nevertheless, it shows his sympathy with one whose misfortunes were the direct outcome of the activities of the Catholic party.

On 27 January 1583 a raid was made upon 'the house of M[ris] Hampden of Stocke (? Stoke) in the County of Bucks,[2] and an inventory was drawn up 'of suche things as were found and caryed away from there by M[r] Pawle Wentworth'. This seems to have been a mean and wanton act of robbery. Lists of pictures, books, beads, and other things taken from 'M[ris] Hampdens bed Chamber', 'the maides chamber', 'M[r] Fyttons Chamber', 'M[r] Carletons Chamber', 'the gentilwomens Chamber', and 'The little gallery', occupy the first two pages. In 'the Chamber over

---

[1] This certificate is in the possession of Mr. W. Westley Manning, who communicated it to *The Times*, together with the letter, on 12 Jan. 1933. A photographic reproduction is filed with the original letter in the Public Record Office.

[2] P.R.O., *Domestic State Papers*, *Eliz.* clxvii. 47.

the stable' was 'one lynnen bagge havinge in yt dyverse wrytten papers' and 'a coppie of the popes letter'.

On the third page we read that 'one whose name is reason' arrived on horseback, not knowing what was happening; and becoming suspicious when he caught sight of the raiders, attempted to escape:

comynge to the gate while the house was in searchinge he conceavinge sum suspecte of the company wch he sawe began to ryde backe agyane apace but he was overtaken and searched ther was founde aboughht hym one old prynted songe booke wch was sent unto Carleton as appeard by a letter sent therw^t all and one other letter sent unto Mr Fytton from one Mr Byrde of the Quenes Maties Chapple ther was also fonde aboughht hym the Officin beate marie wch he sayd was hys owne prayer book.

'One whose name is reason' can almost certainly be identified as John Reason, Byrd's servant, who had probably ridden over from Harlington taking the song-book and letters from his master to Fytton and Carleton. It is an error to suppose that this was a secular song-book. Being described as an *old* printed song-book in 1583, it was probable a foreign missal dating perhaps as early as 1500.

Another list of houses to be searched was drawn up and dated 21 August 1586.[1] Here there is mention of 'Mr Birdes house at Harmansworth or Craneford'. This rather vague statement may be intended to indicate his Harlington house; for it may have been made by some one who knew that he lived in that neighbourhood but was uncertain about precise details. Harlington lies between these two villages and joins on to them.

In this same summer of 1586 the Jesuits were under special observation; Father William Weston,[2] in his autobiography has much to say, both as to the celebration of the Divine Mysteries at gatherings in private houses, and also about the experiences the Jesuits underwent in hiding-places to avoid the imminent danger of arrest.

On 7 July 1586 Henry Garnett and Robert Southwell, two notable Jesuit priests, landed in England and were met by Weston. Next day they went to a gentleman's house

[1] Ibid. cxcii. 48.
[2] Morris's *Troubles of our Catholic Forefathers*, ii. 142.

in Berkshire, some ten leagues from London, where they stayed for a week, celebrating the Mass regularly in the private Chapel attached to the house. Among the party, says Weston, was

Mr Byrd, the most celebrated musician and organist of the English nation, who had been formerly in the Queen's Chapel, and was held in the highest estimation; but for his religion he sacrificed every thing, both his office and the Court and all those hopes which are nurtured by such persons as pretend to similar places in the dwellings of princes, as steps towards the increasing of their fortune.

There is otherwise no known evidence that Byrd ever gave up his place in the Chapel Royal, nor any entry in the Cheque Book to suggest that he did so. Weston may have been misinformed, or he may have been led by enthusiasm into an exaggerated statement. The house is thought by Father Morris to have been that of Mr. Bold or Bolt,[1] who was organist to Sir John Petre. Bolt was arrested as a papist in 1594, and went later to Brussels, spending the rest of his life abroad.

Morris has related this incident in a manner that has led to some pardonable confusion. The letter preserved at Stonyhurst College, to which Morris alludes, refers to another matter altogether. It is dated 30 June 1601, and was written by Henry Garnett to Father Strange. It has no reference whatever to this meeting in 1586, fifteen years earlier, nor to Byrd.

In a letter dated 28 May 1594[2] there is mention of a brother of William Byrd in connexion with certain people who as Catholics were under the observation of the authorities. This letter was written from Greenwich by Benjamin Baird, or Beard, and addressed to 'Mr Joanes' (Morgan Jones, of Gray's Inn).

Morris, in *Troubles of our Catholic Forefathers*,[3] is in error in saying this letter was written by Benjamin Tichborne to the Lord Keeper Puckering. Baird was Tichborne's nephew.[4]

---

[1] Ibid., p. 142.
[2] P.R.O., *Domestic State Papers*, ccxlviii. 118.
[3] *Troubles of our Catholic Forefathers*, ii. 143.
[4] P.R.O.. *Domestic State Papers*, ccxlviii. 83.

Mr Peter. Meetyng you lately in aldersgat strete at
Sr John Petres house. I moved you for the payment
of the Annuitye dew unto Mris Dorothe Tempest
at Michaellmas last past. for ye quarter before passed.
And then you promised me. yt aboute a fortnight
after yt she came unto you. I shuld receyve yt for
her. bringing a Certificat. yt she is alyve. So yt
is Sr. yt my attendance heere at the Courte is so
Requisite as I can not have as yet any spare tyme
to come to London. for the Receipt of the same.
But this is most hartely to desyre you. to accept of the
Certificat under my hand. as you have verye frendlye
done heeretofore. And to deliver unto ye partye yt shall
Bring the same unto you (wch I thinke wilbe the
gentlewoman her selfe) suche somme as is now dew.
And you shall ever Commande me. in any thing wherein
I may pleasure you. or any frend of yours. whilst I lyve.
And thus with my verye hartye Commendations. I
Comit you to God. fro the Courte this xxvijth of
octobre. 15[illegible]

Yo assured poore frend to Comande
William Byrde

Holograph letter written by Byrd to William Petre

Baird writes that he was

lodged with one Patrick Masons house a notable bold knave by whom I understood many matters and among the rest, of one Hill a seaman who cometh shortly from beyond seas and is a co͞mon conveyer of Seminaries in this land. . . . meeting wth one Bird Brother to Bird of the Chappell I understand that M^ris Tregion M^ris Charnock and M^ris Sibile Tregion will be seen at the Court on this day. By whose . . . adventure some good may be done.

Among other people mentioned in this letter are Phillips, who is described in another letter from Baird to Jones as 'Tregion's man'; and 'John Currye who useth about Hogsdon (Hoxton) n^r London . . . an accomplese of John Cornelius lately taken'. The Tregions and Charnocks were well-known Catholic families.

Among the *Cecil Papers* at Hatfield[1] is a statement made in French by one Charles de Ligny to Sir Thomas Parry, the English ambassador in Paris. This manuscript is undated, but Mr. Salisbury, who edited these Papers for the Historical MSS. Commission, gave reasons for assigning it to November 1605.

De Ligny stated that a certain Jesuit, named Dr. Noiriche, came to England in the suite of the Vice-Admiral. Subsequently he was taken to a house some distance from London, where he found Garnet in company with several Jesuits and gentlemen who were playing music. Among them was Mr. William Byrd, who played the organs and many other instruments. Fearing for his safety among such people he took leave of them. Shortly after this, being lodged near the Tower at the sign of the Fleur-de-Lys, he was arrested on account of certain Papistical books in his possession, written by William Byrd and dedicated to 'Seigneur Henry Howardo', Earl of Northampton and a member of the Privy Council. De Ligny soon afterwards left England for Paris.

'The Papistical books' mentioned by de Ligny must have been the part-books of the first book of *Gradualia*, published early in the same year (1605) and dedicated to Lord Northampton.

'Garnet' was, no doubt, Father Henry Garnett.

[1] Vol. 191 (147) quoted here by kind permission of the Marquis of Salisbury.

The Records of the Archdeaconry of Essex, now kept at Chelmsford, show that throughout the period of Byrd's residence at Stondon he and his family were regularly presented as recusants. They seem, in fact, to have been more stubborn in their attitude here than at Harlington, where, it will be remembered, Byrd himself was but rarely named.

The earliest entry is in 1595, when a statement of the Churchwardens to the Archdeacon reads: 'We answere that Mr W Bird and his wife his son and his wife and his two daughters doe not and have not come to õr Churche since they came to õr pish to dwell.'[1]

Several similar entries cccur from time to time in the Archdeacon's Registers. For instance, in 1603 we read 'Stondon Massie: Willielmum Byrde generosum et eius uxorem Presentat for not receyvinge the communion and for not cominge to Churche. Christopherum Byrde generosum et eius uxorem simile. Mariam Byrde simile.'[2]

On 11 May 1605 the Archdeacon cited the whole of the Byrd family in a very informing minute of unusual length:[3]

Willimũ Bird et Eleñã eius ux̃ psentat for Popishe Recusants he is a gentleman of the Kings Maties Chapell and as the minister and churchwardens doe heare the said Willm̃ Birde with the asistance of one Gabriel Colford who is nowe at Antwerp hath byn the Chiefe and principall seducer of John Wright sonne and heire of John Wright of Kelvedon in Essex gent and of Anne Wright the daughter of the said John Wright thelder. And the said Ellen Birde as it is reported and as her servants have confessed have appoynted busines on the Saboth daye for her servants of purpose to keepe them from Churche and hath also done her best indeavour to seduce Thoda Pigbone her nowe mayde servant to drawe her to poperie as the mayd hath confessed And besids hath drawen her mayde servants from tyme to tyme these 7 yeres from cominge to Churche and the said Ellen refuseth conference and the minister and Churchwardens have not as yet spoke with the said Wm Birde because he is from home—and they have been excommunicate these 7 yeares.

Xpofer̃ Bird et Catherine eius ux psentat for popishe Recusants they doe utterlye refuse conference and they have stood excom-

---

[1] Chelmsford Diocesan Registry. Essex Archidiaconal Records. E. 36. fo. 124.
[2] Ibid. E. 26. fo. 292.   [3] Ibid. E. 27. fo. 136ᵛ.

municate these 7 yeares and they are maynteyned as the minister and Churchwardens doe Thinke by the said Wm Birde.

Thomas Bird Psentat for a popishe Recusant he hath stood excommunicate these 7 yeares and is manteyned as the minister and churchwardens doe thinke at the charges of the said Wm Birde & he doth resorte often tymes to the house of the said Willm Birde

Mariam Birde simile

Elizabetha Jackson viduã simile

Catherina Hooke ux Johñis Hooke ab Stanford Ryvers simile

The Wrights were seated for many years at Kelvedon Hall and were near neighbours of the Byrds. Thoda Pigbone is evidently to be identified with Rhoda Pickbone, as she is called elsewhere in the Archdeacon's Registers in association with one of the Kelvedon Hall servants. Byrd at this date seems to have been supporting the whole of his family at Stondon Place, including his son and his wife, his widowed daughter, and his other married daughter and her husband. The mention of Catherine Hooke is clearly in error for Rachel, whose first husband was John Hooke. This entry in the Registers supplies his Christian name, which was otherwise unknown, and the fact that he came from the neighbouring village of Stanford Rivers.

Later in this same year, 1605, there is mention in the Registers of Byrd and 'his wief'; but this is the last time her name occurs, and as it is known that she predeceased her husband it seems more than likely that she died in 1605 or 1606.[1]

Byrd's name continued to be mentioned frequently. For example, in 1612 it is stated that 'Wyllyam Byrd gent hath been a recusant a long tyme no less than xvj yeares as the churchwardens doe thinke'. In the same year he was presented 'for that he will not paye to the rate for his land lyinge in the parish to the reparations of the Churche and bells which some is xx^s.'[2]

In 1615, when Byrd was again presented, his daughter-in-law Catherine was described as a widow, showing that his son Christopher died before that date.[3]

---

[1] *The Essex Review*, Oct. 1923, article on Byrd by E. H. L. Reeve.

[2] Ibid.

[3] Chelmsford Diocesan Registry, Essex Archidiaconal Records E. 51. fo. 150^v.

We have thus a continuous record to show that throughout his life Byrd remained consistently true to his personal convictions on religious matters. Musicians of all schools of religious thought to-day may rejoice that he suffered so little molestation from the authorities, and especially that his musical work was so little disturbed. As a composer of Church music, quite apart from his secular and instrumental works, he has provided churchmen of all Christian denominations with music of the very highest quality. Other composers of his day wrote Masses and Latin Motets that are comparable with those of Byrd; but none of these produced also such splendid examples of Anglican Church music as he did: to mention only his 'Great' Service, his 'Short' Service, and such anthems as 'This day Christ was born', 'Sing joyfully', and 'Praise our Lord all ye Gentiles'. True, as he was, to the older traditions of the Church, his mind was above controversy. For him the beauty of Christian worship, as adorned with music, knew no limitations as defined by this or that phase of doctrine. It is for this reason that Byrd's Church music, both Latin and English, so nobly achieves its purpose.

CHAPTER IV

THE MASSES

THE term 'Tudor', as applied to a particular school of English musical composition, has in recent years come into very general usage. It has met with such universal acceptance that it is not to be suggested here that it should be superseded or displaced. Yet it is misleading that any single term should be employed to cover so long a period when it is realized what immense developments in the art of music took place within its limits. For it is scarcely going beyond the mark to say that the progress made between the time when Robert Fairfax reached manhood and the date of the death of Orlando Gibbons was quite as great as that made in the century and a half that followed, even though that period extends as far as the days of Haydn and Mozart.

The Tudor dynasty of the English monarchy is measured from the accession of Henry VII until the death of Queen Elizabeth; and since in music, as in literature and architecture, the style which characterized the work of the closing decade of Elizabeth's reign survived throughout the reign of the Stuart king James, and even beyond it, it has become customary, regardless of strict accuracy, to extend the use of the term Tudor to the music of such composers as Orlando Gibbons and Thomas Tomkins; and indeed much of the work of Wilbye and Dowland, to mention no others, belongs to the reign of James I. Tomkins, moreover, lived on until the period of the Commonwealth, writing music in the true Elizabethan manner until his enforced retirement from Worcester Cathedral in the Civil War.

Consideration of these facts leads to the conclusion that the period to be dealt with is not in reality that which is defined by the limits of the Tudor dynasty, even if that is permitted to include the reign of James I, but rather the period that lies between the two devastating Civil Wars; that is to say between 1485, when the battle of Bosworth

Field brought victory and the throne of England to the Tudor king Henry VII, and 1642, the date of the battle of Edgehill, which opened the armed conflict which was to cost King Charles I his life and throne. It was in this period that medieval England came to an end and modern England was evolved.

This fundamental change can be seen as clearly in the realm of music as in other branches of art and culture. And in all its aspects it can be attributed to two outstanding influences: firstly, the spread of the Renaissance movement to England, and secondly, the policy of Henry VII, which had such a stimulating effect upon the middle classes of the community. As regards music this last was perhaps the more powerful influence of the two, for it led to a growing taste for good music on the part of the laity; and it was the secularization of music that constitutes such a conspicuous feature of its progress in the sixteenth century.

In the closing years of the fifteenth century Robert Fairfax was the pre-eminent figure of musical England. He wrote no music of any importance except for the Church, and this bears the distinct stamp of medievalism. He and his contemporaries, for instance, were only then beginning to discard that principle of musical structure which depended upon the employment of a plainsong melody laid out in long notes in one of the voice-parts, while the composer exhibited his skill and taste in ornamenting this melody with other voice-parts, introducing fragments of it with contrapuntal devices, and in various ways weaving round it a texture of combined sounds that should produce a pleasurable effect upon a listener. This was essentially a medieval idea. It is true that Byrd occasionally worked upon this very principle, but it is not suggested that even he completely freed himself from medievalism.

A generation later than Fairfax came John Taverner, who was selected by Cardinal Wolsey to be the first organist of Christ Church, Oxford. Taverner was in reality the last of the English medieval composers. That he was also the greatest of these is frankly admitted. As was stated in the detailed survey of this period which was printed in the Carnegie edition of *Tudor Church Music*,[1] 'he sums up all

[1] Vol. i, Preface, xxiv.

the qualities of his precursors and contemporaries and expresses all their ideals. Where they were bold, he is bolder; where they were skilful, he shows more skill; where they spoke clearly, his voice is clearer yet.' Nevertheless, a glance at any page, chosen at random from Taverner's work and compared with that of Byrd, chosen alike at haphazard, will at once reveal the cleavage between the medieval and the modern. Just as Taverner is the last of the medieval composers, so Byrd is first of the moderns; not modern in the sense that we use the word in relation to twentieth-century music, but none the less he does belong to the modern world; Byrd's vocal music can be performed to-day without explanation or apology both in the church and on the concert platform.

When Henry VII was proclaimed king the art of musical composition still belonged exclusively, or nearly so, to the Church. When Byrd died secular music had not only come to birth, but in some directions it had reached maturity. It had found its highest form of expression in the madrigal; keyboard music, chamber-music for stringed instruments, and the solo art-song had been evolved, while the earliest experiments in the direction of opera were being made; the violin, viola, violoncello had reached perfection in design[1] and were superseding the viol family. Some of these developments were being carried still further before the Civil War broke out. The progress since the end of the Wars of the Roses had been immense, and it becomes abundantly clear, when we contemplate it, that in England, at least, during that period the gulf between medieval and modern music had been bridged.

Byrd himself played a great part in this story of progress; for whereas Fairfax, Taverner, Tye, Tallis, Marbeck, and Robert White in succession were almost exclusively Church musicians, Byrd explored and excelled in every branch of composition known in his day, both sacred and secular, while in the realm of instrumental music he ventured into entirely new fields. As a Church musician he was even greater than the rest, but he has a further claim to supremacy for the versatility with which his gifts were used, and for the genius which enabled him to extend so

[1] Andrea Amati was making perfect violins as early as 1565.

widely the scope of musical composition. It is this that especially distinguishes him as the first of the moderns.

Nevertheless, Byrd's finest work was that which he wrote for the Latin rites of the Church, and it is that branch of his music which claims first consideration. He had the good fortune to be born at a most favourable moment in relation to the development of the polyphonic style of composition as applied to the Mass and the Motet. At the date of the Council of Trent Byrd was just twenty years old. The famous decree issued by that Council in 1563 had practically ruled out of use most of the music which had been written up to that time for the Latin rites of the Church. The reason for this drastic resolution was that it had been a common practice to build up a piece of Church music, and more especially the music of the Mass, upon some well-known popular melody treated as a canto fermo. These melodies were usually those of secular songs and were often associated with words of a light or even frivolous nature. A good instance of such use of a popular tune is to be seen in Taverner's 'Western Wynde' Mass, in which the tune is repeated over and over again in all the sections of the Mass. It can cause no surprise in these circumstances that the ecclesiastical authorities took drastic steps to deal with what amounted to a serious abuse.

A few years before the issue of this decree, and before Marcellus became Pope, Palestrina had written the Mass now known as *Missa Papae Marcelli*. This Mass was produced in accordance with the expressed views of Marcellus with whom Palestrina was at that time closely associated; and incidentally its style was in conformity with the decree which was subsequently issued, but not, as so often stated, as a result of it. It set a new standard and served as a model for all future work of this nature.

When Byrd first set himself to compose music for the Mass this new model had established itself; for, unlike the English composers of a century earlier, who showed a definite unwillingness to profit from the successful efforts of the Netherland musicians in the direction of new developments, Byrd was wise enough to take advantage of the lead which Palestrina had given to Church musicians of all nationalities, and to follow his methods of construction.

Byrd composed no more than three Masses, as far as is known. These were published in his lifetime, but no title-page exists in the few rare exemplars that have survived, and in consequence no exact date can be assigned to them. That they should have been published at all at this period is no small wonder.

It is possible that no publisher could have dared to issue them under the title of *Masses*, or even to associate his name with their publication. It is strange that, whereas all the music-books printed at this period were registered, in accordance with regulations, in the books of the Stationers' Company, a careful search of the registers reveals no entry referring to Byrd's Masses. That they were printed in England is beyond doubt. That they were printed by Thomas East is practically certain, as may be judged by the type employed, and more particularly by the elaborate initial letters which are identical with those which East used in printing Yonge's *Musica Transalpina* in 1588.

In 1609 East published a sheet Catalogue of *Musick bookes printed in England*. Rimbault knew of a copy,[1] but unfortunately none can be found to-day; neither can Clavel's catalogue be found, which, according to Rimbault, was issued in 1675 and incorporated East's list. Playford also published a similar catalogue about 1650,[2] and in it Byrd's three Masses are mentioned under the title of 'Kirries'. No dates of publication or names of publishers are given in this catalogue, but it may fairly be assumed that the 'Kirries' were found by Playford in East's Catalogue of 1609.

An earlier list of East's musical publications is recorded in the Stationers' Registers, dated 6 December 1596.[3] This includes Byrd's four important sets issued in 1588, 1589, and 1591, but not the Masses.

H. B. Collins drew attention to the fact that in his four sets just mentioned Byrd employed the half-circle as the time-signature, and that this is also found in the three-part and four-part Masses.[4] In the five-part Mass the barred half-circle is used, and this is also employed by Byrd in

---

[1] Rimbault's *Bibliotheca Madrigaliana*, p. 14.
[2] B.M., Harl. MS. 5936, no. 421.
[3] Arber's *Transcript of the Stationers' Registers*, iii. 76.
[4] *Mus. Assoc. Proceedings*, 39th Session p. 7.

the two books of *Gradualia* and the *Psalms, Songs,* and *Sonnets* of 1611. Mr. Collins tentatively put forward the inference that the first two Masses belonged to the 1588–91 period and the five-part Mass to the 1605–11 period.

The complete text of the three-part Mass is to be found in Baldwin's manuscript in the Royal Collection, now in the British Museum. This is dated 1603.

The most probable suggestion is that all the three Masses were issued in conjunction with the first book of *Gradualia* in 1605. After James I had succeeded Elizabeth there was a better prospect of such a publication being permitted; and, indeed, the publication of so distinctively a Catholic collection of motets as the two books of *Gradualia* would probably have been impossible during the reign of the Queen. But even so, a separate . title-page, announcing music for the celebration of the Mass, might have involved too grave a risk. On 1 January 1605 'Master Easte' registered with the Stationers[1] 'A sett of songes called Gradualia ac Cantiones sacrae' by Byrd. Could the Masses have been included in this set, thinly disguised under the title of *Cantiones Sacrae?* No exemplar of the first edition of the first book of *Gradualia* is known to exist. In the year of its publication the Gunpowder Plot resulted in more stringent measures against the Catholics. It may perhaps be inferred that the *Gradualia* and the Masses were consequently suppressed, but that a few copies of the Masses survived to be bound up eventually with the second edition of the two books of *Gradualia*, both of which were published in 1610; for the British Museum exemplar is not alone among the rare survivors that have been found bound up in this manner.

The three Masses are of the highest quality and must be considered here in some detail. The three-part work is marked throughout by simpler treatment than the other two. It opens with the threefold *Kyrie eleison*. It is noteworthy that in all three Masses Byrd set the *Kyrie* to music, for this was not the usual practice, especially before his day. For example, there is no *Kyrie* in any of the settings of Taverner, Tallis, Tye, or Robert White.

This short setting of the *Kyrie* is of much beauty, although

[1] Arber, op. cit. iii. 279.

it is of extreme simplicity and brevity. Beginning in the key of F it closes in A.

The *Gloria in excelsis* is planned for the most part in short isolated sections, punctuated with a minim rest in all three voices before the succeeding sections open with homophonic phrases. The lowest of the three parts in this Mass seems to have been intended for a tenor or a high baritone voice, the middle voice being too high in places for a tenor; for both these parts are occasionally taken to a very high range if assigned to tenors and basses. Yet Byrd was evidently thinking of his voices as being in their high register at the words 'Domine Deus rex coelestis', where the lowest voice sings with great effect:

and again

A very similar treatment of the three voices is to be seen in the *Credo* at the words 'et ascendit in coelum'. After some imitative counterpoint at the words 'cum sancto spiritu' and 'in gloria Dei patris', the concluding 'Amen' is set with a rich flowing phrase for the tenor and baritone, while the alto sustains a single note and then takes up the baritone phrase in the final cadence. The 'Amen' seems closely to anticipate the *Sanctus* of this Mass.

The *Credo*, like the *Gloria in excelsis*, is divided into very clearly defined sections, similarly punctuated with a minim rest; the sections, however, are of greater length, and the use of homophonic phrases is reserved for passages which they are intended to enforce with special emphasis, for instance, such points in the *Credo* as 'et in unum Dominum'; 'et iterum venturus est'; and 'Qui cum patre et filio'. Byrd's artistry is well illustrated in his handling of the section 'Et incarnatus est', where, having just closed a florid passage with the chord of F major, he passes simply to B flat, employing an E flat with telling effect in the tenor part on the third syllable of the word 'incarnatus', and subsequently one in the baritone. This particular note is introduced again with similar value in the succeeding phrase 'ex Maria Virgine', and nowhere else in the whole of the Mass, with the sole exception of the *Agnus Dei*, where again its telling effect is enhanced by the composer's art in keeping it in reserve for such purposes.

A characteristic example of word-painting is to be found at the words 'qui ex patre filioque procedit', where two voices alone are employed following each other in canonical style though not actually in canon. Many lesser composers with this idea in their minds would have carried it out in strict academic form. 'Qui cum patre et filio', as already mentioned, follows this phrase, by contrast, note against note; and the triple rhythm is suggestive of the Trinity in Unity:

The *Sanctus*, in comparison with the other numbers in this Mass, is elaborated at rather greater length. The triple repetition of the word is expressed in phrases of great splendour and dignity. The rest of this number is treated with various contrapuntal imitations working up to a fine climax, with the concluding 'Osanna in excelsis' much reinforced by the use of shorter notes and the high range of the lower voices.

The *Benedictus* is simple in character and quite short. The *Agnus Dei* opens with the same phrase as the *Benedictus*. The purposeful employment of E flat in this number has already been mentioned. It adds poignancy to the 'miserere nobis' and also to the beautiful passage which the tenor voice sings in the third *Agnus Dei*.

The four-part Mass is constructed upon a more developed scheme. The *Kyrie* is, in fact, the most extended of Byrd's three settings of this number. The repetitions within the limits of each of the three sections suggest that the composer was regarding this as a ninefold rather than as a threefold setting of the *Kyrie*. In each section a simple short phrase is employed as the foundation of the whole structure; this is repeated in the various voice-parts while more elaborate counter-subjects are embroidered upon it in imitative style.

The third section closes with an extended melismatic passage, which rounds off the whole number with a true sense of balance, while the soprano voice sings the original simple phrase in the dominant key.

The *Gloria in excelsis* opens with the two top voices alone, and the phrases that follow are given to the four voices answering each other in pairs. Throughout this number Byrd secures and maintains interest by the variety with which he groups the voices. From 'Domine Deus' down to 'deprecationem nostram' he uses only three voices at a time: first the alto, tenor, and bass; then the soprano, alto, and bass; and lastly the soprano, tenor, and bass. Both the rhythmic and melodic treatment of 'tu solus altissimus' and 'cum sancto spiritu' are somewhat reminiscent of the setting of these passages in the three-part Mass. The modulations in this number are of some interest. Beginning in G minor, a full close in C major is reached at 'glorificamus te'. At 'pater omnipotens' there is a full close in F major, and at 'Jesu Christe' the music has modulated to D major. Starting afresh in the original key of G minor, F major is once more reached, and in the main this key prevails for a long period until 'tu solus Dominus'; ultimately it reaches the dominant, D major, at 'Jesu Christe', to close with a plagal cadence in G major.

As is the case with every number in this Mass except the *Sanctus*, the *Credo* opens with the soprano and alto voices alone. Subsequently the four voices are employed almost continuously, except in two passages where special emphasis is secured by the use of three. The first of these is at 'Qui propter homines'. This passage opens effectively in B flat major following a full close in D major. Here the composer introduces a characteristic touch of realism in a melismatic phrase representing flight as that of a bird, with its waving rise and fall in the process of descent.

de - scen - dit   de   coe - - - - - - - - - - - - - lis

This phrase is imitated in the bass voice-part.

The *Crucifixus* is the other passage written for only three voices, the bass being silent here. Byrd secures the necessary solemnity at this point by using the voices homophonically as far as the word 'Pilatus'; and at the cadence on the word 'nobis' a special effect is produced by the three voices singing the note D unharmonized at the three different octaves. Throughout his work Byrd showed wonderful resource in employing subtle touches of this character.

'Et unam sanctam' is set with great vigour:

The *Sanctus* opens with phrases of beautiful outline, taken up by all four voices in turn. These phrases are not unlike those of the *Sanctus* in the three-part Mass. At the words 'pleni sunt coeli' the bass voice remains silent, so that it comes in with added force in the final 'Osanna', where it leads a series of strong phrases working up to a noble climax with which this movement ends. The 'Osanna' in the *Benedictus* is different in character, and it concludes in a rather more florid style.

The *Agnus Dei* is of wonderful beauty. The opening passage is identical with that of the *Gloria*. The two voices in duet finish the first 'miserere' with a poignant phrase on D an octave apart; and while these notes are sustained the tenor breaks in with F and the bass follows with B flat.

In the second 'miserere' there is a striking sequential passage for the bass voice:

The first *Agnus* having been set for two voices, and the second for three only, all four voices join in the third *Agnus* with rather more florid material; and this adds a feeling of insistence to the repeated petition. The concluding bars of this Mass are among the most beautiful in the whole realm of music; they give the impression towards the end of being written on a dominant pedal, owing to the frequent sustained use of D in the bass voice. The final cadence, closing in G major, is of supreme loveliness.

Although there is reason for supposing that the five-part Mass is a later work than the other two, yet it is somewhat more modal in character than these. The opening of each movement, which is almost identical throughout the work with the exception of the *Sanctus* and *Benedictus*, has a decidedly modal flavour.

The three sections of the *Kyrie* are treated without much elaboration, and the sequence of keys gives a perfect sense of balance. The first section begins in D minor, ending with the conventional 'tierce de Picardy'. The second opens in B flat and closes in G. The third is slightly longer; it opens also in B flat; then it passes through G to D, to close with a plagal cadence in A.

Throughout the *Gloria* the voices are grouped with much variety. After the opening sentence the short verbal phrases are handled compactly with varying vocal combinations, all five voices entering homophonically after a minim rest at the words 'Gratias agimus'. 'Domine Deus' is similarly punctuated a few bars later. The section extending from 'Domine Deus, Agnus dei' down to 'deprecationem nostram' is varied with groups of three voices; and only four are employed for 'qui sedes' down to 'miserere nobis'. This arrangement adds great force to the entry of the full chorus at the words 'Quoniam tu solus'.

The texture of the *Credo* is more closely woven; there are fewer clear-cut cadences here than in the *Gloria*, but the grouping of the voices is again handled with variety and good effect. The section 'Qui propter nos homines' is for alto, 2nd tenor, and bass. It opens in F, following a full close in A major. This passage is treated simply in contrapuntal style, with some diatonic runs in tenths between the alto and bass voices at 'de coelis', which, by contrast, give solemnity to the more sustained notes at the words 'et incarnatus est'. This section is sung by another group of three voices. At 'Crucifixus' all the voices combine in D minor, moving to a cadence in B flat. Great vigour is infused into 'et resurrexit', not only by means of the crisp melodic phrases with which the passage opens, but still more by the quick changes of key. Following a cadence in D major, the modulations run rapidly through G, B flat, F, and A, ultimately arriving at a full close in C major at the word 'patris'. The little realistic touch in introducing a triple measure for the words 'tertia die' may also be noticed. A splendid climax to this entire section of the *Credo* is achieved at 'non erit finis'.

Byrd then reverts to his groupings of three voices, reserving the full strength of the choir for 'et unam sanctam Catholicam et Apostolicam ecclesiam'; and from here to the end of the movement full pressure is sustained with a vigorous climax, close imitations being rapidly taken up from part to part at the final phrase 'et vitam venturi saeculi'. A short but beautiful 'Amen' follows.

The opening of the *Sanctus* is built upon a phrase of three long notes, given in turn to each of the voices, and ornamented by contrapuntal phrases in the other voices. The *Benedictus* is quite short, and the 'Osanna' is identical with that of the *Sanctus*.

As in the four-part Mass, the *Agnus Dei* excels all the other movements in beauty. The three sections are treated quite distinctly; the first is given to three voices, the second to four, and the full complement of five is reserved for the third, and final, section. An unusual dissonance, characteristic of Byrd's work, occurs in the second section, where the alto voice holds an F in suspension against the E in the bass:

The closing passages are of entrancing loveliness. The key of F major here brings a sense of absolute repose, with F reiterated in long notes in the bass. The modulations then pass to D minor, A major, and D major. Instead of being reserved in the conventional manner for the final chord, the 'tierce de Picardy' is employed in the penultimate cadence, which is authentic, thus enhancing the beauty of the concluding bars and the final plagal cadence.

CHAPTER V

THE CANTIONES SACRAE

THE publication by Tallis and Byrd jointly of a set of *Cantiones Sacrae* in 1575 was an interesting venture. Very little music had been printed in England before that date, apart from early missals by Pynson and others at the beginning of the sixteenth century. In 1530 Wynkyn de Worde produced a set of songs of which the Bassus part alone survives. In 1560 John Daye published his *Certaine Notes*, containing English Anthems and Services, and these were followed by Daye with Versions of the Psalms. In 1571 Thomas Whythorne's *Songes of three, fower and five voices* were issued. These publications alone preceded the Tallis and Byrd set of *Cantiones Sacrae*, which were the first Latin motets to be printed in England. It is remarkable that a set of Latin motets should have been issued at this date, when the use of the reformed Liturgy had become securely established while the Latin rites had been made illegal. It is more remarkable still that Queen Elizabeth should have accepted the dedication of them. Yet it will be noticed that these motets were carefully chosen as having no reference to anything that could offend the strictest Reformer; even Tallis's *O sacrum convivium* was no exception to this.

The full title of the work was: 'Cantiones, Quae ab | Argumento Sacrae Vocantur, | Quinque et Sex Partium, Autoribus | Thoma Tallisio & Guilielmo Birdo Anglis, Serenis|simae Regineae Maiestati a priuato Sacello ge|nerosis, & Organistis. | Cum Privilegio | Excudebat Thomas Vautrollerius typographus Lon|dinensis in claustro vulgo Blackfriers | commorans, | 1575.'

The prefatory matter is more lengthy than was usual in such publications. An anonymous set of ten Latin elegiac verses, headed 'De Anglorum Musica', follows the title-page. The long Latin dedication to Queen Elizabeth bears the signature of 'Tho. Tall. & Guil. Birdus', and this was, no doubt, their own composition. As stated in a former chapter, they speak in terms of high praise of the Queen's skill and taste in music; and when due allowance has been made for the flattery that came inevitably from two members of her 'Chappell', it is probable that Elizabeth inherited her father's gifts and was no mean musician.

Two very long sets of Latin elegiacs are added. Richard Mulcaster wrote 'In Musicam Thomae Tallisii, et Guilielmi Birdi'. He too praised the Queen as:

> aetatis gloria nostrae . . .
> Nec contenta graues aliorum audire labores
> Ipsa etiam egregie voce manuque canit.[1]

The second set was by Ferdinand Richardson 'In eandem Thomae Tallisii et Guilielmi Birdi Musicam'. It is this set of verses that contains the lines quoted in a former chapter,[2] mentioning Tallis as the veteran musician and Byrd his pupil.

At the end of the set are six lines of Latin elegiacs addressed to the Reader: 'Autores Cantionum ad Lectorem'. These are followed by 'The Extract and Effect of the Quenes Maiesties letters patents to Thomas Tallis and William Birde, for the printing of musicke'.

As being the joint production of two composers, this book of *Cantiones* resembles the book of *Ayres* which Rosseter and Campian published at a later date; but whereas the songs of these last-named were printed in separate sections, the motets of Tallis and Byrd were mixed up, for the most part, in groups of three. There are thirty-four motets in the set, seventeen by each composer; but some of these are designed in two or more sections which are separately indexed in the original edition.

Eleven of Byrd's motets in this set are for six voices; one is for eight, and the remainder are for five voices.

The first of Byrd's motets in this book, *Emendemus in melius*, is among the most beautiful of all that he wrote. It is comparable with his *Ave verum*, *Justorum animae*, and the *Agnus Dei* of the four- and five-part Masses. Like the

---

[1] 'The glory of our age . . . not content with listening to the serious performances of others, she sings quite exceptionally both with voice and hand.'
[2] p. 2.

Ave verum it is almost entirely homophonic in design, and each short sentence is self-contained. Its beauty lies mainly in a wonderful succession of simple chords. The opening of the second section in E flat after the close in G major agrees exactly with the spirit of the words, which changes at this point from penitence to pleading: Adiuva nos, Deus; with a sure hope of salvation: Deus, salutaris noster. And here Byrd has a splendidly strong cadence in C major to express this confidence.

Ad - iu - va nos, De - - us, sa - lu - ta - ris no - - - ster.

The next cadence is even more beautiful at the word 'honorem':

ho - - no - - - - - rem

Siderum rector (No. 19) is another of this set constructed on simple lines. It is classified as a hymn in the original edition. The melody is given to the soprano in the first verse, and it is transferred to the tenor for the second verse. This is a very effective little work and not difficult.

Both *Attollite portas* (No. 11) and *Laudate pueri* (No. 17) are vigorous and bright in character. In *Attollite portas* Byrd secures much variety by the contrasted grouping of the voices. At 'Quis est ipse Rex gloriae?' he repeated the phrase three times in different keys, using three different pairs of voices. An English version of this motet is found in early manuscripts at Durham and Peterhouse, Cambridge, among Byrd's special 'Preces and Psalms for Ascension Day at Evensong'. This English version was almost certainly made in Byrd's lifetime, but the underlaying of the English words as found in these manuscripts is not wholly satisfactory. The words of *Laudate pueri* are chosen from three different psalms. This motet is constructed in three separate sections, the music of each of which is repeated though the words run on. In each repeated section the two altos and the two basses inter-change parts. The third section is constructed on a simple phrase, very similar to the opening of the canon *Non nobis*, although there is no reason whatever to connect the two. It is a phrase that might be found anywhere in any composer's work:

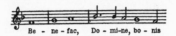

Be - ne - fac, Do - mi-ne, bo - nis

Another example of coincidence in musical phrases occurs in *Libera me, Domine*, Byrd's second motet in this set, where the bass has a phrase identical with that in Morley's *It was a lover and his lass*:

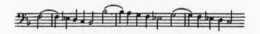

The remarkable canons in *O lux beata Trinitas* (No. 12), *Miserere mihi* (No. 29), and *Diliges Dominum* (No. 25) will be more fully discussed in a later chapter dealing with other compositions of this type. The composers of this period, especially those on the Continent, were fond of displaying their skill in this direction by introducing elaborate passages in strict canon. The last number in this book, *Miserere nostri*, by Tallis, is a typical example of a display of academic skill in intricate canonical composition. Byrd's skill in this matter was unsurpassed; and no doubt as a young man, no more than thirty-two years of age at this date, he felt the desire to demonstrate his ability to compete with the rest on these lines. But even the best canons are not wholly free from academic flavour, and Byrd's riper judgement in later years evidently revealed this fact more clearly to his mind; for, although his marvellous contrapuntal skill enabled him to handle all manner of imitative devices with fluent ease, yet he seldom introduced passages of any length in strict canon after 1575.

Any comparison of Byrd's work at this date with what he wrote later must necessarily be of a tentative nature, because the style of polyphonic writing in the ninety years that had elapsed since the battle of Bosworth had wellnigh reached its full development, and the subsequent differences are so narrowed down as to be difficult to define. Yet it can be said clearly that the 1575 *Cantiones* do not in a general way compare with Byrd's more mature work. This is not so apparent in those motets of this set which are constructed on simpler lines. *Emendemus in melius* and *Siderum rector*, for example, are of the highest quality of their kind. But in the motets of more ambitious design there is undoubtedly less sureness of touch than is found so conspicuously in most of the subsequent motets. The general appearance of a page of the score of these earlier works offers fewer features to catch the eye than with the later compositions. There are imitative contrapuntal entries without number, it is true, yet the general texture is less varied.

And as regards harmonic treatment, this subject will be more fully discussed in a later chapter; but it may be said here that although Byrd continued to employ unexpected dissonances throughout his life, some of those in these earlier works seem harsher and more experimental in character than those which he wrote in later days. For instance, it would probably be difficult to find in the subsequent books of *Cantiones Sacrae* or the *Gradualia* anything quite so severely dissonant, or an example of such awkward part-writing, as is shown in the following phrases from *Domine, secundum actum meum* (No. 24):

and a few bars later:

The first book of *Cantiones Sacrae* was entitled: 'Liber Primus | Sacrarum Cantio-|num Quinque vocum. | Autore Guilielmo Byrd Organista | Regio, Anglo. | Excudebat Thomas Est ex assigna-|tione Guilielmi Byrd. | Cum privilegio. | Londini. 25. Octob. 1589.'

This book was dedicated to Edward, Earl of Worcester, Byrd's intimate friend and patron. It has been stated in a former chapter that at the time of his death Byrd had a 'lodginge' in Lord Worcester's house in the Strand, furnished with his own belongings. Worcester was ten years younger than Byrd. He succeeded his father as fourth Earl in the year in which this book of *Cantiones* was published. Throughout his life he was a Catholic; yet in 1604 he was placed on the Commission for the expulsion of the Jesuits, and he was one of those who examined the conspirators in the Tower after the Gunpowder Plot. As Byrd's dedication states, he was a man of letters. He graduated M.A. at Oxford in 1592. He was created a Knight of the Garter in 1593. His second daughter, Katherine, married William, son of John, first Lord Petre of Writtle, another Catholic patron of Byrd. Worcester died in 1628.

The dedication, neatly expressed in Latin, was no doubt written by Byrd himself. It is of greater interest than many of the conventional addresses of the period. It should be read in conjunction with the corresponding English address to Sir Christopher Hatton in Byrd's *Psalmes, Sonets and Songs* published a year earlier. Byrd's purpose is stated in both instances in very similar language, and it is made clear that he had accumulated a large number of compositions both Latin and English; also that many were already in circulation in manuscript, and that errors had crept into the text through careless transcription. There was, in fact, such an unsatisfactory medley (*farrago*) ot his works being circulated that he determined, as far as his time would allow, to arrange them in books and publish them.

The four important publications of this period are thus shown to be the outcome of a definite scheme. The *Psalmes, Sonets and Songs* were published in 1588; *Songs of Sundrie natures* in 1589; the first book of *Cantiones Sacrae* in 1589; and the second book of *Cantiones Sacrae* in 1591. It may be inferred that a large number of the compositions in these

four books were already known, even if the text in circulation was often faulty; and, in fact, many of the manuscript
versions of earlier date than the printed books survive to-
day. They must indeed have been widely known, because
Byrd had already established a very great reputation as a
composer as early as 1575.

Byrd's dedication to Lord Worcester opens as follows:

Nonnulli, certa mihi necessitudine coniuncti, solideque existi-
mationis homines, cum nuperrime perspiceret, meas quasdam cantiones Musicas, per scriptorum in delineandis autographis incuriam,
vicii aliquid contraxisse, quod ex nostro Museolo in autographis
minime prorepserat: ut ipsas, sed ad tornum prius redactas & castiga-
tiores iam praelo submitterem, suo tandem rogatu impulerunt.
Caeterum tanta fuit earum farrago, ut ipsam (sicuti per otium licuerit)
in varios libros distribuendam esse duxerim, suisque in lucem tempori-
bus exponendam. Primam itaque partem huius laboris (nobilissime
Comes) Tibi, ut auspicatissimo bonarum litterarum, & virtutis
Patrono ex officio inscribendam putavi.

The rest of the address is concerned with elaborate com-
pliments of a conventional kind, customary at this period.

Since we have Byrd's own authority for stating that the
two books of *Cantiones* represent an orderly collection of
works that had accumulated over a period of years, the
suggestion that this first book reflects the depressed state
of Byrd's mind, caused by the increased misfortunes of
the Catholics at this date, falls to the ground. There are,
it is true, in this first book of *Cantiones* a large proportion
of motets of a penitential character, but there is no reason
to suppose that *Deficit in dolore vita mea*, the opening number, *Vide, Domine, afflictionem meam*, and *Deus, venerunt gentes*
were included by Byrd with any special reference to contemporary events; whereas *In Resurrectione tua*, *O quam
gloriosum*, and *Laetentur coeli* are examples of unrestrained
joy associated with praise and thanksgiving.

There are sixteen complete motets in this set, but seven
of them are laid out in two separate sections, independently
indexed in the original edition. *Tribulationes civitatum* is
divided into three sections and *Deus, venerunt gentes* into
four. As announced on the title-page, all these motets are
for five voices; but Byrd varied his combinations of voices,

although the greater number are for S.A.A.T.B. *Deficit in dolor*, for example, can be effectively sung by men's voices (A.A.T.T.B.) if it is transposed down a tone. Even in the original key the range of the two upper voices is too low for sopranos.

On turning to the 1589 book immediately after studying the 1575 *Cantiones*, even allowing for the fact that some examples from the later book may have been composed quite soon after 1575, the smoothness and precision of the writing clearly reveal a more perfected technique.

The choice of particular motets for special notice here must necessarily be limited. *Tristitia et anxietas* (Nos. 6–7) is a motet of great beauty. A feeling of deep contrition is expressed throughout in a characteristic manner. The treatment of 'Moestum factum est cor meum' is typical of Byrd's work, and the concluding passages of the motet are full of pathos. *Vide Domine* (Nos. 9–10) stands out among the finest things in the set. The subject of this motet is also of a penitential character. It provides a striking example of Byrd's use of modulation. The main key is D minor, but the opening phrases are in D major, soon leading to a close in F major. After passing through B flat, a plagal cadence in E flat is reached which gives a very sombre colouring to the words 'desolata Civitas electa', the chords being very remote from the principal key:

Other interesting details in this motet must be passed over, but the final phrase should be mentioned with its very remarkable cadence, which will be discussed further in a later chapter.[1]

John Alcock, the early-eighteenth-century organist of Lichfield Cathedral, who did fine work in collecting and scoring Church music of the earlier periods, has recorded with reference to *Domine, tu iurasti* (No. 15) that 'This

[1] p. 228.

EDWARD, FOURTH EARL OF WORCESTER, K.G.

Reproduced by permission of the Trustees of the British Museum

Peice in yᵉ opinion of Mʳ Bird himself is yᵉ best he ever Compos'd'.[1] It could be wished that Alcock had given his authority for this statement, for it suggests that some document of rare interest was in his hands. Nevertheless it is difficult to find any special degree of excellence in this motet, and it seems likely that if Byrd left any such comment it may in the process of transcription have become attached to the wrong motet.

Vigilate (No. 16) is characterized by great vigour and a number of touches of realism, notably the imitations on a descending scale passage at the word 'sero'; and the effect of the cock crowing at the phrase 'an galli cantu'. The setting of the words 'Ne venerit repente' gives an impression of breathless haste, by means of the rapid and detached repetition of the word 'repente' in all the voices in close imitation. And finally, by contrast, the syncopated falling scale at the word 'dormientes' inevitably calls to mind the experience of being involuntarily overcome with sleepiness.

The Easter motet *In resurrectione tua* (No. 17) is a short and brilliant piece of work. By the gradual introduction of shorter notes a climax is reached at 'exultet', and this is outdone by the dazzling and complex 'Alleluia' with which the motet concludes. *O quam gloriosum* (Nos. 22–3) has splendid dignity. *Laetentur coeli* (Nos. 28–9) opens very vigorously with a fine example of imitative counterpoint; the word 'exultet' in this motet is treated in precisely the same manner as in *In resurrectione tua*, with identical rhythmic and imitative devices. *Aspice, Domine* (Nos. 18–19) gives the impression of being an earlier work than the rest. It is singular in this book, as being constructed upon a plain-song melody which is placed in the tenor part. There are also some of the severer dissonances in this motet which are reminiscent of the 1575 compositions.

[1] B.M. Add. MS. 23624, fo. 99.

It remains to mention *Ne irascaris* (Nos. 20–21), perhaps to be regarded as the finest piece of the set. It is well known owing to the fact that the second section, *Civitas sancti tui*, in its English version, has a place as a favourite anthem in all English cathedrals. Throughout this motet Byrd secures special effects by the varied distribution and combination of the voices, and more particularly by the occasional use of the three lower voices in low range. For example, he opens with three voices in closely confined harmony, in a very low register; and the phrase is repeated an octave higher, also in three parts. A similar effect is produced, but with four voices, at the words 'Sion deserta facta est'; here he uses the higher voices first, and the lower ones repeat the phrase an octave lower. The E flat chord at the repetition of the word 'deserta' in the low register of the voices produces an effect of utter desolation and despair.

The plaint for 'Jerusalem desolata' increases in intensity and beauty throughout the numerous repetitions of the phrase, reaching its climax in a state of exhausted grief at the final cadence. One very unusual chord occurs in this motet near the beginning of the second section, on the word 'deserta'. The D sharp might have been thought to be a printer's error but for the fact that there are three more examples of this chord to be found in Byrd's two books of *Cantiones Sacrae*,[1] and one in his madrigal *Penelope ever was praised*. Byrd's particular request that the printer was not to be blamed if any unexpected dissonance is found in his work[2] is in itself a valid reason for the opinion that this chord was deliberately introduced in each of these instances.

---

[1] *Tristitia et anxietas*, Bk. I, no. 6; *Domine exaudi*, Bk. II, nos. 10–11 (twice).

[2] Byrd's Epistle to the Reader in *Psalmes, Sonets and Songs* (1588).

Byrd chose Lord Lumley as the patron of his second book of *Cantiones Sacrae*. Lumley was his senior by ten years. He succeeded to the title at the age of three, when his father was executed for taking part in Aske's insurrection. By his marriage to a daughter of Henry, Earl of Arundel, he strengthened his ties with the Catholic party; and with his father-in-law he was deeply implicated in the Ridolfi Plot, with the result that he was imprisoned in the Marshalsea. In later years he was restored to favour, and he entertained Queen Elizabeth at Lewes in 1591, the year in which Byrd's second book was published. Lumley sat on the commission under which William Shelley was indicted for high treason in 1585, thus forming another link with Byrd's personal history.

The book was entitled 'Liber Secundus | Sacrarum Cantionum, | Quarum aliae ad Quinque, aliae verò ad | Sex voces aeditae sunt. | Autore Guilielmo Byrd, Organista | Regio, Anglo. | Excudebat Thomas Este ex assigna-|tione Guilielmi Byrd. | Cum privilegio. | Londini, quarto Novemb. 1591.' It contains thirteen complete motets for five voices, and eight for six voices. Counting the separate sections, as indexed in the original edition, there are thirty-two compositions in all. The second of the three sections of the first motet in the book, for no apparent reason, is not included in the index as an independent number.

The opening number is one of the finest. The words are a free paraphrase of Psalm 150 in Latin elegiac verse. It consists of three sections. A feature of this motet is the frequent use of triple rhythms to give brilliance and force, while the principal measure is square. The opening bars are for three voices only; then the whole choir bursts in with splendid vigour: 'Firmamenta sonent inclyta facta Dei'. In the second section complex triple measures are employed in a characteristic manner, giving tremendous rhythmic vitality to the line 'Laude Dei resonent resonantia tympana summi'.

The climax of the motet is reached in the third section with 'Halleluia canat'. a glorious example of smooth and flowing counterpoint, expressing a joyous outburst of praise.

With a fine sense of proportion Byrd concludes this motet, designed on a larger scale than anything up to that date, and foreshadowing some of the great motets of Bach, with a passage broadened out in long notes. He thus gives massive dignity to the final phrase 'tempus in omne Deo'.

It should be observed that this motet provides one of the rare examples in Byrd's work in which his original notevalues must be retained in a modern edition designed for practical use. Byrd in this instance seems certainly to be writing with the crotchet unit in his mind, rather than that of a minim. *Cantate Domino* (No. 29 in this same book) is another such example.

In *Domine exaudi* (Nos. 10–11) there are the two examples of the use of the augmented sixth referred to in connexion with *Civitas sancti tui* in the first book. *Haec dicit Dominus* (Nos. 13–14) is of a penitential character and very

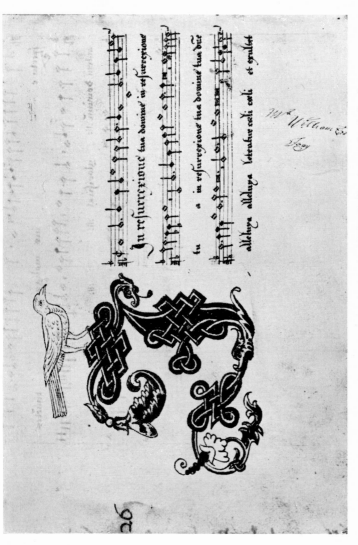

A page from a MS. part-book in the hand of John Sadler (1591), lately in the collection of Miss Willmott

Reproduced by permission of Captain R. G. Berkeley

beautiful. At the original pitch it is perfectly suited to men's voices (A.T.T.B.B.). The chord of E flat at the word 'lamentationis', following a sustained chord of D major, has a remarkable effect; and the succeeding passage, 'Rachael plorantis filios', is an example of Byrd's power of tender expression and pathos such as has, perhaps, never been surpassed by any composer.

Other fine numbers in the five-part section of the book are *Recordare, Domine* (Nos. 17–18), especially the second section, *Exsurge, Domine* (No. 19) and *Miserere mei* (No. 20).

The following passage in *Recordare, Domine* is noticeable as a typical piece of expressive writing, in which the simplicity and dignity of the bass part are conspicuous.

The structure of *Exsurge, Domine* may be analysed as consisting roughly of five short sections, the second and fourth of which are very similar in character: 'et ne repellas me', and 'et tribulationis nostrae'. Both these musical phrases lend themselves very easily to contrapuntal treatment, and Byrd seems for once to have been tempted to prolong their development unduly; this impression is emphasized owing to the lack of contrast between them. The phrase employed for 'et tribulationis' is very similar to that for 'et animalia' in *O magnum misterium* (*Gradualia*, Bk. II, No. 8), and again for 'prae multitudine iniquitatis' in *Peccavi super numerum* (one of the manuscript motets). This offers one of the very few instances of Byrd repeating himself. Nevertheless, this motet as a whole is saved by the brilliance of the other sections and also by individual vocal phrases, such as:

and the three lower voices are combined in the following phrase:

Miserere mei is a setting of the first verse of Psalm 51. This is one of those pieces which Byrd constructed on a harmonic rather than a contrapuntal plan. The opening passages are definitely homophonic, and the beauty of this short motet lies largely in the succession of keys through which it modulates. Opening in G minor, a half-close in D major is soon reached, to be followed by an authentic cadence in F, and a return to D minor; the first half of the verse ends with a definite close in D major. The second

section opens with another homophonic phrase in B flat
leading to a full close in C major. The final sentence 'dele
iniquitatem meam' is treated contrapuntally, the original
key of G minor being quickly restored.

Passing to the motets for six voices, *Domine, non sum
dignus* (No. 23) is an outstanding piece of writing. The
vocal score (especially in an edition in which the note-
values have been halved) reveals at a glance the intricacy
of the contrapuntal devices and the even distribution of the
part-writing. The subject is the Miracle of the healing of
the nobleman's son. The eager intensity of the man's
appeal is represented in the numerous repetitions of the
word 'Domine' at the outset, and again at 'sed tantum dic
verbum', where the contrapuntal imitations become more
and more complex. The phrase for 'et sanabitur' is stated
first in quick notes, and then in notes double as long,
suggesting a growing confidence in the man's mind that
his pleading would be answered. There is a very surprising
resemblance here to a passage in Brahms's *Requiem*, especially in relation to the syncopations:

Infelix ego (Nos. 24–6) differs from other motets in that
the words are neither biblical nor liturgical. It is of great
length and of a penitential character; it includes some moving passages and has a lovely ending. It was very popular
in Byrd's own time, if we may judge from the fact that it finds
a place in an unusually large number of the early manuscripts.

Many interesting and beautiful features of these motets

must necessarily be passed over within the limits of this chapter, but *Cantate Domino* (No. 29) and *Haec dies* (No. 32) should be mentioned as glorious examples of Byrd's work in his most joyous mood, while *Cunctis diebus* (No. 30) and *Domine, salva nos* (No. 31) are profound expressions of penitence and prayer. *Domine, salva nos* is an exceptionally fine specimen of six-part counterpoint, full of variety and interest quite apart from its special ingenuity. The repetitions of the words 'perimus' and 'impera' should not pass unnoticed.

Haec dies, with which this book concludes, is an Easter Day motet. Byrd wrote three motets beginning with these words, although only two of them have identical text. This is the most brilliant of the three. The splendid 'Alleluia' with which it concludes is built up upon a fivefold repetition of what in later years came to be known as a 'Rosalia' sequence, in the bass voice. The 'Rosalia' sequence derives its name from an old Italian song beginning 'Rosalia mia cara', which was constructed on the principle of repeating a short musical phrase each time one degree higher in the scale. Schumann was fond of these sequences, and they are to be found in the works of Handel, Mozart, and Beethoven. Examples of fivefold repetitions are rare, but there is a sixfold 'Rosalia' sequence in the *Sanctus* of Taverner's *Small Devotion* Mass, and even an eightfold sequence in the same composer's *Gloria tibi Trinitas* Mass.

Cantiones Quae ab Argumento Sacrae Vocantur

1575

4.	Emendemus in melius	. . .	.	5 voc.
5. {	Libera me, Domine, et pone. 1 *pars.*		.	5 voc.
	Dies mei transierunt. 2 *pars.*			
6.	Peccantem me quotidie	. . .	.	5 voc.
10.	Aspice, Domine, quia facta	. .	.	6 voc.
11.	Attollite portas	. . .	.	6 voc.
12 {	O lux beata Trinitas. 1 *pars.*	. .	.	6 voc.
	Te mane laudem carmine. 2 *pars.*	.		
	Deo Patri sit gloria. 3 *pars.*	. .		

17. Laudate, pueri, Dominum . . . 6 voc.
18. Memento homo quod cinis es . . . 6 voc.
19. Siderum rector . . . . . 5 voc.
23. Da mihi auxilium . . . . . 6 voc.
24. ⎰ Domine, secundum actum meum. 1 *pars* . 6 voc.
    ⎱ Ideo deprecor. 2 *pars*.
25. Diliges Dominum . . . . . 8 voc.
29. Miserere mihi, Domine . . . . 6 voc.
30. Tribue, Domine . . . . . 6 voc.
31. Te deprecor supplico . . . . 6 voc.
32. Gloria Patri, qui creavit . . . . 6 voc.
33. Libera me, Domine, de morte . . . 5 voc.

N.B. The remaining numbers in this book were composed by Tallis and are omitted here.

Contents of the First Book of Cantiones Sacrae
1589

⎰ 1. Defecit in dolore. 1 *pars*.
⎱ 2. Sed tu, Domine, refugium. 2 *pars*.

⎰ 3. Domine, praestolamur. 1 *pars*.
⎱ 4. Veni, Domine. 2 *pars*.

5. O Domine, adiuva me.

⎰ 6. Tristitia et anxietas. 1 *pars*.
⎱ 7. Sed tu, Domine, qui non. 2 *pars*.

8. Memento, Domine.

⎰ 9. Vide, Domine, afflictionem 1 *pars*.
⎱ 10. Sed veni, Domine. 2 *pars*.

⎰ 11. Deus, venerunt gentes. 1 *pars*.
⎜ 12. Posuerunt morticinia. 2 *pars*.
⎜ 13. Effuderunt sanguinem. 3 *pars*.
⎱ 14. Facti sumus opprobrium. 4 *pars*.

15. Domine, tu iurasti.
16. Vigilate, nescitis enim.
17. In resurrexione tua.

⎰ 18. Aspice, Domine, de sede. 1 *pars*.
⎱ 19. Respice, Domine. 2 *pars*.

⎰ 20. Ne irascaris. 1 *pars*.
⎱ 21. Civitas sancti tui. 2 *pars*.

⎰ 22. O quam gloriosum. 1 *pars*.
⎜ 23. Benedictio et claritas. 2 *pars*.
⎜ 24. Tribulationes civitatum. 1 *pars*.
⎜ 25. Timor et hebetudo. 2 *pars*.
⎱ 26. Nos enim pro peccatis. 3 *pars*.

27. Domine, secundum multitudinem.

⎰ 28. Laetentur coeli. 1 *pars*.
⎱ 29. Orietur in diebus. 2 *pars*.

All these are for five voices.

Contents of the Second Book of Cantiones Sacrae
1591

Of Five Voices

1. Laudibus in sanctis. 1 *pars.* Magnificum Domini. 2 *pars.*
2. Hunc arguta. 3 *pars.*
3. Quis est homo. 1 *pars.*
4. Diverte a malo. 2 *pars.*
5. Fac cum servo tuo.
6. Salve Regina. 1 *pars.*
7. Et Jesum benedictum. 2 *pars.*
8. Tribulatio proxima. 1 *pars.*
9. Contumelias et terrores. 2 *pars.*
10. Domine, exaudi orationem. 1 *pars.*
11. Et non intres in iudicium. 2 *pars.*
12. Apparebit in finem.
13. Haec dicit Dominus. 1 *pars.*
14. Haec dicit Dominus. 2 *pars.*
15. Circumdederunt me.
16. Levemus corda nostra.
17. Recordare, Domine. 1 *pars.*
18. Requiescat, Domine. 2 *pars.*
19. Exsurge, Domine.
20. Miserere mei, Deus.

Of Six Voices

21. Descendit de coelis. 1 *pars.*
22. Et exivit per auream portam. 2 *pars.*
23. Domine, non sum dignus.
24. Infelix ego omnium. 1 *pars.*
25. Quid igitur faciam. 2 *pars.*
26. Ad te igitur. 3 *pars.*
27. Afflicti pro peccatis. 1 *pars.*
28. Et eruas nos a malis. 2 *pars.*
29. Cantate Domino.
30. Cunctis diebus.
31. Domine, salva nos.
32. Haec dies.

CHAPTER VI

THE GRADUALIA

PUBLISHED in 1605 and 1607, the two books of *Gradualia* represent not only a different period of Byrd's work, as compared with the *Cantiones Sacrae*, but also a somewhat different aim. The motets published hitherto had served for general purposes; the *Gradualia* were specially designed for the liturgical use of those who adhered to the old Catholic traditions of the Church. Many English Catholics had fled to the Continent, and it is likely that Byrd hoped that, partly through their influence, his Latin Church music might make its way in foreign countries, if not in England. It would seem that his hopes were to some extent realized, for his reputation was certainly recognized abroad; indeed Byrd and Dowland seem to have been alone among Englishmen of the great Tudor School of composers to win wide fame outside their native country. It is noteworthy also that whereas Byrd's first book of *Gradualia* was published in 1605, he found it worth while to issue his second book only two years later; and in 1610 there was a demand for a second edition of both books.

No copy of the first edition of the first book is known to have survived, but a transcript of it, made in 1774, now in the Library of the Royal Technical College at Glasgow, points to the existence of a copy at that date. It was entered in the Registers of the Stationers' Company[1] by Thomas East on 10 January 1604/5, as 'A sett of songes called Gradualia ac Canciones sacrae, quinis, quaternis, trinisque vocibus concinnatae. Aucthore Gulielmo Birdo Organista Regio Anglo'. East died before the second edition was issued; and on 22 December 1610 'the first graduation', as it was described in the Registers, with other publications of Byrd, was assigned by Mistress East to John Browne.[2] The second edition was printed by Richard Redmer.

[1] Registers at the Stationers' Hall.
[2] Arber's *Transcripts of the Stationers' Registers*, iii, 450.

On the title-page of the second edition, and presumably on the first edition also, is printed a couplet of elegiac verse quoted from Martial:

> Dulcia defecta modulatur carmina lingua
> Cantator Cygnus funeris ipse sui.

Byrd followed up this reference in the opening words of his dedication of the book to Lord Northampton: 'Cygnum; aiunt, imminente iam morte, suauius canere. Huius ego AVIS suauitatem, in hac extrema aetate mea, Cantionibus istis, quas tibi dedicandas censui . . .' And towards the end he again alludes to the same idea: 'Vides . . . quibus incitamentis adductus volui (si modo potui) Cygnum imitari.'

Byrd was no more than sixty-two years old at this date; it is therefore a little difficult to understand why he should make these allusions to swan-songs and to speak of himself (AVIS) as being in extreme old age. He did, in fact, live another eighteen years after this.

The dedication is in Latin and is of unusual length. It contains much of interest. It is here, for instance, that Byrd, commenting on the beauty of the words to which he set his music, modestly attributed any success that he might have, not to his own skill, but to the inspiration of the words themselves; 'for',[1] he added, 'there is a certain hidden power, as I learnt by experience, in the thoughts underlying the words themselves; so that, as one meditates upon the sacred words and constantly and seriously considers them, the right notes, in some inexplicable manner, suggest themselves quite spontaneously'. Byrd knew that the basic test of good vocal music is that it should be 'framed to the life of the words',[2] to quote his own expression. His own gifts were superlative in this important matter, and it was due to these, more than to any others, that his work is characterized with such rare dignity. It was, moreover, his 'serious and constant meditation upon the words' that caused that 'certain hidden power' to be revealed to him, enabling him to keep on inventing new musical phrases with a fertility of imagination that is quite amazing, seeing that in his immense output there is scarcely any duplication of his phrases, and that his work

---

[1] The present author's translation from the Latin.
[2] Byrd's *Psalmes, Songs, and Sonnets*, 1611, Title-page.

is almost entirely free from the more conventional contrapuntal devices in vogue in his day.

This book was dedicated to Lord Northampton, who
was Byrd's contemporary in age and his intimate friend.
Byrd called him by his Christian name, Henry, in this
dedicatory address. He expressed his gratitude to him for
his sympathetic interest and kindness in his domestic
troubles: 'Te habui, atque etiam, ni fallor, habeo, in
afflictis familiae meae rebus benignissimum Patronum.' It
is not clear to what this phrase alludes, especially as Northampton had had enough personal troubles of his own
until a year or two before this.

Northampton was the second son of Surrey, the poet,
and a cousin of Edward, 17th Earl of Oxford. He naturally
inherited a taste for letters and the arts. Being admitted to
the household of John White, Bishop of Lincoln and later
of Winchester, he studied widely in philosophy, civil law,
theology, and history, and developed a strong sympathy
with the Catholic cause. He took his degree at King's
College, Cambridge, and at this period he was taught to
play the lute.[1]

For many years he supplied Mary Queen of Scots with
political information, and eventually he was imprisoned in
the Fleet. On being released he travelled abroad, but shortly
afterwards he was reduced to penury; and in 1591 he was
lodged by the charity of the Lord Admiral in a little cell
at Greenwich. In despair he thought of 'retiring to a grove
and a prayer-book'.[2]

On the accession of James I his fortunes were completely reversed; he was given a prominent position at the
Court; he was made a Privy Councillor and Lord Warden
of the Cinque Ports in 1604; and in 1605 he was created
Earl of Northampton and a Knight of the Garter. That was
the year in which this book of *Gradualia* was published.

The purpose of the book is stated by Byrd in his address:
'Veris musicae studiosis.' It was to provide, for those who
delight in praising God in hymns and spiritual songs, 'the
Offices of the whole year, which are proper to the Festivals
of the Blessed Virgin Mary and of All Saints; together with

[1] B.M., Lansdowne MS. 109, fo. 51.
[2] *D.N.B.*, *sub* Henry Howard.

some motets for five voices of the same kind, to words taken from Holy Scripture. Also the Office for the Festival of Corpus Christi with the more solemn antiphons of the Blessed Virgin and some other motets of that kind for four voices, together with all the hymns written in praise of the Virgin. Lastly, there are some motets for three voices for the Easter Festival.'[1]

The first book includes as many as sixty-three separate motets: thirty-two for five voices, twenty for four, and eleven for three. It comprises, besides the Festivals of the Blessed Virgin, All Saints, and Corpus Christi, several motets set to words from the Breviary.

The section for five voices is the most important. It is subdivided into eight groups: (1) In Festo Purificationis; (2) In Nativitate S. Mariae Virginis; (3) Pro Adventu; (4) Post Nativitatem Domini; (5) Post Septuagesima; (6) In Annuntiatione B. Mariae; (7) In Assumptione B. Mariae Virginis; (8) In Festo Omnium Sanctorum.

The contrast between this book and the two books of *Cantiones Sacrae* is readily seen in turning over the pages of the Score. For example, the large majority of the motets are much shorter than the *Cantiones*. And as regards technique, the smoothness of the writing and the richness of the harmonic colouring will at once be apparent, although sudden transitions to remote keys for the purpose of special emphasis are far less frequently employed.

From among so large a number only a few examples can be selected for comment here, and the choice must be somewhat arbitrary, since the general level of the shorter numbers is so evenly sustained. A special feature of the short motets is provided by the *Alleluias* with which so many of them conclude. The variety of invention which Byrd could command is strikingly illustrated in his treatment of this phrase. Notable examples of different types may be seen in *Senex puerum portabat* (No. 3), *Virgo Dei Genetrix* (No. 8), *Felix es, sacra Virgo* (No. 9), *Post partum Virgo* (No. 18), and *Assumpta est Maria* (No. 24).

Diffusa est gratia (No. 22) is a fine work. It is of considerable length, consisting as it does of six separate sections. Each voice-part opens very gracefully, in accordance with

[1] The present author's translation from the Latin.

the spirit of the words, with a triple rhythm although the leading measure is square.

The longer numbers naturally give more scope for the composer. *Gaudeamus omnes* (No. 29) for All Saints' Day is especially brilliant. The first phrase closes in the opening key of F. Then in a festive spirit the voices are grouped homophonically, and the words 'diem festum celebrantes' are repeated to sequences of rising keys, B flat, C and D, followed, in solemn and dignified contrast, with long notes to express 'sub honore Sanctorum omnium'.

The phrase 'Gaudent angeli' provides occasion for another sparkling passage with brilliant contrapuntal imitations, while the bass part has the same musical phrase as the other voices in rhythmic augmentation.

The joyous strain is fully maintained in the short section which follows, and it ends with this phrase:

This great motet ends with a 'Gloria Patri' and a particularly beautiful 'saecula saeculorum. Amen'.

It is interesting to compare with this the *Gaudeamus omnes*
(B.V.M.) (No. 23); the words of the first section are in the
same form. The second section in this case also is written
for three voices.

No. 4 is a setting of *Nunc Dimittis*. The word 'lumen' here
is set to descending and rising scales:

The rising scale of a whole octave seems to have carried
the suggestion of light as well as rising to Byrd's mind, for
he used this phrase with the same rhythm in *Surge, illuminare* (No. 15 in the second book of *Gradualia*).

The part-writing throughout this piece is very 'smooth
and it gives a tranquil effect. This is especially noticeable
at the words 'ad revelationem gentium', where the parts run
in pairs with thirds and tenths.

There is some vivid word-painting in the second section
of *Speciosus forma* (No. 17), where 'the pen of a ready-
writer' pours forth a torrent of notes:

The words of *Plorans plorabit* are from the Book of Jeremiah and are similar in character to the Lamentations. The sombre nature of the subject is reflected in the part-writing. The second and third voice-parts lie in a very awkward register for practical performance, whereas the soprano, tenor, and bass parts lie quite normally for those voices. The second part has a range from ♩ to ♩, and the third voice is taken one note lower still with the same upward range—a compass of nearly two octaves. There is no means of knowing how singers in the sixteenth century managed to meet requirements of this kind, yet instances of vocal writing like this are found occasionally in the works of most of the Elizabethan composers. It would seem that these parts were assigned to tenors, or even baritones, rather than to altos, and that the falsetto was freely employed in the higher register. An example of the dominant seventh taken unprepared may be noticed in the tenor part in the final cadence of this motet.

Justorum animae (No. 31) is placed in the All Saints' group. In dealing with a subject of this nature Byrd stands almost unrivalled among the world's musicians. It is said sometimes that he was austere in disposition. That is probably true. Yet this lovely motet shows that he was also capable of the tenderest possible feelings. The final page reaches the same degree of true pathos, as distinct from sentimentality, that marks his *Ave verum* and the settings of *Agnus Dei* in the four- and five-part Masses; and more could not be said. It ends thus:

Adoramus te Christe (No. 26) differs from all the other compositions in this book, being designed as a song for a single voice with an accompaniment of strings. Byrd wrote a considerable number of songs of this kind to English words, both sacred and secular, which will be discussed in a later chapter, but this is the only known example with sacred Latin words. In accordance with Byrd's usual practice the voice is placed in the second line of the score, the treble viol playing in a higher range.

The group of four-voice compositions includes many beautiful short works of varied character. Outstanding among these is *Ave verum* (No. 5). It is mainly homophonic in construction, and it owes its exquisite loveliness to the perfection of the melodic outline as well as to its harmonic features. The melodic scheme consists of a series of upward and downward curves, the summit of the curves coinciding with the most prominent syllables in the verbal phrases; for example, at the second syllable of 'Maria' in the first sentence. Incidentally, this is the highest note reached throughout the motet and it is only employed once again, namely, at the word 'Jesu'.

Stripped quite bare, the curves may be analysed thus:

and it will be seen that the peaks of the curves are reached on the strong syllable of the important word in each instance.

As regards harmonic treatment, the effect of the chord of F major following immediately on D major at the very beginning is not uncommon in the music of this period. Much more striking is the effect of the chord of C major following the half-close in D major at the words 'cuius latus'. The tenor voice has a superb phrase here; and at the word 'perforatum' there is an unusual discord of great beauty.

in cru - ce   pro   ho - mi-ne   Cu - ius   la - tus per - fo-ra - - tum

Another effective discord unusual at this date occurs on the word 'Maria', and the $^6_4$ $^5_3$ suspension is used in the previous bar. Examples of this suspension are not uncommon in Byrd's work, and there are other instances of its use in this same motet.

O Ie - su, Fi - - li Ma-ri - - - ae,

O Ie - su, Fi - li   Ma - ri - - - ae,

The free use of the dominant seventh, and the telling effect of the clash between F sharp and F natural in the 'miserere' are other features to be noticed in this remarkable composition.

Sacerdotes Domini (No. 3) is an attractive little work, with 'Alleluias' grouped in phrases of consecutive sixths and thirds. *Salve Regina* (No. 2) is of greater length; two sections in this motet are scored for only three of the four voices. There is an example here, at the words 'gementes et flentes', of the chord of the diminished seventh, very rare in the music of this date. *Ave Regina coelorum* (No. 14) shows Byrd, by contrast, in a mood of fervent adoration. The character of this motet is established in the opening phrase of the soprano voice:

A - - - - - ve, Re-gi - - na coe-lo - - - - - - - - - rum,

The rhythm of the opening bar recurs in modified form throughout this piece, and notably in the concluding bars. Byrd's pleasure in writing phrases running simply in sixths and thirds is illustrated at the words 'Salve radix', although nothing quite like this passage is to be found elsewhere in his work.

The first two bars quoted here strongly suggest the keyboard style; and it should be remembered that Byrd was a *virtuoso* performer on the virginals as well as a prolific composer of keyboard music. This passage brings to mind a phrase in Giles Farnaby's *Rosa solis*:

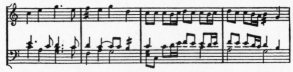

Salve sola Dei Genetrix (No. 17) differs in character from the rest of this collection. It is set for three equal soprano voices and a tenor. It is extremely bright in tone-colour. Another typical little piece of word-painting may be noticed in the final passages of *Senex puerum* (No. 18), a subject also set by Byrd for five voices. The rise and fall in the phrase for the word 'adoravit' is, no doubt, intended to suggest the act of rising and bowing low in solemn adoration.

The group of motets for three voices is of less importance; but these have a value of their own, for the reason that various combinations of voices are provided for. Thus, *Haec dies* (No. 7), *Angelus Domini descendit* (No. 8), and *Post octo dies* (No. 9) among others are suitable for men's voices. In this group is *Turbarum voces in passione Domini secundum Joannem* (No. 10), designed for performance in conjunction with the traditional plainsong to which St. John's text of the narrative was set. The only other known English examples of the setting of the Passion *'turba'* choruses are one by Richard Davy early in the sixteenth century, and two (one imperfect) recently discovered in a manuscript of *circa* 1450 once belonging to St. George's Chapel, Windsor.[1] Byrd, like Davy, wrote these phrases for combined voices in chorus, whereas by the Continental tradition, as exemplified by Orlando di Lasso, they were

[1] This MS. has been acquired by the British Museum but is not yet available for examination.

commonly assigned to a single alto voice. Byrd's settings
are dramatic in character, notably the salutation 'Ave, Rex
Judaeorum' with its mock ceremony in the opening phrase, and
the jeering taunt contained in the little scale passage at the
end. 'Crucifige, crucifige eum' with its overlapping rhythms
vividly represents the vehement anger of the crowd; and
this is intensified by Byrd in the second outburst, 'Tolle,

tolle, crucifige eum'. It must be remembered that Byrd
wrote this setting of the story some sixty years before Hein-
rich Schütz produced his famous 'Passions', and that Schütz
was born exactly a hundred years before Bach and Handel.
Byrd occupies an important place in the early history of the
development of 'Passion Music'.

The second book of *Gradualia* was registered by East
at the Stationers' Hall on 17 February 1607, as 'A booke
called Gradualia, Ac Cantiones sacrae Quaternis, Quinis
et sex vocibus Concinnatae Liber secundus, Aucthore
Gulielmo Burd'. In publication the wording of this title
was slightly altered, the substitution of *seu* for *ac* being one
of the more noticeable changes. It was printed thus:
'Gradualia, | Seu | Cantionum Sa-|crarum: quarum aliae
ad Quatuor, aliae | verò ad Quinque & Sex voces editae
sunt. | Lib. Secundus. | Authore Gulielmo Byrde, Or-
ganista | Regio, Anglo. | Musica Divinos profert modu-
lamine Cantus: | Jubilum in Ore favum in Corde, et in
Aure melos. | Excudebat Thomas Este Londini, ex assigna-
tione | Gulielmi Barley. 1607.'

Byrd's patron this time was another prominent Catholic,
John, first Lord Petre of Writtle. He was the only son of
William Petre of Exeter, who was much in favour with

Queen Mary Tudor, acting as her principal Secretary of State. He held similar office under Queen Elizabeth. John was his son by his second wife, Anne, daughter of Sir William Browne. He was educated at Exeter College, Oxford, of which foundation his father was a liberal benefactor. He was knighted in 1576, and was created Lord Petre by James I in 1603. He died on 11 October 1614. His eldest son married Katherine, daughter of Edward, Earl of Worcester, Byrd's other patron. Seated at Ingatestone in Essex, Lord Petre was Byrd's near neighbour at Stondon.

In his dedicatory address Byrd lamented the recent death of several of his pupils (*viris sanè eâ arte egregiè peritis*). One of these was doubtless Thomas Morley; the others cannot be readily identified. Byrd also recorded his desire that this collection of his works should constitute the testimony of a grateful mind towards God for his divine goodness towards him.

An epigram was printed at the beginning of the book, addressed to Byrd as 'Brittanicae Musicae Parenti' (the Father of British Music), and signed 'G. Ga.'

In this book Byrd reversed his former plan, opening with a section consisting of his fewest number of voices, namely, four, and following it with motets for five and subsequently for six voices. It is considerably shorter than the first book. It contains forty-six motets. Nineteen of these are for four voices, having for their subject *In Nativitate Domini*; *In Epiphania Domini*; and *Post Pascha*. There are eighteen motets for five voices, designed for use *In tempore Paschali*; *In Ascensione Domini*; and *In Festo Pentecostes*. The remaining nine are for six voices; the first seven of these come under the heading *In Festo SS. Petri et Pauli*.

In the four-part section, although a general high level is reached, few of the motets stand out conspicuously among the rest. *Viderunt omnes fines* (No. 2) has a special interest on account of its form. At the end of the second section is the instruction in a footnote 'Chorus (viderunt) sequitur'. This is equivalent to the direction *da capo* at a later period. The motet may thus be regarded as in 'Aria' form. *Beata Virgo* (No. 9) follows the same plan.

Reges Tharsis (No. 11) has no resemblance to Byrd's five-part setting of the same words. A rather curious musical figure is taken up by all the parts in turn at the words 'et insulae munera offerent'; there is nothing quite like it elsewhere in the music of the period:

et in-su-lae mu-ne-ra of-fe-rent.

All the voices have long notes at the words 'et adorabunt eum' in contrast to the previous passage, and this feature, coupled with the descending scale in the bass part, gives the idea of reverent bowing of the knee in adoration. The bass voice here sings:

et ad-o-ra-bunt e-um.

In the final bars of the motet the bass has a scale passage of eleven notes descending from C to G as another little touch of realism, suggesting a final reverential bow.

o-mnes gen-tes ser-vi-ent e - - - - - - - - - i.

Hodie Christus natus est (No. 6) is vigorous and bright, although entirely different in treatment from Byrd's English setting of these words, as printed in *Psalmes, Songs, and Sonnets* (1611). And there are several solemn numbers in this four-part section, of which the most interesting perhaps is *O quam suavis* (No. 18). This motet opens with a striking succession of harmonies:

O quam su - a - vis est, Do - - - - mi - ne

O quam

The hymn *Jesu nostra Redemptio* (No. 19) at its original pitch lies most awkwardly, as regards compass, for modern singers. If transposed down a fourth, or still better a fifth, it is effective for men's voices—two equal tenors and two equal basses. The last verse of the hymn *Tu esto nostrum gaudium* is well contrasted with the earlier verses by its simple homophonic character in triple rhythm.

In the Easter-tide section *Haec dies* is for five voices and

reflects the true Easter spirit. The subject is handled in
quite a different style from the six-part setting in the second
book of *Cantiones Sacrae* and also from the three-part setting
in the first book of *Gradualia*. In this instance Byrd used up
the whole of those words in about fourteen bars, passing on
then to fresh material. The cadence at the words 'quoniam
bonus' may be quoted as showing an example of what is
really the chord of the dominant thirteenth.

Victimae Paschali (No. 22) is another Easter motet that
should be noticed. It is laid out on a fairly lengthy scale,
with great variety in the grouping of the voices. Apart from
the opening and closing passages, the whole of the five
voices are only employed for one short section, namely, at
the words 'Dux vitae mortuus regnat'. Here they enter with
splendid force at the close of the duet *Mors et vita*. This
duet is almost grotesque in its realistic treatment; the two
voices intertwine in a long melismatic passage on the word
'duello'; and the succeeding word 'conflixere' is set in
syncopated phrases so vivid in their dramatic suggestion
that the rapid movements of the two wrestlers, locked to-
gather in mortal combat, seem to be clearly pictured in the
mind's eye. The effect of the passage may perhaps be more
easily appreciated if it is quoted in notes of half the original
value, as in modern notation:

Later in this motet the question 'Dic nobis, Maria, quid vidisti?' is given to the three lower voices and the extended answer to the two sopranos. *Terra tremuit* (No. 23) must be mentioned for the curious little piece of word-painting with which it opens.

All the Ascension-tide motets are fine; notably *Psallite Domino* (No. 29), with its vigorous opening and the diatonic scale-passage of twelve rising notes in the bass voice and eleven in the tenor; this concise little work concludes with a beautiful 'Alleluia'. Of the Pentecostal motets the most important is, perhaps, *Veni Sancte Spiritus* (No. 36). There are nine works in the section for the Festival of St. Peter and St. Paul. All of these are written for six voices and are of very high quality.

In the case of three numbers: *Solve, iubente Deo* (No. 40), *Hodie Simon Petrus* (No. 42), and *Tu es Pastor ovium* (No. 43), no words are printed in the original edition beyond the opening phrase. No satisfactory explanation of this curious fact can be found; for when it is seen that the entire words of these motets fit the musical phrases throughout, with scarcely any instances of uncertainty, it becomes abundantly evident that Byrd was wedding his music 'to the life of the words' no less here than in his other work. Nor can these three motets be compared with *Adoramus te Christe* (No. 26 in the first book of *Gradualia*), in which the entire words are assigned to a single voice, whereas they could not possibly be fitted to the other parts, these being undoubtedly intended for the instrumental accompaniment of the single voice.

Solve iubente Deo, the 'Alleluia' of the Mass of S. Peter ad Vincula, is the most brilliant of these motets; it is perhaps Byrd's greatest achievement in this particular style, and is unsurpassed as a piece of polyphonic writing. The melodic interest is distributed among the six parts with well-balanced equality. The word 'solve' is several times repeated with a florid phrase passed from voice to voice throughout the score; 'iubente Deo' is expressed with more movement still, and this is followed by a very florid treatment of the phrase 'terrarum catenas' with a rapid little run on the second syllable of 'catenas' suggesting the shaking of the chains:

The rhythm of this phrase inevitably calls to mind the G minor fugue of Bach.

The character of the music becomes calmer for 'ut pateant coelestia regna', brightening with a melismatic run in the first soprano part at the final word 'beatis'.

Hodie Simon Petrus is almost, if not quite, as fine. It is of greater length and has a more elaborate 'Alleluia' at the end. Here, also, is some very intricate contrapuntal writing, especially at the words 'clavicularius regni gaudens migravit ad Christum'.

Contents of Gradualia, Book I
1605

OF FIVE VOICES

Post Nativitatem Domini

16. Vultum tuum.
17. Speciosus forma.
    Lingua mea.
18. Post partum.
19. Felix namque es.

Post Septuagesima
20. Alleluia. Ave Maria.
    Virga Jesse floruit.
21. Gaude Maria.

In Annunciatione B. Mariae
22. Diffusa est gratia.
    Propter veritatem.
    Audi, filia.
    Vultum tuum.
    Adducentur regi.
    Adducentur in laetitia.

In Assumptione B. Mariae Virginis

23. Gaudeamus omnes.
    Assumpta est Maria.
24. Assumpta est Maria.
25. Optimam partem elegit.
26. Adoramus te, Christe.
27. Unam petii a Domino.
    Ut videam voluntatem.
28. Plorans plorabit.
    Dic regi.

In Festo Omnium Sanctorum
29. Gaudeamus omnes.
    Exultate, iusti.
    Gloria Patri.
30. Timete Dominum.
    Inquirentes autem.
31. Iustorum animae.
32. Beati mundo corde.

OF FOUR VOICES

1. Cibavit eos.
   Exultate Deo.
   Gloria Patri.
2. Oculi omnium.
   Aperis tu manum.
   Caro mea vere est cibus.
3. Sacerdotes Domini.
4. Quotiescunque manducabitis.
5. Ave verum corpus.
6. O salutaris hostia.
7. O sacrum convivium.
8. Nobis datus, nobis natus. 1 *pars*.
   Verbum caro. 2 *pars*.
   Tantum ergo. 3 *pars*.

9. Ecce quam bonum. 1 *pars*.
   Quod descendit. 2 *pars*.
10. Christus resurgens. 1 *pars*.
    Dicant nunc Judaei. 2 *pars*.
11. Visita, quaesumus.
12. Salve, Regina. 1 *pars*.
    Eia ergo. 2 *pars*.
13. Alma Redemptoris.
14. Ave Regina.
15. In manus tuas, Domine.
16. Laetania.
17. Salve, sola Dei Genetrix.
18. Senex puerum portabat.
19. Hodie beata Virgo.
20. Deo Gratias.

OF THREE VOICES

1. Quem terra, pontus. 1 *pars*.
   Cui luna. 2 *pars*.
   Beata Mater. 3 *pars*.
   Beata coeli nuncio. 4 *pars*.
   Gloria tibi. 5 *pars*.

2. O gloriosa Domina. 1 *pars*.
   Quod Eva tristis. 2 *pars*.
   Tu regis alti ianua. 3 *pars*.
   Gloria tibi. 4 *pars*.

3. Memento, salutis auctor. 1
  pars.
  Maria, Mater gratiae. 2 pars.
  Gloria tibi, Domine. 3 pars.
4. Ave Maris stella. 1 pars.
  Sumens illud. 2 pars.
  Solve vincla reis. 3 pars.
  Monstra te esse Matrem. 4
  pars.
  Virgo singularis. 5 pars.
  Vitam praesta. 6 pars.
  Sit laus Deo. 7 pars.
5. Regina coeli. 1 pars.
  Quia quem merusiti. 2 pars.

Resurrexit. 3 pars.
Ora pro nobis. 4 pars.
6. Alleluia. Quae lucescit. 1
  pars.
  Vespere autem Sabbathi 2
  pars.
7. Haec dies.
8. Angelus Domini descendit.
9. Post dies octo. 1 pars.
  Mane nobiscum. 2 pars.
10. Turbarum voces.
11. Adorna thalamum tuum 1
  pars.
  Subsistit Virgo. 2 pars.

Contents of Gradualia, Book II
1607

OF FOUR VOICES

In Nativitate Domini

1. Puer natus est nobis.
  Cantate Domino.
  Gloria Patri.
2. Viderunt omnes fines.
  Notum fecit Dominus.
3. Dies sanctificatus.
4. Tui sunt coeli
5. Viderunt omnes fines.
6. Hodie Christus natus est.
7. O admirabile commercium.
8. O magnum misterium.
9. Beata Virgo, cuius viscera.
  Ave Maria.

In Epiphania Domini
10. Ecce advenit.

Deus iudicium.
Gloria Patri.
11. Reges Tharsis.
12. Vidimus stellam.
13. Ab ortu solis. 1 pars.
14. Venite, comedite. 2 pars.
15. Surge, illuminare.

Post Pascha
16. Alleluia. Cognoverunt discipuli.
17. Ego sum panis vivus.
18. O quam suavis est.
19. Jesu nostra redemptio.
  Quae te vicit clementia.
  Inferni claustra penetrans.
  Ipsa te cogat pietas.
  Tu esto nostrum gaudium.

OF FIVE VOICES

In tempore Paschali
20. Resurrexi, et adhuc.
  Domine, probasti me.
  Gloria Patri.
21. Haec dies.

22. Victimae Paschali.
  Dic nobis, Maria.
23. Terra tremuit.
24. Pascha nostrum.

In Ascensione Domini

25. Viri Galilei.
    Omnes gentes, plaudite.
26. Alleluia. Ascendit Deus.
27. Dominus in Sina.
28. Ascendit Deus.
29. Psallite Domino.
30. O Rex gloriae.

In Festo Pentecostes

31. Spiritus Domini.
    Exsurgat Deus.

32. Alleluia.   Emitte spiritum
    tuum.
33. Veni, Sancte Spiritus, reple
    tuorum.
34. Confirma hoc, Deus.
35. Factus est repente.
36. Veni, Sancte Spiritus, et
    emitte.
    O lux beatissima.
    Da tuis fidelibus.
37. Non vos relinquam orphanos.

OF SIX VOICES

In Festo SS. Petri et Pauli

38. Nunc scio vere.
    Domine, probasti me.
    Gloria Patri.
39. Constitues eos Principes.
    Pro patribus tuis.
40. Solve iubente Deo.

41. Tu es Petrus.
42. Hodie Simon Petrus.
43. Tu es Pastor ovium.
44. Quodcunque ligaveris.

45. Laudate Dominum.
46. Venite, exultemus Domino.

CHAPTER VII

MOTETS SURVIVING ONLY IN MANUSCRIPT

IT is not easy to realize the conditions under which the daily choral services were performed in the English Cathedrals and Abbey Churches in Elizabethan days. It may safely be said that no Cathedral singer to-day could be found to render his part under the same conditions. There was, of course, practically no printed music available for the use of the singers; and the small selection of Church music provided by John Daye, when he published his *Certaine Notes* in 1560, did little to diminish the need for manuscript part-books as the sole means of supplying choristers with the music to be sung. In consequence, at every one of these establishments there grew up a corpus of Church music, of which no full score existed, but which was nevertheless complete in the separate part-books allotted to the singers in accordance with the compass of their voices. This practice had been gradually evolved from the earliest days of part-singing in the Church, and it continued in a diminishing degree almost down to the present time. That any of the sixteenth- and early seventeenth-century part-books should survive to-day is little short of miraculous when it is recalled that a large proportion of them must have passed out of active service and been lost at a comparatively early date; others survived for a time to be worn out with continuous daily use; many more were ruthlessly destroyed at that disastrous period when under the Commonwealth cathedral choirs were disbanded and Church music was suppressed. Hardly any sixteenth-century music survived in use after the Restoration of the Monarchy, when something new was demanded and supplied.

And considering the active hostility shown to 'papistical books' of all kinds even in Elizabeth's reign, it is yet more surprising that any part-books of Latin music should exist to-day than that a few similar sets of English Church music survive. In many instances, however, these sets of part-books are now far from being complete; and sometimes no more than a single voice-part survives out of a set that should consist of five or six.

It is indeed fortunate that a considerable number of Byrd's motets, not otherwise known, are to be found in rare manuscript part-books.

As will be seen from the references supplied with a list of those works at the end of the present chapter, four libraries together include almost all that is known of their text. Christ Church, Oxford, and St. Michael's College, Tenbury, supply by far the greater part, but an important contribution comes from the British Museum, where John Baldwin's manuscript, belonging to the Royal Collection, is also now to be seen. Only one manuscript in the Bodleian Library (Mus. Sch. E. 423) is of much value in reference to Byrd's motets; and although this is of early date and the text authoritative, it consists of no more than a single part-book. The 'Sadler' MS. (Bodl. Mus. Sch. E. 1–5) includes some motets of Byrd, but none that were not printed in the composer's lifetime. This fine manuscript is dated 1585.

The Christ Church set of part-books (979–83) are also known as the 'Baldwin MSS.', because they are stamped with the initials I.B. on the covers and are perhaps, like the score in the Royal Collection, in his hand; they are of great value and contain as many as twelve of Byrd's unprinted motets, including the *De lamentatione*.

The tenor part-book is unfortunately missing from this set, as also from the companion set of books (984–8). This latter set belonged to one Robert Dow and it provides a beautiful example of musical penmanship.

St. Michael's College Tenbury, is very rich in the owner-ship of early part-books of this character. The most import-ant of these, for the purpose in hand, are those numbered in the Catalogue 341–4, 354–8, and 369–73. The first of these sets lacks the bass part-book; the original covers are stamped with the name of Edward Paston. MS. 389 is the single survivor of a set of six; it includes as many as six of the unprinted motets of Byrd. This book is of unique interest. On the original vellum cover are the initials T.E., repeated in red ink on fol. 2, and the book is not improbably in the hand of Thomas East. On the top margin of the book, when closed, are the initials W.B., and it may have belonged

to Byrd. There is reason to think that John Alcock of Lichfield had before him this set of part-books in its complete-
ness when transcribing the motet *Vide, Domine, quoniam
tribulor* (B.M. Add. MS. 23624). Some manuscripts of first-
rate importance have recently been added to the Tenbury
library. Among them is a splendid bass part-book (1464),
dated about 1575, and a beautiful tenor part-book (1468),
in the hand of John Sadler, dated 1591. It was formerly in
the Braikenridge Art Collection at Brislington near Bristol,
and must have belonged to the same set as an alto part-book
now owned by Captain Berkeley of Spetchley Park and
before that by Miss E. A. Willmott, for the grotesque figures in the initial letters are similar. These Sadler MSS. include several of Byrd's motets, but *Petrus beatus* is the only
one not printed in either of his two books of *Cantiones Sacrae*.

In addition to these part-books certain manuscripts in
lute tablature are of value as text. The lute was a fashionable instrument in the sixteenth and early seventeenth centuries, and although a fair quantity of music was expressly
composed for it, yet a wide demand existed for arrangements
of choral music, both sacred and secular, to play on the lute.
Two large collections of such arrangements are to be seen
in the British Museum.[1] These are in Italian tablature and
include a number of Byrd's motets, some of which are not
found elsewhere. The Tenbury MS. 340 is in the same hand,
and it also includes some of these motets.

It will be observed that practically all of the manuscripts
just referred to are of early date in relation to Byrd's published work. The Christ Church MSS. 984–8 were begun
in 1581 and the companion set very little later, while MS.
45 is earlier still. The British Museum Additional MSS.
17802–5 are dated about 1585, and Baldwin's score in the
Royal Music Collection about 1600. The Tenbury MSS.
belong to the closing years of the sixteenth century, and
the single part-book in the Bodleian Library is not later
than 1580.

From these facts it would appear that most, if not all, of
the compositions to be considered in this chapter were
written before Byrd published his two books of *Cantiones
Sacrae*.

[1] B.M. Add. MSS. 29246, 29247.

It is a matter for regret that the available text of so many of these compositions is incomplete; yet with very few exceptions it has been found practicable to reconstruct the missing parts with a fair amount of satisfaction.

The *De lamentatione* is perhaps the most important of these manuscript works. Byrd chose verses 8–10 of the second chapter of the Lamentations of Jeremiah for his setting. The voice-parts are laid out for an extremely low range of compass, even after allowance has been made for the differences in the matter of pitch that prevailed in Byrd's time as compared with our own. The highest part of the five is low for an ordinary alto, rarely even touching B flat; while the second and third parts are scarcely above baritone register, with an occasional F as the highest note, and ranging down to B flat. The two other parts are correspondingly low. The sombre effect, rightly suited to the subject, is by no means marred if the work is transposed up a third or even a fourth.

The opening section set to the words *De lamentatione Jeremiae prophetae* is extremely impressive. Though it is not written in strict canon, yet the voices follow one another at intervals of some length with the same subject in the manner of a Fugue, the later entries being successively at a higher pitch, so that throughout the section the intensity of feeling is worked up to a climax. These words are, of course, no more than a preliminary announcement, and Byrd's music most suitably produces the effect of a kind of overture. Quite different in character is the setting of the prophet's words when they are reached: 'Cogitavit Dominus dissipare murum filiae Sion.' The five voices follow each other here with entries separated by no more than half a bar, and anxiety and despair are expressed by complex triple measures which overlap in the several voices.

The work throughout is very contrapuntal in style;

scarcely a single homophonic phrase is to be found in it, and the feeling of troubled agitation is maintained with little intermission. The scheme of modulation is interesting. The harmony is, of course, mainly modal; but if it be permitted to speak in terms of keys, the first section opens and ends in D. The interlude (*Heth*) closes in G, in which key the next section begins and ends. The following interlude (*Teth*) closes in C major. The third section opens in C minor and ends in B flat, the subsequent interlude (*Jod*) closing in F; the fourth section closes in A, and the final section, opening in C, closes in the original key of D.

The Hebrew letters (in this instance *Heth*, *Teth*, and *Jod*) were set to music in accordance with the convention of the day. *Teth* and *Jod* are remarkable bits of contrapuntal writing; the standard of note-values here is quite twice as fast as those used in the rest of the work, and rhythms of great variety and complexity are introduced in *Teth*. These sections serve the purpose for which instrumental interludes were designed at a later period.

Among the less important of these manuscript works *Audivi vocem* stands out as a characteristic example. A quiet and reposeful opening ends with a cadence at the word 'dicentem', where all five voices hold the chord of G major on a breve. The soprano then leads off alone at the word 'Beati' on E, and the other four voices join in with the chord of A major. The motet closes with prolonged repetitions of the words 'qui in Domino moriuntur'. The musical figure employed here to express dying is reminiscent of that which Byrd used in *Vigilate* (*Cant. Sac.* i. 16) to express falling asleep.

Christe qui lux is another of the shorter works to be noticed. It is written in simple hymn-form. In the Christ Church MSS., where alone this motet has survived, no mention is made of the first verse of the hymn; the text begins with the second verse 'Precamur sancte Domine', and it is taken for granted that the first verse should be sung to the plain-song melody unharmonized. In the subsequent five verses each voice in turn is given the melody, the remaining voices supplying new harmonies for each verse.

Noctis recolitur provides a striking contrast to *Christe qui lux* in the method of dealing with the plain-song melody of a hymn. Byrd, in this instance, selected three verses from the hymn *Sacris sollemniis*, and gave the plain-song melody to the soprano throughout, while the other four voice-parts are written in imitative counterpoint. As the form of the melody involves repetition, in order to cover the whole of the words in each verse, Byrd's exceptional gifts in devising new harmonies and fresh melodic material for his counterpoints are amply illustrated here, seeing that this section of the plain-song recurs six times in all.

Domine Deus omnipotens is designed on more important lines. It contains a fine passage in homophonic treatment, which is in sharp contrast with the rest of the work, more particularly with the appeal for mercy at the words 'miserere mei secundum misericordiam tuam'. Another motet of a pentitential character is *Peccavi super numerum*. Byrd always excelled in this style of work. The grief of 'a contrite heart' is fully expressed in the opening bars:

This motet ends, in the same spirit of deep penitence, with close imitations on the words 'iniquitatis meae'.

Complete text of *Petrus beatus* is found only at Tenbury, though a single voice-part is also in the Willmott MS. in Sadler's hand. A vigorous spirit is maintained throughout the three separate sections into which the motet is divided. It is constructed on a plain-song melody given to the alto voice. The imitative contrapuntal style in which the other four parts are written is unbroken by any homophonic phrase. The 'Amen' with which the 'Gloria' concludes is of a smooth and flowing character; short-scale passages are carried from voice to voice, so that at one point a continuous scale of two octaves and five notes runs right across the vocal score from the bass to the soprano.

One of the finest 'Amens' in any of Byrd's motets is that with which *O salutaris hostia* concludes. It is for six voices. It extends over some fourteen bars of well-moulded phrases, providing at the same time an example of ingenious writing, three of the parts being in strict canon.

Reges Tharsis, set for five voices, is quite distinct from the four-part setting of the same words included in the second book of *Gradualia* (No. 11). The only known text of this motet is that of the Christ Church MSS. 979–83; but the text as scored from these part-books seems to be full of error, a fact that is difficult to explain, seeing that these books are otherwise remarkably accurate. Nor can satisfactory emendations be proposed without a drastic re-writing of certain passages. It is impossible to entertain the suggestion that the text as it stands represents the work of Byrd, even as a child; the crudities and many elementary grammatical faults cannot be regarded in the light of deliberate experiments. The text was scored without any attempt at emendation in *Tudor Church Music*,[1] and the problems which it raises must remain unsolved. It should be mentioned, however, that since the publication of the score in *Tudor Church Music* it

[1] Vol. ix, p. 295.

has been discovered that the missing tenor part is to be supplied by the plain-song melody in the Sarum Proces-sional.[1] There is a splendid phrase in triple measure in the soprano part of this motet which seems characteristic of Byrd at his best:

Among the compositions for six voices *Circumspice Jeru-salem* is extremely fine. This is another of the motets that has survived only in the Tenbury MSS. Two of the inner voice-parts are missing in the part-books, a strange mis-fortune, because all the six books of the set are complete and the omission of this motet in two of the books seems to have been quite fortuitous, the pages being left blank at this point. Fortunately, however, there has survived, also in the Tenbury collection, a contemporary adaptation of this motet for the lute,[2] and with its aid it has been possible to reconstruct the text of the two missing parts with a fair hope that they correspond closely with what the composer wrote. This motet ends with great dignity.

Deus in adiutorium is remarkable for its great length; it extends to more than 250 bars of four minims each. There is something very realistic in the sneer of those 'that cry over me There, there', as the English version of the Psalm has it, where the vulgate has 'Euge, euge'.

Byrd probably found it difficult to include in his printed volumes any eight-part motets of the size of his *Ad Domi-num cum tribularer* and *Quomodo cantabimus*, while *Domine, quis habitabit?* is for as many as nine voices. All these are superb examples of polyphonic writing of a complicated kind, as a glance at the score of any page chosen at random will show, especially if the value of the notes has been halved in a modern edition.

---

[1] Information communicated to the author by Mr. H. B. Collins
[2] Tenbury MS. 340.

Quomodo cantabimus is noteworthy from several points of view. In the first place the exact date of the composition is known, and the circumstances under which Byrd wrote it are also of particular interest. Philippo de Monte had set the opening verses of this Psalm for eight voices and sent his motet to Byrd in the year 1583. Byrd thereupon composed *Quomodo cantabimus* also for eight voices and sent it to de Monte in the following year, 1584. It was John Alcock, organist of Lichfield in the eighteenth century, who recorded these facts[1] and he evidently had some authoritative manuscript in his hands, giving the score of both these anthems as well as these details concerning them.

The association of Byrd and de Monte is another matter of interest, not known apart from Alcock's note; it adds strength to the surmise that Byrd was held in high esteem by contemporary musicians on the Continent.

Alcock's score of *Quomodo cantabimus*, late though it is in date, has all the appearance of representing an accurate text; and it has some advantages in this respect when compared with that of John Baldwin in the Royal Collection, now in the British Museum.

Baldwin's text, which is in full score, is given without any of the words. The words are found in the Tenbury MS. 389; but of the eight parts the first tenor alone survives in that set. There are indications that the complete set to which this single book belongs was the manuscript in Alcock's hands. It happens, for instance, that de Monte's *Super flumina* immediately precedes Byrd's *Quomodo cantabimus* in the Tenbury part-book, as it also does in Baldwin's MS. Baldwin seems to have made some slight alterations in regard to note-values; for example, occasionally he substitutes a dotted crotchet and a quaver for a minim. And there is one serious error in Baldwin's score: the first entry of the second alto part is made six beats too soon, the defect being compensated by additional rests some eight bars later, after which the text is correct. Unfortunately this error, which violates the strictness of the canon and fails to fit in with the other parts, was copied into *Tudor Church Music*.[2]

---

[1] B.M. Add. MS. 23624, ff. 101 and 107.
[2] Vol. ix, p. 283.

In *Tudor Church Music*[1] attention was directed to a fragment, set to the words 'Quia illic interrogaverunt nos', which Samuel Wesley inserted in the score which he made[2] of a large part of Byrd's second book of *Gradualia*. With reference to this short piece Wesley added a footnote, since erased but nevertheless legible, in which he expressed regret that he could find 'only this one verse of *Super flumina Babilonis* composed by our Author' (meaning Byrd). Wesley was evidently copying a manuscript now in the Fitzwilliam Museum at Cambridge,[3] dated *circa* 1740, where this *Quia illic* fragment is similarly placed between *Jesu nostra Redemptio* and *Quotiescunque manducabitis*. The note already alluded to in Alcock's manuscript finally disposes of any suggestion that this fragment was a portion of the first part of *Quomodo cantabimus*. And, in point of fact, this *Quia illic* is by Victoria, being part of his motet *Super flumina*. The complete Psalm, as set jointly by de Monte and Byrd, may be performed as one work. Another example of a composite work is provided in the setting of alternate verses of Psalms 113, 114, and 115, of which Shepherd composed the first section (*Sit nomen Domini*), Byrd the second (*Similes illis fiant*), and W. Mundy the third (*Benedixit omnibus qui timent*). The same plain-song bass was used throughout the three sections.

As a composition *Quomodo cantabimus* is remarkable not only for the general skill and interest of the contrapuntal writing, but also for the introduction of a complicated example of strict canonical writing, described in Alcock's manuscript as 'Canon tres partes in una in octavo et unisono arsin et thesin'. In this connexion it will be discussed with other canons in a later chapter.

A few bars of the motet for nine voices, *Domine, quis habitabit?*, may be quoted here in score, as showing Byrd's masterly handling of the contrapuntal style in many parts. It will be more easily read by modern eyes if printed in notes of half their original value, and transposed up a minor third to the pitch at which it is obviously best suited to the several voices.

[1] Ibid., Preface, xv.
[2] B.M. Add. MS. 35001, fo. 139.
[3] Fitzwilliam MS. 30 *b*. 17.

Attention has sometimes been drawn to the value of the rising seventh in the bass part of the 'Hallelujah' Chorus in Handel's *Messiah* at the passage:

The king-dom of this world

Byrd uses the same interval in the phrase 'non movebitur in aeternum' in *Domine, quis habitabit?*, as may be seen in a compressed arrangement of the nine-part score transposed up a minor third:

non mo - ve - bi-tur   in ae-ter - - num,

The task of compiling a list of motets by Byrd, or by any other composer of the period, that are to be found only in manuscript is far from easy. In many of the part-books no composer's name is given, and erroneous ascriptions are far from uncommon even in association with authentic early text.

Incola ego sum, ascribed to Byrd in the Tenbury MSS. 354–8, is not by Byrd but is the second part of *Retribue servo tuo* by Robert Parsons, to whom it is correctly attributed in Brit. Mus. Add. MS. 32377, Christ Church MSS. 979–83 and 984–8. The whole of Parsons's motet is erroneously ascribed to Byrd in the Tenbury MSS. 354–8. Similarly, *Dies illa, dies irae* is wrongly ascribed to Byrd in Baldwin's MS. in the Royal Collection. It is the second part of *Libera me, Domine* by Parsons. Both these motets were incorrectly included in *Tudor Church Music*, vol. ix.

Decantabat populus has no ascription in Christ Church MSS. 984–8, but it is ascribed to Byrd in each of the part-books in Brit. Mus. Add. MSS. 37402–6, where, however, no words are given. For this reason it has been wrongly placed among the instrumental works in the British Museum catalogue. Although it is somewhat different in style from Byrd's other work, there is no valid reason why the British Museum ascription, which is of early date, should be disputed.

With sounder reason, on the evidence of style alone, doubt might have been cast upon the ascription of *Vide, Domine, quoniam tribulor*. This motet is not only unlike anything else that Byrd wrote, but it can scarcely be matched, in its special features, in the whole realm of Tudor vocal music. Yet the ascription in such a manuscript as Tenbury 389 cannot lightly be set aside, especially when it is recalled that this manuscript may actually have belonged to Byrd. Moreover, John Alcock, who in 1762 had in his hands text of undoubted authenticity, also ascribed this work to Byrd.

As a piece of chromatic writing, with dazzling modulation, it ranks with Weelkes's *O Care, thou wilt despatch me*, Farnaby's *Construe my meaning*, and Dowland's *From silent night*; and, as the evidence of the Tenbury MS. shows, it is of earlier date than these.

The motet opens in E flat major, and the chord of G flat major is reached as soon as the fifth bar. This same chord occurs again in this work, and these are perhaps the only examples of its use at this period. Another original harmonic feature in this motet is the modulation to F major, taken suddenly in succession to a plagal cadence in D flat.

Very few bars later, following a close in C major, at the words 'subversum est cor meum', the 'troubled heart' finds expression in the sharp keys:

Two bars later the chord of A flat is reached, and the first section of the motet closes in F. The second section starts straight off in A major; and, following a half close in C major, the next phrase opens in A flat, returning again to C, and then to G. The word 'gladius' is repeated in homophonic phrases with restless modulations, expressing extreme terror: E flat, G flat, D flat, and through G to C again; then, in the concluding passage, the keys of E flat, D major, and A major are touched in succession, leading to a final authentic cadence in F.

leading to:

Whether this motet is by Byrd or not, and it may reasonably be accepted as his, it is a very remarkable piece of writing in view of its date.

Ad punctum in modico, of which only the two bass parts are known to survive, is, as far as can be judged from these, an important composition for five voices written in Byrd's best manner.

It remains to mention some smaller compositions which were written on plain-song melodies, and apparently designed for performance on viols rather than voices. There are several of these pieces in the set of Tenbury part-books numbered in the catalogue 354–8. Some of them are also found adapted for performance on the lute. A number of these are preserved in two manuscripts in the British Museum,[1] very neatly written in Italian tablature. These books are in the same hand as the Tenbury MS. 340. The compositions belonging to this class are for the most part designed in the *In nomine* style, which will be discussed more fully in a later chapter. The opening words of the plain-song melodies, upon which they are severally constructed, are usually quoted in the manuscripts with the musical text, and for this reason they have been wrongly classified in certain lists and catalogues as vocal compositions.

The lute-books also include many adaptations of undoubted vocal works. For example, Byrd's *Infelix ego*, from his second book of *Cantiones Sacrae*, seems to have been a very popular piece as arranged for the lute. It appears three times in one collection,[2] each time in a different key, with the result that it has been wrongly noted as three independent compositions in the catalogue.

Motets surviving only in Manuscript

Of three voices

Alleluia. Confitemini Domino.	B. M. Add. 18936-9; Baldwin's MS., fo. 160; Ch. Ch. 45.
Sanctus.	Ch. Ch. 45.

[1] B.M. Add. MSS. 29246, fo. 13; fo. 20; 29247, fo. 53ᵛ.
[2] B.M. Add. MSS. 29246, fos. 13 and 20; 29247 fo. 53ᵛ.

Of four voices

Miserere (short score, words partly indicated).	B.M. Add. 21403, fo. 31.
Precamur, sancte Domine (wanting words).	B.M. Add. 30480-4; Add. 29246, fo. 46 [4th verse and there entitled *Christe qui lux*]; Tenbury, 354-8.
Similes illis fiant.	B.M. Add. 17802-5.

Of five voices

{ Ad punctum in modico (1st and 2nd Bass parts only). In momento indignationis. 2 *pars*.	Bodl. Mus. Sch. E. 423; Petre MS., Essex County Record Office, Chelmsford, fo. 24.
Audivi vocem de coelo.	B.M. Add. 29247, fo. 15ᵛ; Bodl. Mus. Sch. E. 423; Ch. Ch. 979-83, 984-8; Tenbury, 341-4; 369-73; 389. Petre MS., Essex R.O.
Benigne fac (wanting tenor part).	Bodl. Mus. Sch. E. 423; Ch. Ch. 979-83.
{ [Christe, qui lux] (not given in the MS.). Precamur, sancte Domine.	Ch. Ch. 984-8.
{ De lamentatione Jeremiae. Heth. Cogitavit Dominus. Teth. Defixae sunt. Jod. Sederunt in terra. Jerusalem, convertere.	B.M. Add. 32377; Ch. Ch. 979-83; Tenbury, 369-73.
Decantabat populus.	B.M. Add. 37402-6; Ch. Ch. 984-8.
{ Domine Deus omnipotens (wanting tenor part). Ideo misericors. 2 *pars*.	Ch. Ch. 979-83.
Domine, exaudi orationem meam (medius part only)	Tenbury, 389,
{ Ne perdas cum impiis. Eripe me. 2 *pars*.	Bodl. Mus. Sch. E. 423. Baldwin's MS., fo. 75; Ch. Ch. 979-83.
{ Noctis recolitur (wanting tenor part). Dedit fragilibus. 2 *pars*. Panis angelicus. 3 *pars*	Ch. Ch. 979-83.

{ Omni tempore benedic. { Memor esto fili. 2 *pars*.	Bodl. Mus. Sch. E. 423; Baldwin's MS., fo. 73; Ch. Ch. 979-83; Tenbury, 389.
Peccavi super numerum.	B.M. Add. 29247, fo. 33ᵛ; Bodl. Mus. Sch. E. 423; Ch. Ch. 979-83; Tenbury, 389.
{ Petrus beatus. { Quodcunque vinculis. 2 *pars*. { Per immensa saecula. 3 *pars*. { Gloria Deo. 4 *pars*.	Tenbury, 341-4, 369-73; 1464; Willmott MS. No. 12.
Precamur, sancte Domine (*see* Christe qui lux).	
Reges Tharsis (1st tenor: Plainsong from the Sarum Processional).	Ch. Ch. 979-83.
Sponsus amat sponsam (Plainsong and cantus only).	B.M. Add. 32377; Bodl. Mus. Sch. E. 423; Tenbury, 389.
{ Vide, Domine, quoniam tribulor. { Quoniam amaritudine. 2 *pars*.	B.M. Add. 23624; Tenbury 389.

Of six voices

{ Circumspice Jerusalem (two inner parts incomplete). { Ecce enim veniunt. 2 *pars*.	Tenbury, 379-84, 340.
{ Deus in adiutorium (wanting tenor part). { Avertantur retrorsum. 2 *pars*. { Exultent et laetentur. 3 *pars*. { Ego vero egenus. 4 *pars*.	Ch. Ch. 979-83; Tenbury, 389.
Domine, ante te omne desiderium (wanting tenor part).	Ch. Ch. 979-83.
O salutaris hostia.	B.M. Add. 31390, fo. 17ᵛ; Ch. Ch. 979-83; Tenbury, 389.

Of eight voices

{ Ad Dominum cum tribularer (wanting words, all voices). { Heu mihi, Domine. 2 *pars*.	B.M. Add. 31390.
{ Quomodo cantabimus? { Si non proposuero. 2 *pars*	B.M. Add. 23624; Royal Mus. Lib.; Baldwin's MS., fo. 26; Tenbury, 389.

Of nine voices

Domine, quis habitabit?	Royal Mus. Lib.; Baldwin's MS., fo. 40ᵛ.

The following seem intended for instrumental performance having no words except for the plain-song;

Of three voices

Salvator mundi.	B.M. Add. 18936-9; Add. 29246, fo. 14^v (there entitled *Sermone blando*).

Of four voices

Christe qui lux (identical with 4th verse of Precamur. à 4) (*see* vocal list).	B.M. Add. 29246, fo. 46.
Christe Redemptor.	Tenbury, 354-8.
Christe Redemptor (another setting).	B.M. Add. 29246, fo. 48^v; Tenbury, 354-8.
Miserere mihi.	B.M. Add. 18936-9; Tenbury, 354-8.
Miserere mihi (another setting).	B.M. Add. 18936-9; Add. 29246, fo. 48^v.
Precamur, sancte Domine.	Tenbury, 354-8.
Salvator mundi.	B.M. Add. 18936-9; Add. 29246, fo. 14^v.
Salvator mundi (another setting).	B.M. Add. 29246, fo. 47.
Sermone blando.	Tenbury, 354-8.
Sermone blando (another setting).	Tenbury, 354-8.
Te lucis.	Tenbury, 354-8.
Te lucis (another setting).	B.M. Add. 29246, fo. 14^v.
Te lucis (another setting).	B.M. Add. 29246, fo. 46.

CHAPTER VIII

ENGLISH LITURGICAL MUSIC

IN order to understand the value and importance of Byrd's work for the English forms of Church worship, it is necessary to say something of the conditions under which he worked in this field of composition. It must also be realized how vital were the needs of the Reformed Church in relation to music at this period, and that they presented problems which could only be solved by musicianship of the highest class coupled with exceptional originality of imagination.

No one can say, at this distance of time, and in the absence of any contemporary record with reference to this particular branch of the subject, what was the precise effect upon the choral establishments of the English cathedrals at the moment when the ordering of the Services in accordance with the Book of Common Prayer was definitely substituted for the time-honoured Latin rites. It is not proposed to discuss here the ecclesiastical or clerical aspects of the Reformation movement, but it may be useful to state that the majority of those who advocated Reform at that time looked in the main for two leading measures: firstly, the elimination of Papal influence from the control of English politics, both civil and ecclesiastical; and secondly, the substitution of English for Latin as the language of the Church services.

It was the carrying of this latter point into practice that had such a profound effect upon the history of English music; for it meant that the whole repertory of Church music, with the great weight of tradition behind it, had to be discarded, and something immediately substituted for it which at the moment was practically non-existent. The change created a position of stupendous difficulty for the Church musicians of the day. It must not be supposed that the change was made suddenly and completely between two consecutive days. It did, in fact, come about somewhat gradually. English forms of Liturgy had begun to appear some time before 1549. Indeed, a form of Litany with English words had existed as early as the fifteenth century. In 1544 the Litany was revised by Cranmer and printed almost in its present form, and Cranmer adapted each clause to the music of the traditional Latin plain-chant. Another of the earlier steps towards the use of English in the Services was taken when the Primer of Henry the Eighth was issued in 1545.

Evidence that Services on a cathedral scale were being performed in English some time before the publication of the Prayer Book is provided by certain music manuscripts. The most important of these is a set of three part-books in the Bodleian Library,[1] known as the 'Wanley' manuscripts because early in the eighteenth century they belonged to Humfrey Wanley. The date usually assigned to these books is 1546–7. They include nearly one hundred compositions set to English words, including the Morning and Evening Canticles, harmonized settings of Cranmer's Litany, a large number of Anthems, and, what is more remarkable, several settings of the Office for the Holy Communion, complete with *Gloria, Sanctus, Benedictus,* and *Agnus Dei.* Two of these are English adaptations of Masses by John Taverner. Without doubt the musicians of that day had perceived what was coming, and were already seeing to it that the great traditions of English Church music should not fall into decay, whatever changes might be forthcoming at the hands of the Crown, Parliament, or the Clergy. And the musicians moved uniformly in the direction of harmony as opposed to unison. It would seem that they associated plain-song and unison-singing with the hated Latin language. It is perhaps for this reason that the practical use of Marbeck's *Book of Common Prayer Noted* did not long survive the issue of the Second Prayer Book, except for the incorporation of his 'noting' of the Responses, &c., in the various harmonized settings.

The Act of Uniformity was passed in 1549; it ordered that 'the Book of Common Prayer and none other' was to be used on and after the Feast of Pentecost, which fell on 9 June that year. The book had been in the hands of the Clergy for several weeks before this date, and no doubt

[1] Bodl. Mus. Sch. MSS. E. 420–2.

the musicians also were fully occupied during that short
period in preparing for an adequate performance of the
Services in all 'quires and places where they sang'.

But the work of constructing a repertory of English
Church music of first-rate merit could not be accomplished
in a moment, and for some years after the passing of the
Act of Uniformity it had advanced little beyond the experimental stage. It may be interesting to recall who were
prominent in English music in the year 1549. Taverner had
recently died. Tye and Tallis were well advanced in middle
age. Shepherd, Marbeck, and Robert Johnson were in the
prime of life. White and Richard Farrant were still youths;
and among lesser lights Robert Parsons and Osbert Parsley
were in early manhood. Byrd at this date was six years old.

The English work done by most of these composers
was of much less importance than what they wrote for the
older Latin rites of the Church. Three of them, however,
apart of course from Byrd, stand out in different ways as
having contributed something vital to the new movement
at its most critical period: namely, Marbeck, Tallis, and
Farrant. Marbeck's work in 'noting' the Book of Common
Prayer has a special value of its own, seeing that it forms
the basis of all the most familiar settings of the *Preces and
Responses*, not to mention the well-known original melody
which he composed for the Nicene Creed. Judged solely
upon its artistic merits the Latin work of Tallis stands far
above his English; yet it was perhaps a greater achievement
that as a pioneer, with no traditions to follow, he succeeded
in producing work of high class to meet entirely novel requirements; and this was done at the actual moment of
crisis, because his 'short' Service, his five-part *Te Deum*,
and some of his small anthems were almost certainly written
before the death of Edward VI. Moreover, these works are
of sufficient merit to have survived in constant use in English cathedrals for nearly four centuries since they were
composed. It was his sure technique, developed in earlier
days in his Latin work, that enabled him to infuse vitality
and religious expression into his English work in a far
greater degree than his contemporaries at that period.
Richard Farrant's compositions cannot easily be dated;
they may not be earlier than Elizabethan, and their style

certainly suggests that they were not. Yet he also must be accounted among the more important pioneers of English Church music. His music, small as it is in quantity, represents a contribution in the direction of melodic beauty and tenderness which were new to the English Church at that date.

It remained for Byrd to lay the true and enduring foundation. He was born at precisely the right moment. He was only fifteen years old when Elizabeth came to the throne, and much had happened since the passing of the Act of Uniformity in 1549. By the time that he reached the first stages of maturity as a composer much had already been done by his elders in the way of experiment from which he could profit; and, moreover, he had the exceptional advantage of being a pupil of Tallis. When he took up his appointment at Lincoln Cathedral in 1562 he must at once have turned his attention to writing English Services and anthems. The surviving fragments of his Morning Service in F and *Jubilate* in G, both of which have the appearance of being early work, may belong to his Lincoln period. In due course his riper experience, coupled with his supreme genius, enabled him to produce work which has served as a model for all time in this department of composition, passing far beyond the region of experiment into complete maturity.

Tallis has been styled the 'Father of English Church Music', and perhaps rightly, because he did his great work as a pioneer when Byrd was still a child. Byrd in the course of his life earned the even wider title 'Brittanicae Musicae parens'—Parent of British Music—excelling, as he did, not in Church music alone, but in every branch of musical composition known in his day.

From what has just been said it will be realized that musicians of that day were required not only to supply Anthems and settings of the Canticles for the daily choral services in the cathedrals, but also to set music to the Versicles, Responses, and Litany, and to solve the problem of singing the Psalms in the English Version as set out in the Prayer Book. Tallis's musical settings of the *Preces*, *Versicles, and Responses*, and of the Litany are well known. It is less generally known that other musicians, and among them Byrd, essayed the same task at this period.

Byrd's complete version of the *Preces and Responses* is to be found in the manuscripts at Durham Cathedral and at Peterhouse, Cambridge. It was composed for five voices, and the traditional principle of placing the plain-song melody in the tenor part was followed as in Tallis's *Responses*. There are two other versions of Byrd's *Preces* without the *Versicles and Responses*, and these are described in the manuscripts as Byrd's 'First' and 'Second' *Preces*. The setting of 'O Lord, make haste to help us', as found in the complete version and also in the 'Second' *Preces*, has been made familiar because in the eighteenth century, or possibly earlier, it became spuriously incorporated in Tallis's *Preces* to replace the rather dull response which Tallis wrote; and it still retains its place there.

BYRD    TALLIS

Byrd's *Preces and Responses* seem to have been popular and widely used, and deservedly so, for they are beautiful and should be restored, as occasional alternatives to those of Tallis, in cathedral and collegiate choirs.

Byrd's Litany is for four voices, with Cranmer's version of the plain-song melody in the tenor. It will be remembered that Tallis placed the plain-song melody in the treble for the greater part of his setting of the Litany. It is interesting to notice that Byrd set music to the whole of Cranmer's Litany, including the section that follows the Lord's Prayer. Tallis set no farther than the 'Lesser Litany' (Lord, have mercy upon us).

The Anglican chant was unknown before the seventeenth century; such chants as are now assigned to Tudor composers are adaptations. In the absence of any definite evidence it is not possible to say how the Psalms were rendered at the daily morning and evening services in the cathedrals in the early years that followed the appearance of the Book of Common Prayer. In spite of the Act of Uniformity a great variety of usage prevailed. Grindal,

Bishop of London, wrote a memorandum,[1] dated 14 February 1564/5, concerning the 'Varieties in Service and yᵉ Administracion used'. He stated that 'Some kepe pcysely yᵉ ordʳ of yᵉ booke othʳˢ intermedle Psal: in meter'. Several versions of the whole book of Psalms in metre were issued in the latter half of the sixteenth century, apart from that of Sternhold and Hopkins; and it is quite likely that the psalms of the day were ordinarily sung to one of these metrical versions in cathedral and collegiate choirs; and that in Parish churches, where choirs rarely functioned, the Prayer Book version was recited by Parson and Clerk alternately. But on the great Festivals it seems to have been the custom in cathedrals to sing a few verses of each of the special Psalms for the day to a form of music closely allied to the Anglican chant of later days. Tallis, Byrd, and Gibbons were among the famous musicians who set Festival Psalms in this manner. These Psalms are remarkably interesting, for they represent in English use the old Latin practice of singing *Salmi concerti* on special occasions. Many of the Latin *Salmi concerti* may be seen in Proske's *Musica Divina*. It is a peculiar circumstance that these composers should have written anything in the nature of *Salmi concerti* for the English services, whereas there are no such settings for the Latin rite by any English composer, so far as is known.

The Psalms in this form were closely associated by these musicians with their Festal settings of the *Preces*, although the reason for this is not now apparent. Some of the Psalms are proper to Easter Day, Ascension Day, and Whit-Sunday; but some are of a comparatively penitential character: for example, *Save me, O God* (Ps. 54) and *Hear my prayer* (Ps. 55) are among those set in this style by Byrd; and this suggests that these particular psalms may also have been sung in this manner in the course of the monthly cycle. Byrd's treatment of *Teach me, O Lord* (from Ps. 119) was quite novel at that date. It opens with a short passage for organ before the voice enters; and the verses of the psalm are sung alternately by a solo voice and the full choir, the solo being accompanied by an independent organ part.

In the Durham and Peterhouse manuscripts Byrd's

[1] B.M. Lansdowne MSS., 8, fo. 16.

'Second' *Preces* are given in conjunction with Psalm 24, verses 7–10 (*Lift up your heads*). In this instance the verses are set, not in chant form, but as a full anthem for six voices in contrapuntal style, this being an adaptation to English words of his motet *Attollite portas* (*Cant. Sac.*, 1575, No. 11).

Perhaps the most difficult problem with which the musicians were faced in connexion with the new Anglican rites was presented by the morning and evening Canticles. The difficulty of setting the Communion Service was far less arduous, because the sections of that Office for which music is required correspond closely with those of the Mass. And as regards the anthem the model was provided by the motet. For the English Canticles, however, there was little guidance to be derived from anything that had gone before. It is true that the Latin text of *Te Deum*, *Magnificat*, and *Nunc Dimittis* had been set by numbers of the earlier Church musicians, both English and foreign, but not on a sufficiently simple plan to serve in the English daily Matins and Evensong. The model for these settings had to be created.

In the latter days of the Latin services in England, and still more on the Continent, the vogue of writing very florid music for Church use had become pronounced. This was especially the case in the music of the Mass; and it is exemplified, for instance, in Taverner's Masses, where long phrases of music are set to single syllables of the words in such a manner that the several voices, proceeding independently, build up an elaborate structure just as in instrumental music, giving great scope for contrapuntal ingenuity, and often producing fine effects. At the Council of Trent in 1562 decrees were issued in very general terms with the purpose of suppressing certain undesirable features which were being introduced into Church music, especially those of an over-elaborate or secular character.

It was several years earlier in England that Cranmer wrote a letter to Henry the Eighth, dated 7 Oct. [1544], which has been the subject of much careless mis-quotation.[1] When the writer used the phrases 'a devout and solemn note', and 'for every syllable a note' he was referring to his

[1] *Cranmer's Letters*, Parker Soc. Publications, Letter 276, p. 412.

own experiments in adapting music for 'certain processions', which he and the king were planning to include in an English *Processionale*; and more particularly to his English adaptation of *Salve festa dies*, with which he was not satisfied. No order or injunction was contained in the letter. Moreover it was written some five years before the issue of 'the Book of Common Prayer'. It is true however that the earliest settings of the English canticles were designed more or less on the principle of 'for every syllable a note', as may be seen in the Dorian Service of Tallis, and this type was known as the 'Short' Service. It was left to Byrd almost a generation later to demonstrate how beautiful in a rather freer style this 'short' form might be. But neither he, nor even Tallis were under the restriction of any injunction, as witness the splendid five-part *Te Deum* of Tallis, and still more the elaborately extended settings of Byrd and others which came to be styled 'Great' Services.

The complete 'Service' in Byrd's day consisted of *Venite, Te Deum, Benedictus* (with *Jubilate* as an occasional alternative), *Kyrie, Creed, Magnificat,* and *Nunc Dimittis*. As already mentioned, music for the entire Office of the Holy Communion, including *Sanctus, Benedictus qui venit, Agnus Dei,* and *Gloria in excelsis* had been produced before the Book of Common Prayer was published. But by the time that Byrd reached manhood the *Sanctus, Benedictus, Agnus,* and *Gloria* had passed out of use, as regards musical performance. The singing of *Venite* in 'Service' form has long dropped out of practice, and it is unfortunate that there should now be no ordinary opportunity of hearing such works as Byrd's short *Venite*.

Byrd wrote two complete Services, one in each style. His 'Short' Service has never been surpassed as an example of the simpler form of setting the English Canticles for voices without accompaniment. With the exception of a few passages it is written for four voices, and it conforms very largely with the principle of note against note, with a single note to each syllable of the words. In this work Byrd relied for his effect upon short melodic phrases, beautifully outlined and fitted with rare subtlety to the verbal rhythm. In the following phrase from *Venite* it will be noticed how effectively he employs the antiphonal feature, of traditional usage in choirs, and how neatly he expands the musical material of the phrase, as used for 'For he is the Lord our God', to fit the corresponding phrase in reply to it.[1]

There are in this Service two settings of the *Kyrie* in the Anglican form. The Creed is perhaps the most elaborate number. Certain phrases in it are for five and six voices, and the voices are distributed with greater variety here than in any other part of the Service. The melismatic passage in the tenor part at the words 'the Lord, and Giver of life' may be noticed as a characteristic little piece of word-painting.

The only known text of the *Sanctus* has been found, uncatalogued, in a manuscript in the British Museum.[2] It gives only the treble and bass parts, and its authenticity has been questioned. It has been completed and published in five parts by the present writer. It appears to be in keeping with the style of the rest of the Service, and may reasonably be authentic. The gem of Byrd's 'Short' Service is the *Magnificat*. The short melodious phrases follow each other with a remarkable sense of proportion and balance, and the interest is sustained by frequent modulation; indeed, this little composition may be aptly quoted to disprove the statement, so often made, that Tudor compositions are devoid of modulation. One feature in this *Magnificat* serves to illustrate Byrd's artistry in a subtle way: the highest note he uses for the treble voice is D (in the original key) and

[1] Transposed up a minor third and note-values halved.
[2] B.M. Add. MS. 34203, fo. 8ᵛ

he reserves the use if it for one single moment throughout the Song, namely, for the word 'exalted' in the phrase 'and hath exalted the humble and meek', thus giving it special emphasis.

The *Gloria* of the *Magnificat* is brilliant in colour. The Song itself closes in the conventional way with the tonic major triad, the Service being in the minor key. The *Gloria* opens in the key of the subdominant and then reaches a full close with a major triad on the flattened seventh, passing on to two closes in the tonic major before the final phrase is reached. The scheme involves the use of a large preponderance of major triads, and especially of the tonic major triad. The effect is quite unusual in the music of this period, for it was customary when writing in a minor mode to reserve the use of the tonic major triad for the final chord. Wilbye adopted a similar device towards the close of his madrigal *Sweet honey-sucking bees*. The final phrase of this *Gloria*[1] outshines what goes before and ends it triumphantly.

Byrd's 'Great' Service comprises the same seven numbers as his 'Short' Service. It is to be classed with his three Masses among his greatest compositions. It is written in an elaborate contrapuntal style for a double choir, consisting of five voices on each side; there are also passages in six, seven, and eight parts, and one short one in ten. The rhythmic complexity and freedom of writing are very remarkable, and each part moves with complete independence. Indeed, as has been pointed out by conductors, the rhythmic independence of this work constitutes its chief difficulty in performance as well as one of its greatest charms. It is noteworthy that there is less modulation from the main key than in much of Byrd's work, yet this point has been somewhat overstressed.

The tradition of the Anglican 'Service' has always been to set each canticle in the same key, just as in an instru-

[1] Transposed up a minor third and note-values halved.

mental 'Suite'. It must also be remembered that the purpose of the music is purely liturgical, and that the several
numbers were never designed to be performed consecutively
without intermission.

The *Venite* opens with this phrase, harmonized for two
trebles and two altos:

O come let us sing un-to the Lord:

Byrd may have had a fragment of plain-song melody in his
mind. It is, in fact, not wholly unlike one of the traditional
phrases with which the *Te Deum* is precented.

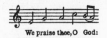

We praise thee,O God:

This opening, with slight modifications, is employed several
times in various parts of this Service, thus binding them
all together. The *Benedictus*, the *Creed*, *Magnificat*, and
Nunc Dimittis begin with it, and in each instance it is
harmonized for four voices, the bass voice being always
omitted. Moreover, much of the Service is written round
this phrase; for example, in the Creed it is repeated twice
at the words 'And he shall come again with glory'; and a
few bars later the third main section of the Creed opens:

And I be-lieve in the Ho-ly Ghost

The *Venite* is, perhaps, the simplest number in this work.
It contains some elaborate contrapuntal writing, but at
several points the voices enter homophonically with much
force, as at the words 'To-day'; 'Forty years long'; and 'It
is a people that do err'.

The *Te Deum* is set with fuller development than *Venite*,
yet without excessive repetition of verbal phrases, so that
it is not made unduly long. Much of it is in five parts, but
there are also passages for six, seven, and eight voices.
Byrd works up to his first climax at 'Also the Holy Ghost,
the Comforter'. This passage is written in seven real parts,

and the following verse, 'Thou art the King of Glory, O Christ', is set for eight voices. In the closing section of this movement the words 'Day by day we magnify thee' are treated with simple homophony, and the final climax is approached with some eight-part counterpoint to the repeated phrase 'have mercy upon us'. The concluding sentence is worked up at considerable length with intricate contrapuntal imitations in six parts, ending gloriously with a plagal cadence.

*

The *Benedictus*, after the opening phrase already alluded to, proceeds characteristically in five parts. The section 'That we being delivered' begins with a long passage in six parts designed for 'verse', or solo voices, producing a rather uncommon effect. Another 'verse' passage is introduced at the words 'And thou, Child'; and here again an unusual group of voices is in combination—three altos and a tenor. The *Gloria* of this canticle is developed with much artifice. It begins fairly simply in five parts, and the counterpoint becomes gradually more complex, the latter part being in seven parts. The scale-passage at 'world without end' is treated with ingenious imitations, and it strongly resembles the corresponding phrase in the *Gloria* of the *Nunc Dimittis*.

A typical example of Byrd's methods may be noticed in the Creed. At the words 'And was crucified' he secures his effect in the simplest manner by going straight from the

* Transposed up a minor third and note-values halved.

main key of the work, C major to B flat major, and the
value of this chord is enhanced by the fact that it is employed nowhere in the Creed apart from this paragraph.

man, And was   cru-ci-fied al - so   for   us   He   suf - fer-ed

The phrase 'He suffered and was buried' is laid out for
a double choir of five voices each.

In the short 'Amen' at the end of this movement the
scale passages are reminiscent of those in the *Gloria* both
of the *Benedictus* and the *Nunc Dimittis*, and it is evident
that Byrd aimed at linking together the different numbers
of this Service by these methods.

The two evening canticles are very similar in style to the
earlier numbers. There is a fine bit of eight-part writing in
the *Magnificat* in the verse 'He hath put down the mighty';
but the outstanding feature of both these is the splendid
treatment of the *Gloria*. In that of the *Magnificat* Byrd employs a series of downward scales, not only for the words
'As it was in the beginning', but also for the concluding
'Amens'. And he used a very vigorous phrase for 'world
without end', which is taken up by one voice after another
with an energy that almost seems to call for reinforcement
with drums.

The *Gloria* of the *Nunc Dimittis* is probably the finest
and the most beautiful ever written for the English use.
The Canticle itself ends in G, and the *Gloria* opens homophonically with great force on the chord of F. It is developed at great length. The phrase 'and ever shall be'
is passed contrapuntally from voice to voice, while the bass
sings the same phrase in augmentation. Then begins the
series of rising scale passages, taken up by one part after
another with cumulative interest and surpassing beauty, till
ultimately an authentic cadence in the original key of the
service is reached. The final four bars are of the nature of
a coda, ending with a plagal cadence; all the five voices in
turn come into prominence here, as if competing to outshine
each other in the beauty of expression.

The return of the A flat (F in the original key) in the third bar quoted here, which thus restores the principal key of the Canticle, is a beautiful feature in the final building up of the harmonic scheme.

The history of the loss and recovery of the 'Great' Service is of no small interest. The scarcity of text, even after allowing for loss and destruction, suggests that it was never widely used. There is, however, no reason for supposing that it was written for any special occasion, because no occasion can be imagined which would have called for the performance of all the seven numbers included in it. No doubt it was intended, like the 'Great' Services of other composers, for use on Festivals. It seems certain that it was in regular use at Durham, York and Worcester where text of it survives; and the fact that some short passages of the *Te Deum* and *Benedictus* exist in the hand of John Baldwin of Windsor,[1] points to it having been sung in St. George's Chapel.

Perhaps it was on account of its length that it dropped out of use and passed into complete oblivion for at least two and a half centuries, until the present author had the good fortune to rediscover and transcribe it for practical use again, with the result that it was performed in its entirety, for the first time after this long lapse, in 1924,

---

* Transposed up a minor third and note-values halved.
[1] Royal Music Library (British Museum), Baldwin's MS.

under the conductorship of Dr. W. Gillies Whittaker in Newcastle Cathedral.[1]

The larger part of the text was found, almost accidentally, at Durham Cathedral, where the Decani alto part is entirely wanting. Subsequently this part for the Evening Canticles was found at Peterhouse, Cambridge; and some fragments of the Morning Canticles are, as just stated, in Baldwin's MS. The remaining missing passages for the alto voice have been reconstructed by the present author.

Byrd wrote two other Evening Services, both of which were printed by Barnard.[2] Like the 'Great' Service they passed completely out of use for many generations, but they have now been restored to the repertory of most cathedral choirs. The 'Second' Service is interesting as being probably the earliest example of a 'Verse' Service. It includes several passages for solo voice with organ accompaniment. Some striking cross-rhythms are introduced at the words 'He hath scattered the proud'. The *Gloria* of the *Magnificat* is unusually spirited and original in conception, as the following excerpt will show:

The 'Third' Service, like the 'Second', is for five voices. Being mainly in triple measure, it was entitled by Barnard 'Master Bird's Three Minnoms'. In the *Magnificat* there is one beautiful passage, which by contrast is in square measure, at the verse 'He remembering his mercy'. The triad on the flat seventh of the key has a very telling effect

---

[1] The Evening Canticles had previously been performed at Evensong at St. Michael's College, Tenbury, on Michaelmas Day, 1923.

[2] *First Book of Selected Church Musick*, John Barnard, 1641.

* Transposed up a minor third and note-values halved.

on the word 'mercy'. This modulation is quite common in the music of this period, but here its value is enhanced because it occurs nowhere else in the composition. This is a typical example of Byrd's artistry, similar to his treatment of the word 'exalted' in his 'Short' *Magnificat*. In the verse 'He hath filled the hungry' the tenor is in canon with the soprano at the octave.

A four-part setting of *Te Deum* and *Benedictus* in F, probably an early work, survives only in fragments among the Peterhouse manuscripts. The alto part is complete and the upper voice-part of half the *Te Deum*. This is sufficient to show the character of the work; and, indeed, half the *Te Deum* can be reconstructed from these fragments with some degree of confidence. In design it is rather more extended than 'Short' Service form. It is not impossible that the missing parts may yet be discovered, perhaps among the works to which no composer's name is assigned in the manuscript.

The bass part of his *Jubilate* in G, probably also an early work, is among the Lambeth MSS. This seems to be quite a simple setting in the 'Short' form. It must be remembered that *Jubilate* was introduced as an alternative to *Benedictus* in the Second Prayer Book of Edward the Sixth. It was ordered to be used at least on those four days in the year when *Benedictus* was read in the second Lesson at Morning Prayer. It is an error to suppose that no Tudor musician set *Jubilate* in Service form. Apart from this example of Byrd, the settings of John Farrant (of Salisbury) and Thomas Weelkes may be called to mind among others.

English Liturgical Music

First Preces and Psalms 47 and 54.	Barnard; Peterhouse, 35, 42; St. John's Coll., Oxford, 180; Lambeth Palace, 764.
Second Preces and Psalms 114 (1-6), 55 (1-8), 119 (33-40), 24 (7-10).	Barnard; Peterhouse, 33, 34, 38, 39; Ch. Ch. 6; St. John's Coll., Oxford, 180; Durham, C1; E. 4-11; Lambeth Palace, 764.
Preces and Responses (2nd alto partly wanting).	Peterhouse, 35, 37, 42-5; Durham, A 1.
Litany for four voices (alto wanting).	Ely, 4; Tenbury, 1382.

Short Service.	Barnard; B.M. Add. 17784;
Venite.	Add. 29289; Add. 34203;
Te Deum.	Royal Mus. Lib., Cosyn's
Benedictus.	score; Peterhouse, 35-45; Ch.
Kyrie No. 1.	Ch. 1001; St. John's Coll.,
Kyrie No. 2.	Oxford, 180; Durham, C 8;
Sanctus.	Ely, 28; York, Gostling's
Magnificat.	MS.; Wimborne Minster;
Nunc Dimittis.	Lambeth Palace 764; R.C.M.,
	1045-51.
Second Service.	Barnard; St. John's Coll., Ox-
Magnificat.	ford, 180; Ely, 4; Wimborne
Nunc Dimittis.	Minster; Lambeth Palace,
	764; Tenbury, 791.
Third Service.	
Magnificat.	Barnard; Ch. Ch. 1001; St
Nunc Dimittis.	John's Coll., Oxford, 180.
Great Service (Decani alto partly	B.M. Add. 17792-6; Add.
wanting).	31443; Royal Mus. Lib.,
Venite.	Baldwin's score; Peterhouse,
Te Deum.	33-5, 38, 39, 42, 46; Dur-
Benedictus.	ham, A 1; C 13, 18; E. 4-11;
Kyrie.	Worcester Cathedral, Mus.
Creed.	MSS.; Tenbury, 791; York
Magnificat.	Minster MSS.
Nunc Dimittis.	
Service in F (fragments only).	Peterhouse, 34, 38, 39.
Te Deum.	
Benedictus.	
Jubilate in G (bass part only).	Lambeth, 764.

CHAPTER IX

ENGLISH ANTHEMS

IN turning from one class of Byrd's composition to another, it is impossible not to be impressed with the wealth of his output. There are more than sixty anthems in the list given at the end of the present chapter; and this number does not include a dozen or more sacred songs which have appeared in catalogues under the heading of Anthems, although they should more strictly be grouped together with the secular songs for solo voice.

In the course of his long life Byrd saw many changes, not only in music, not only in matters of religious observance and worship, but in almost every aspect of social life. The England of Henry the Eighth became the England of Charles the First during Byrd's lifetime. And as regards music, the whole outlook was enlarged with the dawn of the seventeenth century. In the first years that followed the Reformation the English anthem differed little from the Latin motet as regards form and construction. But the stereotyped motet, perfect as it was for its purpose in its own time, was ripe for development in the surroundings of the reformed Anglican services. The same impulse which looked for further opportunities of self-expression, and found it in the realm of secular music in the form of solo singing, led inevitably to the introduction of solo-song in English anthems. Byrd was among the first to experiment with the anthem on these lines; but the bulk of his work in this department followed the older tradition.

By far the greater part of his anthems was printed in his lifetime. His two sets of *Psalmes, Sonets, and Songs* and his *Songs of sundrie natures* contain a fair proportion of sacred numbers that should rightly be classed as anthems. And four more were printed by Sir William Leighton in his *Teares or Lamentacions of a sorrowful soul* in 1614. The list is completed by a comparatively small number that have survived only in manuscript.

It must be frankly stated that many of Byrd's anthems fall below the high level of the rest of his Church music. For example, the *Seven Penitential Psalms*, as set for three voices among his *Songs of sundrie natures*, are disappointing in effect; nor are the ten five-part Psalms in the 1588 set much more attractive. And his four short contributions to Leighton's book are of comparatively small interest. No doubt all of these suffer considerably from the wretchedly poor verbal text, mostly drawn from metrical versions of the Psalms, to which the music is set. Byrd's own statement that beautiful words inspired him inevitably with suitable musical ideas, will explain his comparative failure where this source of inspiration was so conspicuously absent.

On the other hand, there are several of his English anthems which without doubt will bear comparison with his highest standard of excellence. Curiously enough, it is in the spirit of praise and joyfulness, rather than in that of penitence and solemnity, that Byrd excels with the English anthem; this contrasts with what may be seen in his Latin motets. It is also curious that whereas little of value in this department is to be found in the publications of 1588 and 1589, there are several splendid examples of the English anthem in the 1611 set. This fact seems to suggest that as old age approached, between the years 1590 and 1610, when these compositions would have been written, Byrd became more in sympathy with the English words of Scripture. This is not to suggest any fading of his love of the Latin text.

Turning to the 1611 set, which will be more fully discussed together with the publications of 1588 and 1589 in connexion with the madrigalian compositions, the brilliance of *Sing ye to the Lord* (No. 6) at once arrests the eye, in contrast to the dullness of the three-part anthems alluded to above. Still better is the four-part setting of these two opening verses of Psalm 115 to the version *Come, let us rejoice* (No. 16). It ends very gaily with several repetitions of the words 'let us make joy to him' set to a musical phrase very similar to that of 'Halleluiah canat' in *Laudibus in sanctis* (*Cantiones Sacrae*, Bk. ii, No. 1).

Arise, Lord, into thy rest (No. 18) is another fine example of polyphonic writing, with considerable complexity of rhythmic treatment towards the end, at the words 'And let the Saints rejoice'.

Make ye joy to God (No. 28) is even more buoyant in spirit. It opens with a characteristic and suitable phrase worked out in the usual polyphonic manner. Then follows this phrase:

serve ye the Lord with   glad - - - - ness,

and later, at the words 'enter ye in before his sight in jollity', each voice takes up the phrase 'in jollity':

in jol - - - - - - - - - - li - ty,   in jol - - - li - - ty.

The highest class is reached in the anthems for six voices included in the 1611 set. *Praise our Lord, all ye Gentiles* opens with great dignity. The second soprano voice has the first bar alone, and then all the voices take up and repeat the phrase more or less homophonically. The interest is then developed in contrapuntal style and the climax reached at the words 'his truth remaineth for ever'. This passage is worked out at considerable length and with added force as the voices respond to each other with the resounding phrase which grows in fervour of expression at every repetition. Byrd, with his rare sense of fitness, perceived that the glorious climax demanded something exceptional for the 'Amen' that should follow it. In the result he succeeded in writing one of the most perfect settings of the word in the whole realm of music. It is worth quoting in full, and it is printed below in modern notation with the crotchet unit substituted for minim, and transposed up a minor third (the expression marks are added by the author).

Turn our captivity (No. 30) is another fine anthem in which Byrd's genius for conceiving musical phrases in accordance with 'the life of the words' is exemplified. There are several picturesque touches here; for instance, the curious little turn of the voices up and down in the first two bars: and the contrapuntal entries of the voices 'casting their seeds'. The advancing multitudes at the words 'but coming', and the joyous outburst that follows when all the voices sing note against note in triple rhythm, are features that are represented with dramatic effect.

In this same volume is the brilliant number entitled by Byrd 'a Caroll for Christmas Day', *This day Christ was born*. It is interesting to compare the same composer's *Hodie Christus natus est* (*Gradualia*, Bk. ii, No. 6), which has been discussed in a former chapter. Throughout this English setting of the words the joy of Christmas is expressed with glowing fervour. 'The Archangels are glad'—'The just rejoice'. Then, with greater restraint and cumulative dignity, 'Glory be to God on high' is sung in ascending scale-passages by voice after voice, working up to a great climax. The 'Alleluia' with which the anthem concludes forms a kind of coda.

One of the few compositions of Byrd that has helped to keep his name alive in cathedral circles during the past three centuries is his six-part anthem *Sing joyfully*. This is mainly due to the fact that it was printed in the collections of cathedral music both by Barnard[1] and by Boyce.[2] It is a fine example of polyphonic writing, though perhaps lacking something in the way of variety of style. The second section, *Blow up the trumpet in the new moon*, is set to music in a conventional manner which was followed by several other composers with whom these words have been popular; but it must be remembered that Byrd was first in the field in writing music to these English words. This anthem must have enjoyed wide popularity, for it is found in a large number of early manuscripts. The text for the phrase 'Blow up the trumpet' as given in the Bodleian MS.[3] differs from all the other known versions, and seems more characteristic of Byrd than the other variants.

It is curious that Byrd should have written another anthem to a slightly different English text of this same Psalm. This other setting, *Sing we merrily*, was included by him in his 1611 set (No. 20). It is designed for a very unusual lay-out of voices: three sopranos, all ranging up to high G, an alto, and a tenor. It is likely that this was composed to meet some special conditions.

Other anthems to be noticed are *Arise, O Lord, why sleepest thou?* the first section of which is for five voices, and the second (*Help us, O God*) for six. This anthem must not be confused with the contemporary adaptation to English words of *Exsurge, Domine*, nor with *Arise, Lord, into thy rest*. *Prevent us, O Lord*, and *O God, whom our offences* may be mentioned among the simpler anthems of Byrd; both of these have survived only in manuscript.

O praise our Lord, ye saints above is a fine piece of music; but some doubt must be expressed as to whether it can rightly be ascribed to Byrd. It is known in complete form only in one source of text, namely, in the British Museum Additional MS. 17797, where it is ascribed to Byrd. The sections *Praise him on tube* and *The gladsome sound of silver bells* are also found in Additional MSS. 18936–9, and here they are ascribed to 'Alphonso', i.e. Alphonso Ferrabosco,

---

[1] *First Book of Selected Church Music*, 1641.
[2] *Cathedral Music*, vol. ii.
[3] Bodl. Mus. MS d. 212–16.

the elder. The anthem throughout its five sections[1] is unlike
anything else that Byrd wrote, both in design or style, and
it seems probable that the whole anthem was the work of
Ferrabosco.

Bow thine ear, which held its place in English cathedrals
throughout the long period when Byrd's music was neglected, is, of course, an adaptation of English words to
Civitas sancti tui, the second section of the motet *Ne irascaris* (*Cantiones Sacrae*, Bk. i, No. 20). English versions of
this motet were in use in Byrd's day, and they may have
had his sanction. Its great beauty is in no way marred by
translation, but Barnard's English version is not wholly
successful.

It has already been stated that Byrd made experiments
in composing what came at a later date to be known as
'Verse' anthems. In some of these verse anthems short
passages for solo voice were interspersed between choral
sections; others took the form of songs with a choral section
at the end of each verse.

Have mercy upon me, O God (1611 set, No. 25)[2] is a
lovely work of this kind. The first nine bars are for a quartet
of viols; the soprano voice alone then sings the opening
phrase of the Psalm to an accompaniment of viols. The
choir of five voices repeats the same words. Each subsequent phrase is treated alternately by soloist and chorus in
a similar manner until the words 'Wash me clean' are
reached. After this verse has been sung by the solo voice,
the soprano joins with the other voices in the repetition,
making harmony in six parts. The concluding 'Amen' is
also for six voices. The viols were, no doubt, intended to
duplicate the voices in the choral sections. Although there
is no printed instruction on the point in the original part-
book, it would almost seem that in the final verse, and
perhaps in the 'Amen' also, the soloist alone was intended
to sing the top line to the accompaniment of the voices

---

[1] In the edition of this anthem, edited by W. B. Squire, one section was
omitted.

[2] In the Durham MSS. and elsewhere, this anthem is incorrectly assigned
to Gibbons. This error unfortunately found its way into Vol. iv of *Tudor
Church Music*, and into the author's *Orlando Gibbons: a short account of his
life and work*. The opening verse in the MSS. is assigned to two soprano voices.

and viols. If this was actually Byrd's intention, this composition becomes vested with exceptional interest in relation to the history of song-form.

Thou God that guid'st both heaven and earth is an anthem that has survived only in manuscript. It is constructed on a plan closely resembling that of *Have mercy upon me*, except that the manuscripts give the text of an accompaniment for organ in place of viols. This accompaniment is of a very free and independent character. The soprano part of this anthem is definitely labelled 'solo' and the choral sections 'full'. Both these compositions are remarkable as being among the earliest examples of the 'verse anthem'.

Two splendid Christmas anthems are included in *Songs of sundrie natures*. These take the form of songs, with choral refrain repeated at the close of each verse. *From Virgin's womb this day did spring* (No. 35) is a poem of four verses by Francis Kindlemarsh, who flourished about the year 1570. The first and last verses will probably be found sufficient for performance. Each verse has the refrain:

> Rejoice, rejoice, with heart and voice,
> In Christ his birth this day rejoice.

Byrd in this instance was working with words that would have vividly appealed to his musical imagination. For example, the final verse of the song runs:

> O sing unto this glittering glorious King.
> O praise his Name let every living thing.
> Let heart and voice like bells of silver ring
> The comfort that this day to man doth bring.
> Let lute and shalm with sound of sweet delight
> These joys of Christ his birth this day recite.

The song is set for a mezzo-soprano voice within the narrow compass of a seventh upwards from middle C. It may therefore reasonably be sung by a baritone voice an octave lower. The accompaniment is for viols. The chorus 'Rejoice, rejoice' is perhaps the most brilliant little piece of Christmas music in existence. It is written for two sopranos and two altos, but it can effectively be sung an octave lower by tenors and basses. Each voice enters in turn with the vigorous phrase:

Presently the groups of triple crotchets break into four quavers, and the chorus works up to an ecstasy of fervour at the finish:

The other 'Carowle', as Byrd styles it, is also in song-form; but in this case it is designed as a duet for two equal voices, accompanied by viols, with a refrain for a normal mixed chorus of four voices. The song consists of three stanzas, beginning with the words *An earthly tree a heavenly fruit it bare* (No. 40 in the same set). The refrain, to the words 'Cast off all doubtful care', is rather similar in treatment to that of *From Virgin's womb* without reaching quite the same degree of brilliance.

Byrd must certainly be regarded as one of the pioneers of the 'Verse' anthem. It could not be expected that many experiments of this nature should reach a high level. Some of them suffer also from the poverty of the words. Yet the examples quoted here certainly show that Byrd did something more than point to the direction in which the English anthem was destined to develop half a century after his death.

English Anthems

FULL ANTHEMS

Of three voices

Attend mine humble prayer.	Songs of sundrie natures No. 7.
From depth of sin.	„ „ „ No. 6.
I have been young.	Psalmes, Songs and Sonnets (1611) No. 7.

Lord, hear my prayer.	Songs of sundrie natures No. 5
Lord, in thy rage.	„ „ „ No. 1.
Lord, in they wrath.	„ „ „ No. 3.
O God, which art most merciful.	„ „ „ No. 4.
Right blest are they.	„ „ „ No. 2.
Sing ye to our Lord.	Psalmes, Songs and Sonnets (1611) No. 6.

Of four voices

Be unto me, O Lord.	Leighton's Teares or Lamentacions No. 12.
Come, let us rejoice.	Psalmes, Songs and Sonnets (1611) No. 16.
Look down, O Lord.	Leighton's Teares or Lamentacions No. 1.
O Lord, my God.	Songs of sundrie natures No. 22.

Of five voices

Arise, Lord, into thy rest.	Psalmes, Songs and Sonnets (1611) No. 18.
Blessed is he that fears the Lord.	Psalmes, Sonets and Songs (1588) No. 8.
Come, help, O God.	Leighton's Teares or Lamentacions No. 22.
Even from the depth.	Psalmes, Sonets and Songs (1588) No. 9.
Exalt thyself, O God (Bass part only).	St. John's Coll., Oxford 180, and Dunnington-Jefferson MS. York Minster.
Help, Lord, for wasted are those men.	Psalmes, Sonets and Songs (1588) No. 7.
How long shall mine enemies?	B.M. Add. 17792-6; Ch. Ch. 984-8; 1001; Peterhouse, 35, 42, 44; St. John's Coll., Oxford, 180; Durham, A 1; C 4-7, 9-11, 15-17; Tenbury, 1382.
How shall a young man?	Psalmes, Sonets and Songs (1588) No. 4.
I laid me down to rest.	Leighton's Teares or Lamentacions No. 1.
If that a sinner's sighs.	Psalmes, Sonets and Songs (1588) No. 30.

Let God arise (single part only).	Ch. Ch. 1012, fo. 102.
Let not our prayers be rejected.	Tenbury, 1382.
Lord, in thy wrath.	Psalmes, Sonets and Songs (1588) No. 9.
Make ye joy to God.	Psalmes, Songs and Sonnets (1611) No. 24
Mine eyes with fervency.	Psalmes, Sonets and Songs (1588) No. 2.
My soul oppressed with care.	Psalmes, Sonets and Songs (1588) No. 3.
O God, give ear.	Psalmes, Sonets and Songs (1588) No. 1.
O God, whom our offences.	Barnard; B.M. Add. 17792-6; Ch. Ch. 1001; St. John's Coll., Oxford, 180; Lambeth Palace, 764; R.C.M. 1045-7, 1049; Tenbury, 1382.
O Lord, how long wilt thou forget me?	Psalmes, Sonets and Songs (1588) No. 5.
O Lord, who in thy sacred tent.	Psalmes, Sonets and Songs (1588) No. 6.
O praise our Lord, ye saints.	B.M. Add. 17797; Add. 18936-9.
Prevent us, O Lord.	Barnard; B.M. Add. 29372-6; Peterhouse, 35-7, 42-5; Ch. Ch. 984-8; 1001; St. John's Coll., Oxford, 181; Durham, C 4-7, 9, 11-12, 15-17. York, Gostling MSS.; Lambeth, 764.
Prostrate, O Lord, I lie.	Psalmes, Sonets and Songs (1588) No. 27.
Save me, O God.	B.M. Add. 17784; 30478-9; Ch. Ch. 56-60; 1001; 1012; St. John's Coll., Oxford, 180; Durham, C. 4-7, 10-11, 15-17. York, Gostling MSS.; Ely, 4; 28; Wimborne.
Sing we merrily. Blow up the trumpet (*2nd part*).	Psalmes, Songs and Sonnets (1611) Nos. 20-21.

A page from the 'Superius' part-book of a Set belonging *circa* 1600 to Edward Paston, and now at St. Michael's College, Tenbury (MSS. 341–4). It shows the conclusion of Byrd's anthem *Christ is risen* and the beginning of his *Arise, O Lord*

Reproduced by permission of the Warden and Fellows of St. Michael's College, Tenbury

Of six voices

{ Arise, O Lord, why sleepest thou?

[Help us, O God (*2nd part*).

B.M. Add. 30478-9; Egerton 2009, 11, 12; Ch. Ch. 1220, 2; 1001; 1012; St. John's Coll., Oxford, 180; Durham, A 1; C 1, 4-7, 9-12, 15-17; Ely, 1; 28; Lambeth Palace, 764; Tenbury, 341-4; 389; 1382.

{ Behold how good a thing it is.

{ And as the pleasant morning

[dew (*2nd part*).

Songs of sundrie natures, Nos. 38-9.

Behold now, praise the Lord (single part only).

Tenbury, 1382.

Let us arise from sin (single part only).

Tenbury, 1382.

O God, the proud are risen.

Peterhouse, 33-4, 38-9, 46; Ch. Ch. 1001; St. John's Coll., Oxford, 181; Durham, A 1; C 4-7, 11-12, 15-17; Ely, 1.

O Lord, give ear to the prayer.

Peterhouse, 33, 34, 38, 39; Durham, A 1; C 4-7, 11-12, 15-17; Ely, 1.

O Lord, make thy servant Elizabeth.

Barnard; Peterhouse, 34, 36, 38, 39, 44; 46; Ch. Ch. 984-8; 1001; St. John's Coll., Oxford, 180; Durham, A 1; C 4, 6, 7, 11, 12, 15-17; York, Gostling MSS.; Ely, 28; Lambeth Palace, 764; R.C.M. 1045-51; Tenbury, 791; 1382.

Praise our Lord, all ye Gentiles.

Psalmes, Songs and Sonnets (1611) No. 29.

{ Sing joyfully.

{ Blow up the trumpet (*2nd part*)

Barnard; B.M. Add. 17784; Add. 17792-6; Add. 29366-8; Add. 29372-7; Add. 30478-9; Bodl. Mus. Sch. d. 212-16; Peterhouse, 33, 34, 38, 39, 46; St. John's Coll., Oxford, 180; Durham, A 1, 2; C 2, 4-7, 10-12, 15-17; York, Gostling MSS.; Ely, 1, 2; Tenbury, 1382.

This day Christ was born.	Psalmes, Songs and Sonnets (1611) No. 27.
Turn our captivity.	Psalmes, Songs and Sonnets (1611) No. 30.
Unto the hills mine eyes I lift.	Songs of sundrie natures, No. 45.

VERSE ANTHEMS

Alack, when I look back.	B.M. Add. 15117; Ch. Ch. 1001; St. John's Coll., Oxford, 180; Durham, C 4, 5, 7, 9, 10; Lambeth Palace, 764; R.C.M. 1048, 1051, Tenbury, 791; 1382.
{ An earthly tree. { Cast off all doubtful care (*2nd part*).	Songs of sundrie natures, Nos. 40 and 25.
Behold, O God, the sad and heavy case.	B.M. Add. 30479; Durham, A 5; C 1, 4-7, 9, 10.
{ Christ rising again. { Christ is risen (*2nd part*).	Songs of sundrie natures, Nos. 46-7.
{ From Virgin's womb. { Rejoice, rejoice (*2nd part*)	Songs of sundrie natures, Nos. 35 and 24.
Have mercy upon me.	Psalmes, Songs and Sonnets (1611) No. 25.
Hear my prayer.	Barnard; Ch. Ch. 1001; St. John's Coll., Oxford, 181; Durham, C 2, 3, 7, 11, 14, 16; Lambeth Palace, 764; R.C.M. 1045-51; Tenbury, 791; 1382
Lord, to thee I make my moan (a single part only).	Bodl. Mus. Sch. e. 423.
Now may Israel say (a single part only).	Tenbury, 1382.
O Lord, rebuke me not.	Barnard; R.C.M. 1045-51.
O God, that guides the cheerful sun.	Psalmes, Songs and Sonnets (1611) No. 28
Thou God, that guid'st both heaven and earth.	Barnard; B.M. Add. 30478; Ch. Ch. 1001; St. John's Coll., Oxford, 181; Ely, 4; Lambeth Palace, 764; R.C.M. 1046, 48, 51; Tenbury, 791; 1382.

CHAPTER X

MADRIGALIAN COMPOSITIONS

MADRIGAL singing came into fashion in England many years before English musicians turned their attention to the composition of madrigals. The vogue of the madrigal dates from about the year 1535, when the Flemish composer Verdelot published the first set of vocal works that bore the actual title of *Madrigali*. Adrian Willaert, born in Flanders about the year 1480, migrated to Italy and became the founder of the Venetian school of musicians, and Verdelot was probably his pupil. During the succeeding sixty or seventy years the output of madrigals in Italy was immense. Early in the reign of Queen Elizabeth Italian madrigal part-books were finding their way into England, and the practice gradually grew up of singing music of this kind to while away the winter evenings after supper.

It is strange that the coming of the English madrigal was so long delayed. Several reasons for this may be suggested. The English people from time immemorial have been prone to approve the accomplishments of foreign musicians in preference to those of their fellow countrymen. It is no new thing for English musicians to adopt foreign names in expectation that they will have a higher commercial value. John Cooper, born in 1570, thought it worth while to be known as Coperario. And it is likely that madrigal singers in early Elizabethan days thought scorn of the pleasant attempts of such composers as Richard Edwards, possibly preferring some of the less successful Italian madrigals to such a gem as *In going to my naked bed*. It is likely that for some time the English composers were snubbed. It is likely also that the composers were in a position to ignore such treatment, because their time and energies must have been occupied chiefly in supplying the needs of the Reformed Anglican Services. It was also the natural inclination of many of them still to follow the time-honoured forms of composition with Latin text. Another reason may be that music-publishing was unprofitable. Little was attempted in these lines before the granting of the Licence to Tallis and Byrd; and that privilege, on their own statement, for a time brought loss rather than profit.

The year 1588 saw the defeat of the Spanish Armada. It was also an important date in the history of English music; for it was in that year that Nicholas Yonge published a collection of Italian madrigals adapted to English words. These madrigals had become popular with a group of his friends, who were in the habit of meeting at his house in the City of London with the object of singing them. This publication was the first of two collections entitled *Musica Transalpina*. Yonge inserted in it a composition by Byrd, *The fair young virgin*, an English version of *La Virginella*, which Byrd included in his *Psalmes, Sonets, & Songs* published later in the same year. As Yonge used the term 'madrigals', in describing his collection, *The fair young Virgin* stands as the first English madrigal ever printed.

The publication in 1588 of Yonge's collection and Byrd's *Psalmes, Sonets, & Songs* was the prelude to the wonderful output of English madrigals that was produced during the subsequent twenty-five years.

The full title of Byrd's set was 'Psalmes, Sonets, & songs of Sadnes and pietie, made into Musicke of five parts: whereof, | some of them going abroade among divers, in untrue coppies | are heere truely corrected, and th'other being Songs | very rare and newly composed, are heere published, for the recreation | of all such as delight in Musicke: By William Byrd, | one of the Gent of the Queenes Maiesties | honorable Chappell. | Printed by Thomas East the assigne of W. Byrd, | and are to be sold at the dwelling house of the said T. East, by Paules Wharfe. | 1588 | cum privilegio Regiae Maiestatis.|'

The volume was divided into three sections: (1) Psalms, (2) Sonnets and Pastorals, (3) Songs of Sadness and Piety. The Psalms have already been discussed. The Sonnets and Pastorals may be classed as madrigals, but in style they differ in a marked manner from those of Morley, Wilbye, and others of the English School. Several of these compositions were written at an earlier date, being found in such manuscripts as Christ Church 984–8. For example, *Though*

Amaryllis dance in green (No. 12) is included in these Christ Church books in the form of a song with string accompaniment. This incidentally provides the clue to the form of almost all the compositions in the 1588 set. It will be noticed that the phrase 'The first singing-part' is printed in connexion with one of the upper voice-parts, though not always the top part. Byrd had composed these pieces as solo songs in the first instance, and he subsequently adapted the viol parts for voices; yet these lower parts should still hold a slightly subordinate position in the polyphony, so that the prominence of the solo line may not be compromised. In the 'first singing-part' the words of the poem flow on without repetition, and are broken only by short rests between the phrases. This principle of construction is observed with hardly any exception throughout this 1588 set. It also explains why Byrd was able to choose poems of several stanzas for his purpose, whereas madrigalists like Wilbye and Morley found six lines sufficient as a rule. Only the first stanza was printed with the music; but, as in song-form, any number could be sung in succession by repeating the music; yet it is doubtful whether more than two could be effective in performance. In reference to the words, it is remarkable what fine poetry Byrd included in this volume. Philip Sidney, Edward, Earl of Oxford, Edward Dyer, and Thomas Deloney are among poets represented here, while some of the anonymous lyrics are on the same high level. The words of *Constant Penelope* (No. 23) are in hexameter measure, and Byrd has been careful in the first singing-part of this madrigal to scan the lines in accordance with the classical metre. The words are a translation of Ovid's 1st Epistle, 'Penelope to Ulysses', beginning 'Hanc tua Penelope lento tibi mittit, Ulixe'.

No. 24 is *La Virginella*. It was an English version of this that Yonge included in *Musica Transalpina*. Here it is printed with the original Italian words from Ariosto's *Orlando Furioso*, Canto I, v. 42. This madrigal is definitely constructed in song-form, and it will be better appreciated if the soprano part is frankly regarded as the melody.

Among these 'Pastorals' *Though Amaryllis dance in green* (No. 12) stands out as the most attractive. It reveals the lighter side of Byrd's somewhat austere nature. A feature

of this madrigal is the alternative and sometimes simultaneous use of two kinds of triple rhythm, as shown in the first
two bars:

Though A-maryl-lis   dance in green,

Rhythmic variety, and even complexity, is a feature of his
writing, and particularly of the pieces in this set. The first
of the 'Pastorals' opens thus:

I   joy not in no earthly   bliss, I   force not Croesus' wealth___ a   straw.

An extreme example of rhythmic complexity is found in
The match that's made for just and true respects (No. 26).
A number of cross-rhythms are introduced throughout
this song, which make it very difficult in performance; but
in the refrain 'Pari iugo dulcis tractus' that particular form
of sixteenth-century proportion called 'sesquialtera' is introduced in each of the voice-parts in turn, adding much to
the rhythmic complications. At the end of this item there
is printed the quaint formula, 'Heere endeth the Sonets and
Pastoralles and beginneth Songs of Sadnes and Pietie'. In
this last section of the book there are some beautiful things
written in Byrd's best manner. The *Lullaby* (No. 32) is
sublime in its simple loveliness. The refrain has been so
frequently dissociated from the main part of this song, that
it is not generally realized that it forms part of a Carol of
the Holy Child, the subject of the poem being the massacre
of the Holy Innocents. The final cadence of the song as
well as that of the refrain, illustrates how beautiful the
simultaneous clash of C♮ and C♯ can sound.

The refrain ends thus:

my   sweet lit-tle Ba-by, Ba - - - - - - by.

Another splendid 'Song of Pietie' is *Why do I use my paper, ink and pen?* The words were written by Henry Walpole as 'An Epitaph of the Life and Death of the most famous Clerk and virtuous Priest Edmund Campion', who was executed in 1581. It was a subject that would have appealed very directly to Byrd with his Catholic sympathies. Strangely enough, though the poem consists of as many as thirty verses, the second and third of the three which Byrd printed are not found elsewhere. There may have been a political reason for this, for the excerpt, as it stands in Byrd's book, could have given no possible cause for offence; and it may be assumed that these two additional stanzas were also written by Walpole.

The music rises to a noble climax at the words 'their glorious death'. It may also be noticed how Byrd used the dominant seventh freely in its first inversion in this passage.

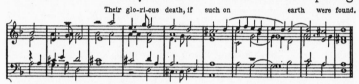

This book concludes with two 'funerall songs of that honorable Gent Syr Phillip Sidney, Knight'. The first of these is absolutely simple in character, and a feeling of deep pathos is completely expressed. Opening in G minor, a short melodic phrase, extending over three bars, is repeated several times; the last of these repetitions is of exceptional beauty:

In this first set Byrd makes his famous appeal to every one to take up singing.

¶ Reasons briefly set downe by th'auctor, to perswade every one to learne to sing.

First it is a Knowledge easely taught, and quickly learned where there is a good Master, and an apt Scoller.

2. The exercise of singing is delightfull to Nature & good to preserve the health of Man.

3. It doth strengthen all the parts of the brest, & doth open the pipes.

4. It is a singular good remedie for a stutting & stammering in the speech.

5. It is the best meanes to procure a perfect pronunciation & to make a good Orator.

6. It is the onely way to know where Nature hath bestowed the benefit of a good voyce: which guift is so rare, as there is not one among a thousand, that hath it: and in many, that excellent guift is lost, because they want Art to expresse Nature.

7. There is not any Musicke of Instruments whatsoever, comparable to that which is made of the voyces of Men, where the voyces are good, and the same well sorted and ordered.

8. The better the voyce is, the meeter it is to honour and serve God there-with: and the voyce of man is chiefly to be imployed to that ende.

omnis spiritus laudet Dominum.

> Since singing is so good a thing
> I wish all men would learne to sing.

In his 'Epistle to the Reader' Byrd expressed a wish that if any should find errors in his compositions they should 'either with courtesie let the same be concealed, or in friendlie sort' tell him of them, so that they might be corrected in any reprint 'remembering alwaies that it is more easy to finde a fault then to amend it'.

The book was dedicated to Sir Christopher Hatton, who was about three years older than Byrd. As a young man he had attracted the notice of Queen Elizabeth by his graceful dancing, and this led to his holding several court appointments. In 1586 he was a member of the Commission for the trial of Mary Queen of Scots. In the following year he was made Lord Chancellor, to the indignation of the legal profession. He was, however, a man of considerable literary culture and a friend to men of letters. He wrote the fourth Act of *Gismond of Salerne*, the first love-tragedy written in English. This play provides a very interesting link between Hatton and Byrd, because Byrd's song *Come tread the path* was also composed for it.

More will be said of this when discussing Byrd's songs in the following chapter. Hatton died in 1591. He must not be confused with his nephew and namesake, Sir Christopher Hatton, K.B., to whom Orlando Gibbons dedicated his set of madrigals.

Byrd's *Songs of sundrie natures* followed in the next year as part of his scheme to produce an accurate text of all his works. He was encouraged also by the success of the former publications, for he wrote: 'Finding that my last Impression of Musicke (most gentle Reader) through thy curtesie and favor hath had good passage and utterance ... I have bene encouraged thereby to take further paines therein'. He also said that since the publishing of the former set, only a year earlier, 'the exercise and love of that Art hath exceedingly encreased'. This illuminating comment supports the theory that English musical taste began to turn definitely towards the native madrigal about the year 1588.

Lord Hunsdon was patron of this book. He was son of William Carey and Mary Boleyn, the sister of Anne, and therefore was first cousin to Queen Elizabeth. Born in 1524, he was raised to the peerage in 1558, and later was created a Knight of the Garter. He is said to have lacked most of the literary culture of his class; but Byrd chose him, as he says in his dedicatory address, in return for the many favours he had shown him in his official capacity at the Court as Lord Chamberlain. In this address Byrd repeats the statement that 'since the publishing in print of my last labors in Musicke, divers persons of great honor and worship have more esteemed & delighted in the exercise of that Art, then before'. Music had suddenly become fashionable. It was no longer dependent solely on the support of City men, like Nicholas Yonge and his friends. The highest people in the land were delighting in it, and in the big country houses the gentry were singing madrigals.

The full title of this publication was 'Songs of sundrie natures, some of | gravitie, and others of myrth, fit for all compa|nies and voyces. Lately made and composed in|to Musicke of 3. 4. 5. and 6. parts: and pub|lished for the delight of all such as take plea|sure in the exercise of | that Art. | By William Byrd, one of the Gentlemen | of the Queenes Maiesties honorable | Chappell. | Imprinted at

London by Thomas | East, the assigne of William Byrd, and are to be | sold at the house of the sayd T. East, being in | Aldersgate streete, at the signe of the | blacke Horse. 1589. | Cum privilegio maiestatis. |'

The book opens with the three-part settings of the seven penitential Psalms that have been already mentioned. But it is interesting to notice that, whereas these are constructed on the principle of song-form, Byrd passes straight into pure madrigalian style in the three-part secular numbers that follow. For example, in *The nightingale so pleasant* (No. 9) each of the three parts has an equal share of the melodic interest. The opening bars, as regards style, might have been written by Wilbye.

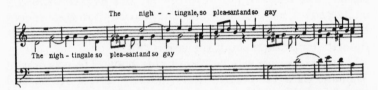

It is true that the words flow on, as in a song, with little repetition; but all three voice-parts are alike in this feature. This small madrigal is one of many that has been overlooked by those who aver that Byrd could not write in the lighter vein. It will be found that almost all of the three- and four-voice madrigals in this set are in the lighter vein. *From Citheron the warlike boy* (No. 19) is developed at some length in three sections; and another pretty madrigal is *While that the sun* (No. 23) with its delightful rhythmic changes at 'Adieu love, untrue love'.

In the five-voice section Byrd reverts fairly strictly to song-form, for instance, in *Weeping full sore* (No. 26), *Compel the hawk to sit* (No. 28), and several other numbers; and in this form his work is less interesting. *I thought that love had been a boy* (No. 32) is one of those in which the soprano part is definitely in song form; nevertheless this gay little piece is thoroughly madrigalian in spirit, and extremely effective in performance, though the cross-rhythms need careful handling. The six-part section of the book is also rather dull, with the exception of *Who made thee, Hob, forsake the plough?* which finds a place among the songs and duets in the next chapter. It is disappointing that Byrd's setting of Sir Philip Sidney's *O dear life, what may it be?* (No. 33) from *Astrophel and Stella* should be so devoid of interest; and it might have been expected that he would have been more successful with the fine anonymous sonnet *Of gold all burnished* (Nos. 36–7); it seems here as if he were tied hand and foot to his ideas of song-form.

With the 1611 set we reach Byrd's last important publication: 'Psalmes, Songs, and | Sonnets: some solemne, others | ioyfull, framed to the life of the | words: Fit for Voyces or Viols | of 3. 4. 5. and 6 Parts | Composed by William Byrd, one of the | Gent. of his Maiesties honourable | Chappell. | 1611 | London | Printed by Thomas Snodham, the assigne | of W. Barley |'

The dedication is to Francis, 4th Earl of Cumberland. In contrast to his brother George, 3rd Earl, whom he succeeded in the Peerage, Francis was a person of small consequence. He lacked the distinction that marked the rest of Byrd's chosen patrons. One writer[1] described him as 'an easy improvident man but otherwise comparatively blameless'. Historians of the Clifford family may have taken too little account of the taste for music which the 4th Earl does seem to have shown; and Byrd in his dedicatory address was definite in his statement that his 'Lordship hath alwayes beene and is a worthy lover and Patron of that facultie', i.e. Music. Evidence of Lord Cumberland's taste in this direction is also provided by the fact that music was a special feature of his entertainment of King James I. This music was published under the title: 'The Ayres that were sung and played at Brougham castle in Westmerland in the King's entertainment given by the Right honorable the Earle of Cumberland and his Right Noble sonne the Lord Clifford. Composed by Mr. George Mason and Mr. John Earsden. London. Printed by Thomas Snodham cum privilegio. 1618'. Francis was born in 1559, succeeded to the earldom in 1605, and died in 1640. Byrd's address to 'all true lovers of Musicke' contains, as these documents usually do, some pithy sayings. Here Byrd desires

---

[1] Whitaker's *History of Craven*, p. 247.

that you will be but as carefull to heare them well expressed as I
have been both in the Composing and correcting of them. Otherwise the best Song that ever was made will seeme harsh and unpleasant, for that the well expressing of them, either by Voyces, or
Instruments, is the life of our labours, which is seldome or never
well performed at the first singing or playing. Besides a song that is
well and artificially made cannot be well perceived nor understood at
the first hearing, but the oftner you shall heare it, the better cause of
liking you will discover: and commonly that Song is best esteemed
with which our eares are most acquainted. As I have done my best
endeavour to give you content, so I beseech you satisfie my desire
in hearing them well expressed, and then I doubt not, for Art and
Ayre both of skilfull and ignorant they will deserve liking.

There are several light madrigalian numbers among the
pieces for three and four voices. *In winter cold* (Nos. 3 and
4) is delightfully humorous, with some quaint touches of
realism, as when the grasshopper explains to the ant how
she 'sung and hopp'd in meadows green'. No. 9 is a four-
part setting of *This sweet and merry month of May*. Attractive as this is, it cannot be compared with the same composer's six-part setting of the same words, which was
included by Thomas Watson in his *First Sett of Italian
Madrigalls Englished*. Watson's high regard for Byrd's
composition is thus expressed on the title-page of this
collection: 'There are also heere inserted two excellent
Madrigalls of Master William Byrds, composed after the
Italian vaine, at the request of the sayd Thomas Watson.'
The madrigal is here described as 'two', because it was
in two sections separately numbered. Though Watson's
collection was published in 1590, it cannot be supposed
that Byrd's four-part setting published twenty years later,
was written after the six-part version in which much of
the same melodic material is used. The six-part version
ranks among the very finest of all the English madrigals
of the brighter kind. The singing of the birds is delightfully portrayed and the clumsy gambols of the heavier
animals are suggested by the triple cross-rhythms in the
tenor and bass voice-parts. The homophonic passage in
quick triple measure at the words 'for pleasure at the joyful
time' is especially gay and spirited. This madrigal, with its
tribute to 'Eliza', may be regarded as Byrd's expression of

homage to the Queen in lieu of a contribution to *The Triumphes of Oriana*. The words of the madrigal are attributed to Thomas Watson.

Awake, mine eyes (No. 12) is a typical bright madrigal with a pretty phrase for the warbling of the birds; and *Come, jolly swains* (No. 13) is another example of Byrd's lighter vein. The lay-out of the voices in both these madrigals is for two equal sopranos, alto, and tenor, a condition which perhaps prejudices their popularity, but *Come, jolly swains* may be suited to men's voices if transposed down a fourth. *Retire, my soul* (No. 17) belongs to the class that Byrd described as 'Songs of piety'; it is for five voices; but the soprano voice is in song-form, and it would seem that Byrd could seldom free himself from this idea in his secular vocal work.

It remains to mention *Come, woeful Orpheus* (No. 19), which differs in character from any of Byrd's secular work and at the same time reaches a high level of excellence. The 'life of the words' in this case inevitably led to unusual harmonies and modulations, and in this feature the madrigal may be compared with Byrd's *Vide Domine, quoniam tribulor*. The opening words are worth quoting though their author is unknown:

> Come, woeful Orpheus, with thy charming lyre
> And tune my voice unto thy skilful wire.
> Some strange chromatic notes do you devise
> That best with mournful accents sympathize.
> Of sourest sharps and uncouth flats make choice
> And I'll thereto compassionate my voice.

The first two lines are treated quietly and simply. The main key being, for practical purposes, G minor, there is a full close in G major on the word 'wire'. In the next few bars A major is reached; and within ten bars the chord of A flat is to be found on the word 'mournful'. In the fifth line the 'sourest sharps and uncouth flats' are brought even closer together by the modulations:

Attention may be drawn to the chord in the second complete bar in the above quotation, where the major third and
minor sixth are used together. Though this chord was in
fairly common use among the English composers of this
date, it is extremely rare in Byrd's music.

The madrigal ends with a dominant pedal-point extending over five bars, while the four upper voices enter with
imitations on the word 'compassionate'; and for once
Byrd's austere nature yields to the expression of a deep
emotion.

No more than five madrigals by Byrd have been found
in manuscript apart from those printed in his lifetime.
Nor are these of outstanding interest. They have the appearance of having been written in the first place as songs,
subsequently adapted for combined voices. The most madrigalian in style are *Sith that the tree* and *O sweet deceit*. This
latter is developed at considerable length.

In 1586 there was published a treatise by John Case,
a Fellow of St. John's College, Oxford, entitled *The Praise
of Musicke*. Copies are now of the greatest rarity. So warm
was Byrd's approval of this little book, that he composed
a madrigal for six voices, planned in two lengthy sections,
as 'A gratification unto Master John Case, for his learned
booke, lately made in the praise of Musicke'. Unfortunately no more than the Cantus-secundus part of this
composition is known to survive. The words, by Thomas
Watson, begin:

> Let others prayse what seemes them best,
> I lyke his lines above the rest
> Whose pen hath painted Musickes prayse

The second part begins:

> There may the Solemne Stoycks finde,
> And that Rude Marsia wanteth skil.

This madrigal was printed as a broadside, and this single
voice-part is in the Cambridge University Library. It has
the appearance of having issued from Thomas East's Press.

A publication entitled *Byrd's Lullabyes* is mentioned
more than once in the Registers of the Stationers' Company. It occurs first in a list of Thomas East's books
assigned by Mistress East to John Browne on 22 Decem-

TENOR.

Pſalmes, Sonets, & ſongs of ſadnes and
pietie, made into Muſicke of fiue parts : whereof,
ſome of them going abroade among diuers, in vntrue coppies,
are heere truely corrected, and th'other being Songs
very rare and newly compoſed, are heere publiſhed, for the recreation
of all ſuch as delight in Muſicke : By *William Byrd,*
one of the Gent. of the Queenes Maieſties
honorable Chappell.

Printed by Thomas Eaſt, the aſsigne of VV. Byrd,
and are to be ſold at the dwelling houſe of the ſaid T. Eaſt, by Paules wharfe.
1588.
Cum priuilegio Regiæ Maieſtatis.

Title-page of *Psalmes, Sonets, & songs of sadness and pietie*, showing the
crest of Byrd's patron, Sir Christopher Hatton
Reproduced by permission of the Trustees of the British Museum

ber 1610, soon after East's death,[1] and later in a list of 'bookes which were M^ris East's', belonging to the printers M. Lownes, John Browne, and Thomas Snodham.[2] In the first list are 'Byrd's latyne sette; Lullabyes; 3. 4. 5 and 6 partes'; 'first graduation'. In the second list are 'Birdes Lullabyes second sett to 3. 4. 5 & 6 partes; 5 partes latyne liber primus'. The 'second sett' must refer to *Songs of sundry natures*, as the *Psalmes, Songs and Sonnets* were not published till 1611. There is little room for doubt that the *Lullabyes* refer to the 1588 publication, which includes the *Lullaby*. It may be inferred that this particular item gained such a degree of popularity that the whole set came to be known by it. Evidence of its popularity is provided in a letter from the Earl of Worcester to the Earl of Shrewsbury, written on 19 September 1602,[3] in which Worcester remarked: 'Wee ar frolyke heare in Court mutche dauncing in the privi chamber of Contrey daunces before the Q. M. whoe is exceedingly pleased therew^th Irishe tunes are at this tyme most pleasing, but in wynter lullaby an owld song of Mr Birde wylbee more in request as I thinke.'

Contents of 'Psalmes, Sonets and songs', 1588

Psalms

1. O God, give ear.
2. Mine eyes with fervency.
3. My soul oppressed with care.
4. How shall a young man?
5. O Lord, how long wilt thou forget?
6. O Lord, who in thy sacred tent.
7. Help, Lord, for wasted.
8. Blessed is he.
9. Lord, in thy wrath.
10. Even from the depth.

Sonnets and Pastorals

11. I joy not in no earthly bliss.

12. Though Amaryllis dance.
13. Who likes to love.
14. My mind to me a kingdom is.
15. Where fancy fond.
16. O you that hear this voice.
17. If women could be fair.
18. Ambitious love.
19. What pleasure have great princes?
20. As I beheld I saw a herdman.
21. Although the heathen poets.
22. In fields abroad.
23. Constant Penelope.
24. La Virginella.
25. Farewell, false love.
26. The match that's made.

[1] Arber's Reprint of the Stationers' Registers, iii. 450.
[2] Ibid. iii. 465.
[3] College of Arms, Talbot MSS., vol. M, fo. 18.

Songs of Sadness and Piety

27. Prostrate, O Lord, I lie.
28. All as a sea.
29. Susanna fair.
30. If that a sinner's sighs.
31. Care for thy soul.

32. Lullaby, my sweet little Baby.
33. Why do I use my paper?

Funeral Songs

34. Come to me, grief, for ever.
35. O that most rare breast.

Contents of 'Songs of sundrie natures', 1589

Songs of three parts

1. Lord, in thy rage.
2. Right blest are they.
3. Lord, in thy wrath.
4. O God, which art most merciful.
5. Lord, hear my prayer.
6. From depth of sin.
7. Attend mine humble prayer.
8. Susanna fair.
9. The nightingale so pleasant.
{ 10. When younglings first.
  11. But when by proof. (*2nd part.*)
{ 12. Upon a summer's day.
  13. Then for a boat. (*2nd part.*)
  14. The greedy hawk.

Songs of four parts

{ 15. Is love a boy?
  16. Boy, pity me. (*2nd part.*)
{ 17. Wounded I am.
  18. Yet of us twain. (*2nd part.*)
{ 19. From Citheron.
  20. There careless thoughts. (*2nd part.*)
  21. If love be just. (*3rd part.*)
  22. O Lord, my God.
  23. While that the sun.
{ 35. From Virgin's womb.
  24. Rejoice, rejoice. (*Chorus.*)

{ 40. An earthly tree.
  25. Cast off all doubtful care. (*Chorus.*)

Songs of five parts

26. Weeping full sore.
27. Penelope that longed.
28. Compel the hawk to sit.
{ 29. See those sweet eyes.
  34. Love would discharge. (*2nd part.*)
30 When I was otherwise.
31. When first by force.
32. I thought that Love.
33. O dear life.
{ 36. Of gold all burnished.
  37. Her breath is more sweet. (*2nd part.*)

Songs of six parts

{ 38. Behold, how good a thing.
  39. And as the pleasant morning dew. (*2nd part.*)
41. Who made thee, Hob?
{ 42. And think ye, nymphs?
  43. Love is a fit of pleasure. (*2nd part.*)
44. If in thine heart.
45. Unto the hills.
{ 46. Christ rising again.
  47. Christ is risen again. (*2nd part.*)

Contents of 'Psalmes, Songs and Sonnets', 1611

A PRINTED BROADSIDE, *circa* 1586-7
For six voices
{ Let others praise what seems them best
{ There may the solemn Stoics find (*2nd part*)

MADRIGALS SURVIVING ONLY IN MANUSCRIPT
For five voices

Let Fortune fail.	B.M. Add. 18936-9.
[1]Mount, Hope.	B.M. Add. 18936-9; Add. 31992.
{ O sweet deceit (*part* i). { Like Harpies vile (*part* ii).	B.M. Add. 29401-5; Egerton 2009-12; Harvard 634.1.703.
Penelope ever was praised.	B.M. Add. 18936-9; Egerton 2009-12.
Sith that the tree.	B.M. Add. 18936-9; Add. 31992.

DRAMATIC CHORUS

Preces Deo fundamus	B.M. Harl. 2412, fo. 75.

[1] Ascribed also to Ferrabosco.

CHAPTER XI

SONGS, SACRED AND SECULAR

IT has not generally been realized what an important part Byrd played in the history and development of song as an art form. Altogether about fifty songs by this composer are known. Of some of these no more than fragments survive, and others are known only through contemporary adaptations for the lute; it is possible that several more which bear no ascription in the manuscripts should be added to the list, since they are very similar in character to others that are definitely ascribed to Byrd. The list includes both sacred and secular songs.

The historical interest of Byrd's songs lies in the fact that at least some of them were written many years before the publication of John Dowland's *First Booke of Songs or Ayres* in 1597; for example, there are several in the Christ Church MSS. 984–8 which date from about 1581–5.

Just as Dowland evolved the solo-song out of the part-song, gradually making the accompaniment, which in the first instance he substituted for the three lower voice-parts, more and more instrumental in character; so also did Byrd evolve his solo-songs from the polyphonic type of composition, substituting string instruments for the lower voices, and gradually developing an instrumental in place of a vocal technique.

But Byrd worked on entirely different lines from Dowland and with a different medium. Dowland used the lute exclusively, albeit reinforced by the bass-viol or gamba, for his accompaniments. Byrd, on the other hand, never wrote for the lute, but designed his accompaniments for viols in the manner of a string quartet.

It is a commonplace to speak of the year 1600 as marking a great development in the evolution of modern music; but it must not be overlooked that much was done earlier than this. Powerful influences were growing in force throughout the last quarter of the sixteenth century. The art of music had lagged behind her sister arts of poetry, painting, and sculpture in responding to the claims of the

Renaissance movement, for it was not until the latter years
of the century that this influence began to have effect upon
music and musicians. At this period, however, when the
desire for self-expression was asserting itself with increasing power in every direction, singers were no longer content to sink their individuality in united vocal utterance, and
satisfaction could only be found by them in the freedom of
the solo-song. When that discovery was made by the singers,
it was inevitable that the composers, caught by the same
spirit, should set themselves to meet their needs. Folk-
songs and all kinds of traditional songs and ballads, great
though their value was, did not in themselves supply quite
what was wanted; the composed song with independent
instrumental accompaniment, in other words the art-song,
alone could do this. The pioneer work of Byrd in this
department and the superlative achievements of Dowland
earn for those two English composers a very conspicuous
position in the history of song, a position that has not been
properly assigned to them by musical historians. This is
true, even though it must be frankly admitted that many of
Byrd's songs are of historical rather than aesthetic interest.
It has already been stated that Byrd's madrigals were constructed more or less in song-form. Conversely it may be
said that his songs are not unlike his madrigals in appearance. Nevertheless, in the case of his songs, it would not be
possible, as a rule, to fit the words to the string parts that
form the accompaniment without considerable modifica-
tion, such as Byrd himself was free to make when adapting
his songs to madrigalian form.

Almost all of his sacred songs suffer from the poverty
of the words, most of these being metrical versions of
psalms. The melodies, as a general rule, follow the metre
of the words line by line almost with the regularity of a
hymn-tune, but with each line separated from the next by
a bar or two of instrumental accompaniment. Byrd shows
his fondness for breaking the regularity of the melodic outline by the introduction of triple measures. It cannot be
denied that there is a fine sense of balance and proportion
in the shaping of all these melodies even when an impression
of dullness prevails, as it sometimes does.

Byrd had no hesitation in taking the string parts above

the voice. The opening bars of his setting of a metrical version by William Kethe of Psalm 112, verses 1–3, will indicate the character of most of these sacred songs:

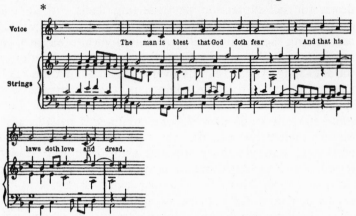

My faults, O Christ, I do confess is in triple measure, and it takes the form of a dialogue, as the words suggest; the voices combine in unison for the final line—'Sing and rejoice, and God above do magnify always'.

Rather different in character is the setting of words by Sidney, *O Lord, how vain are all our frail delights.* Each of the three verses of this song is followed by a refrain ending with a beautiful phrase:

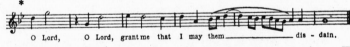

In the secular songs there is much greater variety. Far outshining everything else in this branch of composition at this period is the exquisite *My little sweet darling.* If Byrd is to be adjudged no more than a pioneer in song-writing, he nevertheless reached perfection with this cradle song. And it is important to stress the fact that this song was written some fifteen years or more before the close of the sixteenth century, because the text of it is found in the 'Robert Dow' set of manuscript part-books[1] which were begun in 1581.

As in *Lullaby, my sweet little Baby,* Byrd demonstrates here that he was capable of handling this subject with all

---

* The note-values are halved.   [1] Ch. Ch. MSS. 984–8.

the tenderness and gentleness that it requires; and in its absolute simplicity and freshness it escapes any suspicion of sentimentality. It is the work of true genius. One manuscript ascribes this song to Nicholas Strogers, but the stronger textual support is for Byrd's authorship; and on internal evidence there can be little doubt in deciding between the two claimants. The song at its original pitch is written for a contralto voice. The accompaniment of a quartet of viols is extremely melodious, but it never overshadows the voice. The B flat chord, three bars from the end, has a very telling effect, for the reason, as elsewhere, that the composer has kept it for use here, and here alone. There is no suggestion of madrigalian style in this song, nor are the string parts vocal in character. The song opens thus (note-values halved):

Another of these songs with an alternative and minority ascription is *As Caesar wept when he beheld Pompeius' head.* In the British Museum Add. MS. 31992 it was ascribed to Tallis, but his name was erased in an early hand. The other manuscripts agree in ascribing it to Byrd.

An aged dame is a satirical song with quaint and rather gruesome words, treated by Byrd with some realistic touches.

> An aged dame, in reverence for the dead,
>> With care did place the skulls of men she found
> Upon a hill, as in a sacred bed;
>> But as she toiled she tumbled to the ground.
> Whereat down fell the skulls within her lap,
>> And here and there they run about the hill.

With that quoth she: No marvel is this hap,
Since men alive in mind do differ still;
And as these heads in sunder down do fall,
So varied they in their opinions all.

Ye sacred muses is an elegy on the death of Thomas Tallis. This song opens in the contrapuntal or madrigalian style, all four instruments taking up the phrase and delaying the first entry of the voice for six bars. After this rather academic beginning the theme develops with much pathos. A beautiful melismatic phrase is a feature of the closing bars, 'Tallis is dead, and Music dies'.

Byrd also made experiments in writing for two, and even three, voices in combination with strings, but these are of small interest. So few examples survive that it is likely that he himself recognized there was little satisfaction to be found in this form. The 'Dialogue between two Shepherds' *Who made thee, Hob, forsake the plough?*[1] is constructed on the lines of a solo-song, for the two voices combine in duet only in the final phrase. The composer has caught the exact spirit of rustic humour in this song. The accompaniment is assigned to a quartet of viols; and to be effective the whole song should swing along at a rollicking pace. It is a fine specimen of the composer's lighter style.

Crowned with flowers and lilies is written as a five-part composition for two voices, soprano and bass, or baritone, with string accompaniment. The words are a kind of elegy on the death of Queen Mary—'Mary she hight, of Henry Great the daughter'. The date of her death was 1558, when Byrd was fifteen years old. But there is no reason to suppose that he composed this song at the time of her death, for one of the manuscripts in which this song is found includes several other songs about historical persons, such as Henry

[1] *Songs of sundrie natures*, No. 41.

the Sixth, Thomas Cromwell, and Elizabeth Wydvile, and manifestly the music of these could not be contemporary. It should be mentioned that the string parts of *Crowned with flowers and lilies* are definitely instrumental in character, and it is clear that the words were designed for the soprano and bass parts only. This composition must not be confused with Byrd's five-part madrigal *Crowned with flowers I saw fair Amaryllis* (No. 22 of the 1611 set).

If the study of Byrd's early work in the department of art-song leads to unexpected revelations, what shall be said about his ventures in the field of dramatic song, made perhaps as many as thirty years before the close of the sixteenth century? For it is a fact that Byrd was associating himself with certain dramatic entertainments, composing songs and possibly also incidental music for them. In the year 1567–8 there was acted at the Inner Temple a play entitled *Tancred and Gismunda*. It was written by Robert Wilmot and three other members of the Inns of Court, among whom was Byrd's friend and subsequent patron, Christopher Hatton. Hatton wrote the fourth Act. This was the first love-tragedy produced in English. In two early manuscripts[1] the title of it is given as *Gismond of Salerne*. It was printed as *Tancred and Gismunda* in 1591, but the printed text was altered from the original. In the opinion of such an authority on Elizabethan literature as Percy Simpson there can be no doubt that Byrd's song *Come tread the path* was written for this production, the style of the text being exactly that of the play; and the association of Byrd with Hatton goes far towards confirming Simpson's opinion. Neither the printed text nor the manuscripts have the song, but omission by no means upsets the theory. It is after the murder of her lover Guishardo that Gismond sings:

> Come tread the path of pensive pangs
>   With me, ye lovers true.
> Bewail with me your hapless lot
>   With tears your eyes bedew.
> Aid me, ye ghosts, who loathèd life,
>   Your lovers being slain,
> With sighs and sobs and notes of dule
>   My hard hap to complain.

[1] B.M. Lansdowne MSS. 786; Hargrave MSS. 205.

Farewell, farewell, my lords and friends,
  Farewell, my princely state,
Let father rue his rigour shown
  In slaying of my mate.
Guishardo! if thy sprite do walk,
  Come down thy lover nigh.
Behold, I yield to thee my ghost,
  Ah see! I die, I die.

Byrd set this song for contralto voice with accompaniment of a quartet of viols, and it is an amazing example of dramatic and impassioned declamation. With a true artistic sense of proportion the song opens comparatively quietly, though the very first lines are broken with frequent rests to allow of some emotional expression. The remainder of the first stanza shows more restraint. It is in the second stanza that the heroine's grief reaches breaking point; and it is here that Byrd exhibits his dramatic powers with such astonishing originality, considering that nothing of the kind had been done before this. Three times Gismond invokes her dead lover (note-values halved):

The climax is reached in the final line:

The string parts throughout the song are beautifully melodious.

This was only one of several of Byrd's known compositions for the stage, and it is likely that others he wrote have perished. *If trickling tears of mine* is obviously a stage song. The voice-part has survived at Tenbury,[1] but unfortunately the accompaniment is lost. It is not known to what Play this song belongs. The words are tragic in character and the lines are expressed in broken musical phrases.

More interesting than this, however, is the Latin song *Quis me statim.* The play to which this song belongs has not been identified; it may therefore be well to give the words in full:

> Quis me statim rupto vetat fato mori,
> Crudelis, heu, dum parcis, ah, mors nimis?
> Tuum perforet nostra ferrum viscera
> Amantis ossa dissipes, Hippolyte.

The music of this song also is written with strong dramatic feeling, the word 'Hippolyte' is repeated six times in broken phrases at the end. The accompaniment is for a quartet of viols.

Another Latin play for which Byrd wrote music was *Ricardus Tertius,* by Thomas Legge, sometime Master of Caius College, Cambridge. It was produced at St. John's College in 1579. Contemporary manuscripts of the play are at Clare and Emmanuel Colleges and in the University Library. None of these has any music. Another manuscript is in the British Museum[2]; and in connexion with the closing episode of Act I, Sc. 5, this gives the incomplete text of a musical setting of the chorus with which the Act closes. The scene presents the penance of Jane Shore. The stage directions are partly in Latin and partly in English. 'Processio solemnis' is formed thus:

The show of the Procession

1 A Tipstaffe
2 Shore's wife in her peticote
    having a taper burninge in her hand
3 The Verger
4 Queristers

[1] Tenbury MS. 389, fo. 95.
[2] B.M. Harl. MS. 2412.

> 5 Singing men
> 6 Prebendaries
> 7 The Bishopp of London
> 8 Citizens

The following words are then sung in procession:

> Preces deo fundamus ore supplices
> Ne sit nota polluta mens adultera

> 1. Fidem tuere coniugum
>   Lectumque probro libera;
>   Defende privatos thoros
>   Furtiva ne ledat Venus.

> Preces deo, &c.

> 2. Quemcunque facti poenitet
>   Purga solutum crimine;
>   Exempla favent posteros
>   Furtiva ne foedet Venus.

> Preces deo, &c.

The 'triplex' part of the music for these words is written out in complete form and ascribed to Byrd in the manuscript.[1] No more than three bars and a half of the 'medius' part appear with it, and no other part at all. This fragment of music was printed by J. Stafford Smith[2] in 1812. Seeing the word 'triplex', Smith described the music as a song for three voices. This was an entirely erroneous assumption. The term 'triplex' was commonly employed for the soprano, or top voice, even when the music was written for as many as five or six voices. It is almost certain that Byrd was here writing for five voices; three voices would have been quite unworthy of the occasion, especially as a full choir was available with queristers and singing-men, followed in procession by Prebendaries and the Bishop of London. Moreover, the fragment of the music as given in the manuscript makes it abundantly clear that more than the addition of a bass voice to the triplex and medius is needed to complete the first chord. The style of the music is evidently ecclesiastical, the second section being homophonic in treatment.

---

[1] B.M. Harl. MS. 2412, fo. 75ᵛ (2).
[2] *Musica Antiqua*, iii. 46.

Act II of the play ends with a Coronation procession, and there is a stage direction that the song *Festum diem colimus* is to be sung 'with instruments'. Another song follows the crowning of Henry the Seventh. It seems most likely that Byrd supplied all the music for this play, but not another note has survived. It has been suggested by Dr. E. W. Naylor, who made a lifelong study of the music of this period, that Byrd's piece in the Fitzwilliam Virginal Book entitled 'the Ghost'[1] was written as a Prelude to the entry of the 'Ghoast' of Edward the Fourth in *Ricardus Tertius*. This can, of course, be no more than a conjecture, yet it is an interesting one.

Two single parts of an instrumental piece, labelled *Abradate*,[2] are in manuscript at the British Museum and Tenbury. It was no doubt composed for a play about Abradas, who, as described by Xenophon, fell in battle fighting with Cyrus against the Egyptians. Bewailing his fate the inconsolable Pantheia killed herself. Byrd's music may have been written for a play, printed in 1594, entitled *The Warres of Cyrus King of Persia, against Antiochus King of Assyria, with the Tragicall ende of Panthaea*. This play is probably based on an earlier one, written about 1578 and entitled *Panthea and Abradatas*. This earlier play is sometimes ascribed to Richard Farrant of Windsor, but he probably wrote the music only.

Songs

SACRED

Adoramus te, Christe.	*Gradualia*, Bk. I, pt. ii. No. 26.
Blessed is he.	B.M. Add. 31992; Harvard, 634.1.703, Tenbury 1473.
Have mercy, Lord, on me I pray (*lute arrangement only*).	B.M. Add. 31992.
Have mercy on us, Lord (*wanting voice-part*).	B.M. Add. 18936-9; Add. 31992.

---

[1] No. 162.
[2] Tenbury MS. 389, fo 101. BM., Add. 29427, fo. 101.

I will give laud (*lute arrangement only*).	B.M. Add. 31992.
Lord, to thee I make my moan (*wanting voice-part*).	B.M. Add. 18936-9; Add. 31992; Bodl. E. 423.
My faults, O Christ.	Ch. Ch. 984-8.
O God, but God, how dare I (*wanting three string parts*).	B.M. Add. 31992; Add. 15117; Bodl. E. 423.
O heavenly God (*wanting the three lower string parts*).	B.M. Add. 15117; Add. 31992; Bodl. E. 423; Tenbury, 389.
O Lord, bow down.	B.M. Add. 29401-5; Add. 31992.
O Lord, how vain.	B.M. Add. 29401-5; B.M. Add. 31992; Ch. Ch. 984-8; Bodl. E. 423; Harvard, 634.1.703.
O Lord, how long?	B.M. Add. 31992; Harvard, 634.1.703. Tenbury 1473.
O Lord, within thy tabernacle.	Ch. Ch. 984-8; Tenbury, 389.
O that we woeful wretches.	B.M. Add. 29401-5; Add. 31992; Egerton, 2009-12; Bodl. E. 423.
Remember, Lord (*wanting cantus part*).	B.M. Add. 31992; Harvard, 634.1.703.
The Lord is only my support (*wanting quintus part*).	B.M. Add. 18936-9; Add. 31992.
The man is blest.	B.M. Add. 29401-5. Tenbury 1473.
What unacquainted cheerful voice.	Ch. Ch. 984-8.

SECULAR

Ah, golden hairs.	B.M. Add. 31992; Ch. Ch. 984-988; Bodl. E. 423.
Ah, silly soul.	*Psalmes, Songs and Sonnets* (1611), No. 31.
Ah, youthful years (*lute arrangement only*).	B.M. Add. 31992.
An aged dame.	B.M. Add. 29401-5; Add. 31992; Harvard, 634.1.703.
As Caesar wept.	B.M. Add. 18936-9; Add. 31992; Bodl. E. 423; Harvard, 634.1.703.
Blame I confess.	Ch. Ch. 984-8.
By force I live (*wanting contra-tenor part*).	B.M. Add. 18936-9.

Come, tread the path.	Ch. Ch. 984-8; Tenbury, 389.
Depart, ye furies (*lute arrangement only*)	B.M. Add. 31992.
How vain the toils.	*Psalmes, Songs and Sonnets* (1611), No. 32.
If trickling tears (*voice-part only*).	Tenbury, 389.
In tower most high (*lute arrangement only*).	B.M. Add. 31992.
Look and bow down (*lute arrangement only*).	B.M. Add. 31992.
Methought of late.	B.M. Add. 17792-6; Add. 31992.
My freedom, ah (*wanting cantus part*).	B.M. Add. 31992; Harvard, 634.1.703.
My little sweet darling.	B.M. Add. 17786-91; Ch. Ch. 984-8.
O happy thrice (*contra-tenor part and lute arrangement only*).	B.M. Add. 31992; Bodl. E. 423.
O trifling toys (*voice-part only*).	Tenbury, 389.
Quis me statim.	B.M. Add. 29401-5; Add. 31992; Harvard, 634.1.703.
Sithence that death.	B.M. Add. 29401-5; Harvard, 634.1.703.
The day delayed.	B.M. Add. 31992; Ch. Ch. 984-8.
Thou poets' friend (*wanting contra-tenor part*).	R.C.M. 2049.
Triumph with pleasant melody.	B.M. Add. 30484; Ch. Ch. 984-8.
Truce for a time (*voice-part and lute arrangement only*).	B.M. Add. 31992; Bodl. E. 423.
What steps of strife (*wanting cantus part*).	B.M. Add. 31992; Harvard, 634.1.703; B.M. Harl. 6910.
What wytes (*lute arrangement only*).	B.M. Add. 31992.
While Phoebus used to dwell.	Ch. Ch. 984-8.
While that a cruel fire (*lute arrangement only*).	B.M. Add. 31992.
Whom hateful harms (*wanting contra-tenor part*).	B.M. Add. 18936-9.
With sighs and tears (*lute arrangement only*).	B.M. Add. 31992.
Ye sacred Muses.	B.M. Add. 29401-5; Add. 31992; Harvard, 634.1.703

DUETS *(with string accompaniment)*

Crowned with flowers and lilies.	B.M. Add. 18936-9; Add. 29401-5; Egerton, 2009-12; Harvard, 634.1.703.
Delight is dead.	B.M. Add. 18936-9; 29372-7;[1] 34050.
Who made thee, Hob, forsake the plough?	*Songs of sundrie natures,* No. 41.

TRĪOS *(with string accompaniment)*

E'en as in seas.	B.M. Add. 29401-5.
What vaileth it to rule?	B.M. Add. 31992; Egerton, 2009-12; Harvard, 634.1.703.

In those cases in which the lute arrangement alone survives it is not possible to determine whether they were written as songs with string accompaniment or for voices in madrigalian form.

---

[1] The B.M. Catalogue (Hughes-Hughes) wrongly ascribes this composition in Add. MSS., 29372–7 to Luca Marenzio. All the part-books in that set ascribe it to Byrd.

CHAPTER XII

CANONS AND ROUNDS

IF the canon has rightly been described as the strictest
and most regular species of imitation in music, it may
be added that it is the most academic and artificial form of
musical composition ever devised. To compose a simple
canon in two parts at the octave, or even three, may not
be a task that will heavily tax the skill or inventive faculties
of any musician. And perhaps it was for this very reason
that musicians in the sixteenth century set themselves to
invent all manner of complicated devices which would
come within the range of the strictest laws of imitation,
and thus make an appeal to the cleverest brains, either in
constructing or in solving such musical puzzles. For the
purpose of dealing with a musical puzzle it will be obvious
that a certain amount of musical knowledge is indispens-
able, but for this particular kind of puzzle, ingenuity,
imagination, and patience count for much more than this.

Not only in England, but on the Continent also, musicians in their lighter moments of leisure would meet and
vie with each other in composing intricate canons; and
no doubt they took delight in constructing something
which might baffle a rival musician in his attempts at finding the solution. Orlando di Lasso was one of those who
on the Continent enjoyed this form of recreation. In England no one could approach Byrd at this game, for game in
a sense it was. Another and much easier musical game
played at this time was the writing of descants on a plain-
song melody. To write canons 'two in one' was more difficult; and Thomas Morley has left an account[1] of how
Byrd and Alphonso Ferrabosco competed in friendly
rivalry in making '2 partes in one upon the playne songe
Miserere'. There is always a touch of humanity and humour
in Morley's descriptions. Here he is encouraging his
pupils and readers to play this same game since 'there is
no waie readier to cause you to become perfect, then to

[1] Morley's *Plaine and Easie Introduction to Practicall Musicke*, p. 115.

contend with some one or other'. Yet Morley knew that people were prone to lose their tempers in such conditions and he adjures them in this matter also to copy his 'loving Maister (never without reverence to be named of the musicians) M. *Bird*, and M. *Alphonso*', who strove 'to surmount one another without malice, envie, or backbiting'. Morley goes on to say that his friend George Waterhouse made as many as 'a thousand waies' on the same plain-song *Miserere*. It is likely that these were descants rather than canons.

Some of the results of Byrd's competition with Ferrabosco found their way into a book, intended to be published in 1603 under the title of *Medulla Musicke. Sucked out of the sappe of Two the most famous Musitians that ever were in this land Namely Master* WILLIAM BYRD *gentleman of his Maiestys most Royall Chappell and Master* ALPHONSO FERRABOSCO *gentleman of his Maiestys pryvie chamber either of whom having made 40tie severall waies (without Contention) shewing most rare and intricate skill in 2 partes in one upon the playne songe 'Miserere'. The which at the request of a friend is most plainly sett in severall distinct partes to be songe (with moore ease and understanding of the lesse skilfull) by Master* THOMAS ROBINSON (*and alsoe to the further delight of all suche as love Musique) transposed to the lute by the said Master Thomas Robinson.*

This book was licensed by the Stationers on 15 October 1603 and the fee paid[1]; but it does not seem to have been published. The book, no doubt, contained many of the *Miserere* canons produced in the competition, but it has not been generally understood that the book was Robinson's; and the latter sentences of the title suggest that the canons were freely rearranged and adapted by him 'to be songe'. It is not improbable that Byrd and Ferrabosco disapproved of Robinson's arrangements and stopped the publication as misrepresenting their work.

It is likely that a few of Byrd's *Miserere* canons are included with many far more intricate puzzle-canons in a remarkable collection now in the British Museum.[2] By a slip the compiler of the Museum catalogue miscounted

[1] Arber's Transcripts of the Stationers' Registers, iii. 247.
[2] B.M. Add. MS. 31391.

No. 5 of the canons as two, so that the subsequent numbers
are thrown out by one figure, the right total being twenty-
nine, not thirty.

This little manuscript book is bound in its original vellum
cover. The initials w.b. are written at the end of each canon.
but it is impossible to say whether they are Byrd's autograph. The whole of the twenty-nine are set out in the form
of problems, and in no case is the solution given, although
in many of them the point is indicated at which a fresh
part is to enter.

The first five are constructed on the plain-song *O lux
beata Trinitas*; Nos. 6–10 are '*Per naturam*'; and Nos. 11–29
are on *Miserere*. The last three alone have words for all the
parts; these are for five voices and are set out in the manuscript very neatly in three different coloured inks. In this
way the clue to the solution is hinted at.

Some of the solutions are found in augmentation, some
in inversion, some by combining devices of this kind, and
some are fairly straightforward. In No. 3 the plain-song
is *O lux*; two parts are given to be fitted in as a canon
4 in 2, with a free part. The opening bars will be sufficient
to show the key to the solution:

In this instance the canon is so complete that the first bass
part in diminution is repeated without the slightest alteration in the second half. The most intricate of all these canons
is No. 5. Here the plain-song *O lux* is slightly modified
for the purpose of making 'two parts in one 2 sundry ways';
a bass part also is given to be worked in as 'two parts in one
and agreeth with the sundry ways of plainsong'; and also
a treble and bass are given as free parts (*ad placitum*).

The score in the solution of this puzzle works out in
seven parts thus: (1) The free treble part. (2) The plain-
song as given. (3) The plain-song in canon, entering a bar
later and one degree higher in the scale. (4) The plain-song

as given, and at the original pitch, but backwards. (5) The bass-part as given. (6) This same bass part backwards. (7) The free bass-part.

The solution of No. 14, which puzzled Dr. Pepusch in the eighteenth century, and so clever a canon-writer as Ouseley in the nineteenth, has at last been found[1] in the formula known to the sixteenth-century musicians as 'Digniora sunt priora'. The canon is at the fifth below; all the semibreves in the given part come first, then the minims (including rests), then the crotchets.

It is not suggested for a moment that there is any musical beauty in these puzzle-canons any more than that there is literature in the cross-word puzzles and acrostics of to-day.

[1] By Mr. Hans T. David, of New York.

There is another of these puzzles at Christ Church, Oxford, set out thus[1]:

6 in one

This is easily solved with the aid of the indications as to entry. But the following variety of the same canon has so far eluded all efforts to solve it, or even to understand what it means.

W[t] another conceite contained in the same of 4. parts in two. Who that will fynde it out. 1600.

In contrast to the puzzle canons, composers could, and frequently did, produce melodious and simple-sounding music in this form; and more particularly so when the music took the form of a Round. *Hey ho, to the Greenwood* is as gay and pretty an example as could be found. It is for three equal voices at the unison.

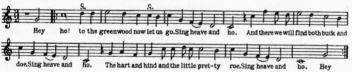

The rhythm of this round has been considerably spoilt in certain printed editions, which give four crotchets to the bar instead of six. The words also have been needlessly altered. Byrd's name is attached to a round entitled *On a game of crib*, and beginning *O hold your hands*, in an eighteenth-century manuscript.[2] It is very unlike Byrd's work, and almost certainly is not by him. *Come, drink to me* is another round attributed to Byrd by the younger

[1] Ch. Ch. MS. 981, fo. 88[v].
[2] B.M. Add. MS. 29386.

Hilton, who printed it in *Catch as catch can* in 1652; this attribution may also be gravely doubted.

Non nobis, Domine is very generally attributed to Byrd, although the actual evidence is not strong. It is not found in any known manuscript earlier than 1651, in which year it was printed by John Playford in *Musick and Mirth*, which forms the third section of his *A Musicall Banquet*. No composer's name is attached to it there. In the following year Hilton included it in *Catch as catch can*, but again anonymously, a fact that is all the more significant, seeing that he attached Byrd's name to *Come, drink to me*, in the same publication. At a later date Blow attributed it to Byrd, and since that time this attribution has been generally accepted. Popular as it is at musical banquets, there is no reason to regard it as a work of outstanding merit, for the simple diatonic phrases lend themselves easily to canonical imitation. Nevertheless, it is remarkable in how many ways this little canon may be solved and sung. There are solutions for two, three, and even four' voices. It will also go in several ways by inversion, and, counting these, there are eleven known solutions. The best-known of these begins:

But the following solution might well be used sometimes for sake of variety. There are musicians who prefer this alternative:

Two *Misereres* and *Pietas omnium virtutum* are among other rounds set to Latin words by Byrd.

Canonical writing was certainly looked upon by composers in the sixteenth century as a display of exceptional skill that should command admiration. The introduction of this device into serious compositions such as Masses, or Motets, or Anglican Church music, is fraught with some danger, because, unless it is accomplished with rare skill, it becomes obvious and self-conscious, and attention is drawn away from the finer aspects of the composition to its material and constructive features. That devices calling for the highest ingenuity and skill can be introduced into a musical composition without affecting the subtle appreciation of its highest artistic qualities, is demonstrated convincingly in the last movement of Mozart's 'Jupiter' Symphony. Similarly, it was found possible by the best of the sixteenth-century composers, both in Italy and in England, to introduce long passages in strict canon without diverting attention from its proper focus. For instance, Byrd's Third English *Magnificat* might be sung numbers of times without singers or listeners noticing that the tenor voice runs in strict canon with the soprano at the words 'He hath filled the hungry'.

Unlike some other composers of this date, Byrd only rarely introduced such a complicated device as strict canon into his greatest work. Free canonical imitation was, of course, a feature of all sixteenth-century polyphonic music; and the amazing skill and variety shown by Byrd in this feature of his work has already been commented on. Almost every page of his music illustrates this; but much careful scrutiny is necessary to discover such passages as do exist in strict canon in his writings on the part of any one who did not happen to know where to look for them. Possessing marvellous skill in canonical writing, it is characteristic of his fine nature that he so seldom gave way to the temptation to display it.

The most remarkable example of strict canon in Byrd's motets is *Diliges Dominum*.[1] It is written for a double chorus of four voices each, and it is constructed in the very intricate form of canon known as 'eight in four Cancrizans'. In practice this means that on reaching the middle of the motet the whole of the music up to that point is sung again backwards, the two choirs interchanging parts. The degree of ingenuity required for such a structure can scarcely be apprehended. This was one of Byrd's early compositions, and it must be admitted that its aesthetic interest is far below his ordinary standard. He evidently

[1] *Cantiones Sacrae*, 1575, No. 25.

learnt early in life that mere cleverness did not indicate the surest road to fame.

There are other important motets in which Byrd introduced some strict and rather elaborate canonical writing. Two more of these are early works, and are included, like *Diliges Dominum*, in the 1575 set of *Cantiones Sacrae*. *Miserere mihi, Domine*[1] is for six voices, and its scheme of construction is unlike anything else in Byrd's work. It is based upon the plain-song melody of *Miserere*, but not in accordance with the usual plan by which the entire melody was laid out in complete form in one of the voice-parts. In this instance the motet opens in the conventional manner with the plain-song in the soprano part, but it breaks off after the word 'Domine', and the bass then takes over the melody, beginning it again, and giving it in complete form. At its conclusion Byrd begins his strict canon four in two, and this final section has the appearance of having been composed separately as a 'miserere canon', for the words are repeated here in complete form. The two top voices are in strict canon, singing the plain-song melody in a somewhat free and disjointed form with some slight embroidery. The tenor and bass are also in strict canon throughout this section, while the two middle voices are *ad placitum* with free parts.

The *Gloria* to *O lux beata Trinitas*,[2] another six-part motet, includes a canon described in the original edition as 'Tres partes in una in subdiapente, aliud in diatessaron'. The three voices not concerned with the canon open the movement with material in free imitation which foreshadows the subject of the canon. The canon is led by the alto voice; the second tenor follows at the interval of a fifth below, and the first soprano enters last at the interval of a fourth above the alto. These voices maintain the canon with the strictest accuracy throughout a rather lengthy development of the *Gloria*. It may be observed that *O lux beata Trinitas* and *Miserere* were the subjects of most of Byrd's puzzle-canons.

O salutaris hostia, one of the motets which survives only in manuscript,[3] provides a very similar example to this

---

[1] *Cantiones Sacrae*, 1575, No. 29.   [2] Ibid., No. 12.
[3] Ch. Ch. MSS. 979–83.

Gloria. This motet is also for six voices, and the canon three in one is worked out in the alto, soprano, and second tenor parts. The second tenor part is wanting in the only known text, and the editors of *Tudor Church Music*,[1] though nearly succeeding in reconstructing the correct text, failed to notice that this part ran right through in strict canon.

Quomodo cantabimus, for eight voices was the motet which Byrd wrote expressly for Philip de Monte; and he may well be pardoned if his national pride induced him on this occasion to exhibit his technical skill in this direction. This canon also is for three voices. The first bass voice leads, followed by the first alto at the interval of an octave above, and the second alto comes last in inversion. Byrd very cleverly, and with fine artistic sense, covers up the canon, which runs with absolute strictness through the whole of the first part of the motet, by borrowing many of the phrases for the other five voices, and using them in free imitation. And in the opening passage he seems to show a desire to disguise and discount any expectation of strict canonical writing by inverting the opening phrase on the word 'Quomodo' in all the parts that do not take part in the canon itself.

Among other motets in which strict canons are to be found are *Petrus beatus* and *Alleluia. Confitemini.* It will be noticed that all the examples quoted here are from Byrd's earlier work, and this clearly indicates that in later life he ceased to regard strict canon as a desirable feature of musical composition.

In quite a different field of composition Byrd has left one fine example of canonical writing in his Fantasy for string quintet.[2] This is a work of greater length than was usual in the Fantasy, but the two upper instruments play in strict canon at an interval of the fourth without a break from beginning to end. Byrd also arranged this Fantasy for the Virginals.[3]

For amazing ingenuity nothing could surpass the Canon (without words) quoted by Morley in his *Plaine and Easie*

[1] Vol. ix, p. 254.
[2] B.M. Add. MSS. 17786–91.
[3] Nevell 29 and Paris Rés. MS. 1122, p. 19.

Introduction.[1] Morley says that this 'waie made by M. Bird for difficultie in the composition is not inferior to anie which I have seene, for it is both made *per arsin & thesin*, and likewise the point or Fuge is reverted, note for note'.

Canons

29 Canons on plain-song melodies.   B.M. Add. 31391.
    O lux beata Trinitas. à 3.
       „   „   à 4.
       „   „   à 6 (2 settings).
       „   „   à 7.
    Per naturam. à 3 (3 settings).
       „   à 4 (2 settings).
    Miserere. à 3 (14 settings).
       „   à 4 (2 settings).
       „   à 5 (3 settings).

3 Canons (*without words*).	
Canon 6 in 1.	Ch. Ch. 981, fo. 88ᵛ.
Canon 4 in 2.	
Canon 2 in 1 'per arsin and thesin bis repetite'.	„ „ Morley's *Plaine and Easie Introduction*, p. 103.

Rounds

Miserere. à 3.	B.M. Add. 29386; Royal Mus. Lib. 24, c. 15.
Miserere (*another setting*). à 3.	B.M. Add. 29386; Royal Mus. Lib. 24, c. 15.
Non nobis Domine.	Playford's *Musick and Mirth* (1651).
Pietas omnium virtutum. à 3.	Royal Mus. Lib. 24, c. 15.
Bless them that curse you. à 3.	Royal Mus. Lib. 24, c. 15.
*Come drink to me. à 4.	Hilton's *Catch as catch can* (1652).
Hey ho! to the greenwood. à 3.	B.M. Add. 31441; Add. 31462, Add. 31463, &c.
*O hold your hands. à 4.	B.M. Add. 29386.

        * Very doubtful attributions.

[1] Page 103.

CHAPTER XIII

CHAMBER MUSIC FOR STRINGS

IN the history of Chamber Music, in its accepted modern sense, no name stands out so pre-eminently as that of Haydn. It was he who, gathering up everything that had gone before him, set up an entirely new standard of form and design, greatly extending the scope for artistic development, and creating a new technique for the instruments of the violin family. To the violinist the technique of Haydn shows as great an advance on that of the thorough-bass school of composers, from Corelli to Bach, as that of Corelli was in comparison with that of the early seventeenth century, And, as regards form and general artistic value, Haydn's quartets are not only the earliest that appeal to modern string-players, but practically nothing earlier than Haydn makes any serious appeal to their interest. Furthermore, in the matter of popularity, the best of Haydn's quartets hold their own to this day in the esteem of performers and listeners alike. This is not to deny that such composers as Mozart, Beethoven, Schubert, and Brahms wrote quartets that are even greater than those of Haydn, but it was upon Haydn's design that they mainly built, and it is for this reason that he has been called the Father of Chamber music.

It is from the historical point of view rather than the aesthetic that the origin and development of chamber music for strings in the sixteenth and early seventeenth centuries should be considered. The aesthetic interest is by no means wholly lacking; but if it be comparatively small when placed beside the works of the great classical composers, the historic interest stands out in conspicuous importance.

The work of the sixteenth-century musicians in this field of composition has never been adequately recognized. Historians have for the most part touched lightly upon it, with perhaps some casual allusion to the technique being of a purely vocal character. The madrigals, it is true, were often stated by the composers to be 'apt for voyces or viols'; and no doubt the string-players of the day were often content to play madrigal music; partly because the repertory of available string music was small; partly because vocal music presented little technical difficulty to the instrumental player; and, moreover, it could be a real source of pleasure, as may still be discovered by string-players who might play such a madrigal as Wilbye's *Sweet honey-sucking bees*.

The earliest developments in instrumental composition, more particularly for strings, date from the middle of the sixteenth century. The organ and the lute were the instruments in the earlier years of the century which created a definite demand for some kind of a repertory. Both in England and Italy composers began to turn their attention in this direction. In England Hugh Aston, born about 1485, was one of the pioneers in writing for the keyboard; and early in the sixteenth century the printer Petrucci produced a few works in lute-tablature in Italy. Almost all of these were transcriptions of vocal pieces. It was not until the latter part of the century that composers began to write original works for strings. The reason for this new departure may be directly traced to the work of the 'luthier' or instrument-maker. The viol, in its various forms and sizes, reached complete maturity as regards scope and design about the year 1550; and within a very few years the violin family had also reached nearly to perfection. There exists a perfect example of the modern violin by Andrea Amati, dated 1565; and long before the end of the century numbers of fine instruments of the whole violin family were being produced at Cremona.

The minds of composers were naturally stimulated by the new and wider possibilities that were thus laid open to them. In Italy Andrea Gabrieli, and later his son, Giovanni, were among the important pioneers in writing for strings. But in this field English musicians played a very leading part. In fact the English school of chamber music for strings has a brilliant continuity, extending from the last quarter of the sixteenth century until the close of the seventeenth, and it includes such names as Byrd, Gibbons, Ward, Dering, Peerson, Tomkins, Jenkins, Sympson, and Purcell.

The wonderful versatility of Byrd's outstanding genius will be recognized when it is stated that there survive among his string works as many as twelve Fantasies, or Fancies, one Prelude, one Pavan and Galliard, eight 'In nomines', and some eight other compositions in the 'In nomine' manner written upon plain-song melodies.

It may be convenient to consider the 'In nomines' first, as being the earlier form of composition, although of less interest than the Fantasy.

The 'In nomine' occupies a peculiar place in the history of musical form, since it seems to have been exclusively an English use. An immense number of 'In nomines' exist, including examples by almost every English composer of note from the time of Taverner, Tallis, and Tye down to that of Orlando Gibbons, and even later. How the term came to be applied to this form of composition is not known. In every instance the traditional plain-song melody of *Gloria tibi Trinitas* is used as a canto fermo, upon which the composer exercises his fancy in writing music for strings in any number of parts. That being so, it seems strange that the words 'In nomine' rather than 'Gloria tibi' should have come into use to denote this form of composition. It has been suggested that as *Gloria tibi Trinitas* is the first Antiphon for Lauds, the instrumental 'In nomine' may have been intended in the first instance to serve as an introduction or Introit before Mass.

Be that as it may, the writing of 'In nomines' became a vogue by the middle of the sixteenth century. Byrd's examples include one for seven parts, but only a single part of this work survives.[1] Four are for five parts, and three for four. In general principle the plan was to begin these movements simply, and to work up interest towards the close, using more rapid notes in the later passages. The canto fermo was placed, at will, in any part; but the bass was usually avoided for the obvious reason that in that position the freedom of the other parts would be more restricted.

The five-part example which is numbered 1 in the appended list at the end of this chapter opens fugally. The subject and answer exactly follow the rules that came

---

[1] B.M. Add. MS. 32377.

to be regarded as paramount in the eighteenth century for controlling this feature of fugal composition.

In the last nine bars Byrd sustains the interest by changing the value of the notes in the canto fermo to triple measure. Thus, in terms of modern notation (halving the note-values) the change has this appearance:

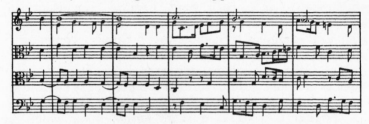

No one could suggest for a moment that the final four bars of this same piece are vocal rather than instrumental in character:

Whereas the compass of many string compositions of this period lies low, having been definitely designed for a consort of viols, it happens that this 'In nomine', and also No. 2 in the list, is of a compass exactly suited for two violins, two violas, and violoncello. It is not unlikely that Byrd had these newer instruments in his mind when he wrote them. No. 2 is very fully scored, and the last sixteen bars are brilliantly worked up with rapid scale passages for all the instruments, excepting, of course, the second violin, which plays the canto fermo. No. 3 in the list seems to have enjoyed great popularity in its day, judging from the large amount of early text of it that has survived. Of all the five-part examples of Byrd it is the most characteristically instrumental, and perhaps also the most musical. Towards the end the following typical bit of string writing occurs (the note-values are halved):

Byrd undoubtedly succeeded in infusing more musical feeling into this rather academic form of composition than any of his contemporaries. The two four-part 'In nomines' are far less interesting; and some of the smaller settings of other plain-song melodies are little more than exercises. But his greatest achievements are found in the Fantasy, or Fancy, which, as the word implies, was a form in which the composer was free to follow wherever his imagination and fancy might lead him.

The fantasy trio and quartet may be passed over without comment, although Byrd thought well enough of the latter to include it in his set of *Psalmes, Songs, and Sonnets,* published in 1611. But the quintet is of great interest. It is developed at considerable length and the two top parts are in strict canon throughout the entire work. Opening in the conventional manner with a quiet subject fugally treated in anticipation of the canon, the growing interest after a while is arrested by another fugal passage, slightly reminiscent of the opening subject. Subsequently Byrd shows his power of invention with a series of phrases of more rapid notes, by means of which fuller and more varied effects are produced, until quite unexpectedly the work ends in a restrained mood in drawn-out notes. The instrumental character of the writing may be judged from such phrases as:

and

In both these quotations the note-values are halved. This quintet appears in *My Ladye Nevells Booke* arranged as a keyboard piece under the title of 'A Lesson of Voluntarie'. There are four Fantasies for sestet. One of these has survived in manuscript at Christ Church, where it is described as being written 'for two basses'.[1] It is more vocal in style than is usual in Byrd's string music. The finest and most interesting of all these works is the sestet which he included in the 1611 set of *Psalmes, Songs, and Sonnets*. This composition has an additional importance because it affords a unique example at this early date of a work constructed in such a way that it foreshadows some of the principles which in Haydn's day became the accepted foundations of Form. It may be said to be divided into three distinct movements, though there is no actual break in the continuity of the piece as a whole. The first is the longest and most important movement. It follows the conventional principles of the Fantasy, beginning with a phrase which is worked in fugal form. The first twenty bars are constructed solely on this phrase, which is repeated continuously by one instrument after another with scarcely any variation, except in the matter of subject and answer (in all the following quotations the note-values are halved):

In the next seven bars the leading phrase is given to the bass instruments in turn, the upper parts playing a florid counter-subject. This phrase is closely allied to the original subject:

The third phrase brings fresh material although it may have some reference to the opening subject with its scale passage. This is taken up in turn by all six instruments:

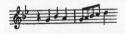

[1] Ch. Ch. MS. 979.

In the subsequent seventeen bars interesting little figures are developed by the upper instruments on a very simple bass; and gradually the key of B flat comes into prominence, G minor having held fairly consistently up to this point; but the close of this movement is in G.

Many of the Fantasies would have ended here; but now an entirely new movement begins. In terms of sixteenth-century notation the rhythm is framed in the proportion called sesquialtera, or three notes to two. The effect in modern notation is that of $\frac{6}{8}$ time (if the note-values are halved). Byrd thus introduces a clearly defined second movement of considerable length in marked contrast to the first, opening with a subject which is clearly shaped upon the third phrase of the first movement, quoted above, though with altered rhythm:

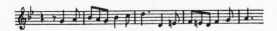

This movement is especially remarkable on account of the scheme of modulations which it follows. Opening in G minor it passes to B flat, and back through C major to a close in G major. Then, through C major, F major is reached, followed by G major and D minor; the final close being in G major. Here some of the principles of sonata-form are definitely suggested.

The string-writing in this bright movement is very characteristic; for example, the reiteration of single notes and the sequential character of the phrases are utterly remote from the vocal style.

Byrd rounds off the composition with yet another movement in complete contrast with the other two. In style this exactly resembles the eighteenth-century minuet. It opens with an eight-bar subject, subdivided into two equal sections. Another six-part Fantasy is written in two clearly

defined movements; and in this composition Byrd introduced some well-known tunes, such as 'Green-sleeves' and
'Walsingham'. A fourth six-part work survives only as
a fragment, but it has the appearance of being another
important piece.

The five-part work described as a 'Prelude' is chiefly
noticeable as an early example of a ground-bass very
curiously constructed. The melody of eight bars is divided
into two sections, at the end of each of which the bass viol
appends a short tag of two bars' length.

There is a short introduction to the composition, and
then these twelve bars of ground bass are repeated eleven
times. Some of the final variations are very elaborate, and
afford a very good example of the type of technique expected of violists at this period. One quotation will suffice
here:

One other work must be mentioned, described as a
Fantasy for five parts, and alternatively, in one manuscript,
as a 'Ground'. It also had the title of 'Browning'. The
reason for this title is not known. It seems to have had a
sort of generic significance, because among John Baldwin's
compositions there is one described as 'a Browning of three
parts',[1] and another by Elway Bevin.[2] The composition is
constructed on the first two lines of a song-tune, the words
of which are:

> The leaves be green, the nuts be brown,
> They hang so high they will not come down.

The term 'Browning' may in some way be connected with
the last word of the first line.

[1] Baldwin's MS., Royal Mus. Lib. 24 d. 2, fo. 121ᵛ.
[2] Ibid., fo. 120ᵛ.

Byrd's 'Browning' was a very popular piece. The melody is used like a ground-bass; and hence the term 'Ground', as applied to this particular setting of the subject. The melody, however, is given to each of the five instruments in turn, beginning with the bass, instead of being kept to the bass throughout. It is repeated altogether twenty times. The variations are extremely dainty and well contrasted. Though violists will prefer the notation of this work as found in the many early manuscript copies of it, the eyes of modern musicians may perhaps more readily appreciate the character of the work if in the following quotation of the opening bars the crotchet unit is substituted for that of the semibreve, and the music transposed up a fourth:

At the conclusion of the score of Browning in B.M. Add. MS. 29996, fo. 157, the words 'laus deo William Byrde' are written. A pencil note, apparently in the hand of John Bishop, states that this is 'Mr Birde's handwriting'. A comparison with his undoubted signature[1] clearly proves this note to be inaccurate.

The Pavan and Galliard for sestet are constructed in regular form and in accordance with these conventional dance measures. Byrd employs the same theme, with the necessary alteration of rhythm, for the two dance forms. This is a very pleasant piece of music and by far the most straightforward of Byrd's compositions for strings.

An 'In nomine' attributed to Byrd in the B.M. Add. MS. 29996, fo. 63, is by Parsons; and another by Baldwin, in the Royal Collection (24. d. 2, fo. 84ᵛ), has been erroneously assigned to Byrd by Dr. Meyer.

The two string parts entitled *Abradate* have already been mentioned.[2] They may be part of an accompaniment to a song in one of the plays.

[1] P.R.O., Exchequer Rolls, E. 407. 72.
[2] See page 169.

Chamber Music for Strings

Fantasies. à 3.
No. 1.   B.M. Add. 34800, fo. 15^v;
                                       R.C.M. 2036, fo. 4^v.
No. 2.   B.M. Add. 29246, fo. 22^v;
                                       R.C.M. 2036, fo. 5^v.
No. 3.   B.M. Add. 29996, fo. 69^v;
                                       R.C.M. 2093, p. 31.

Fantasies. à 4.
No. 1.   *Psalmes, Songs, and Sonnets*
                                       (1611), No. 15; B.M. Add.
                                       29246, fo. 41^v. Bodl. D.
                                       245-7.
No. 2.   B.M. Add. 29246, fo. 39; Add.
                                       29427, fo. 45.
No. 3.   B.M. Add. 29427, fo. 45^v.

Fantasies. à 5.
No. 1.   B.M. Add. 17786-91 (see also
                                       Nevell, 29, and Paris Rés.
                                       1122, p. 19).
No. 2. 'Browning'.   B.M. Add. 17792-6; Add.
                                       29996, fo. 153^v; Add. 31390,
                                       fo. 124^v; Add. 32377, fo. 2;
                                       Bodl. D. 212-16; E. 423,
                                       p. 149; Tenbury, 389, fo. 86.
No. 3. 'Ut my re' (fragment).   B.M. Add. 32377, fo. 5.

Fantasies. à 6.
No. 1.   *Psalmes, Songs, and Sonnets*
                                       (1611), No. 26; B.M. Add.
                                       29996, fo. 213^v; Add. 37402-
                                       37406; Bodl. E. 423, p. 307.
No. 2.   B.M. Add. 17786-91; Add.
                                       29996, fo. 211; Bodl. E. 423,
                                       p. 303; Tenbury, 341-4; 379-
                                       384.
No. 3. 'For two Basses'.   Ch. Ch. 979.
No. 4 (incomplete).   B.M. Add. 29996, fo. 210.

In nomine. à 4.
No. 1.   Bodl. D. 212-16.
No. 2.   Bodl. D. 212-16.

In nomine. à 5.

No. 1.	B.M. Add. 31390, fo. 43^v.
No. 2.	B.M. Add. 31390, fo. 59; Add. 39550-4; Bodl. D. 212-16.
No. 3.	B.M. Add. 22597, fo. 35^v; Add 29401-5; Add. 29996, fo. 68^v; Add. 31390, fo. 120^v; Add. 32377, fo. 8^v; Add. 34049, fo. 47^v; Bodl. D. 212-16; E. 423, p. 182; Ch. Ch. 984-988; Tenbury, 389, fo. 71; R.C.M. 2049, fo. 13^v.
No. 4.	B.M. Add. 32377, fo. 9^v; Bodl. D. 212-16; Tenbury, 389, fo. 72.
No. 5.	Bodl. D. 212-16.

In nomine. à 7.　　　　　　　B.M. Add. 32377, fo. 10.

Prelude and Fantasy. à 5.　　B.M. Add. 17792-6; Add. 32377, fo. 2.

Pavan and Galliard. à 6.　　　Bodl. C. 64.

Abradate (two single string parts). B.M. Add. 29427 fo. 17. Tenbury, 389, fo. 101.

The following are instrumental pieces written in the 'In nomine' style upon plain-song melodies:

Salvator mundi. à 3.	B.M. Add. 18936-9; Add. 29246, fo. 14 (called here *Sermone blando*).
Christe Redemptor, No. 1. à 4.	Tenbury, 354-8.
Christe Redemptor, No. 2. à 4.	B.M. Add. 29246, fo. 48^v; Tenbury, 354-8.
Miserere, No. 1. à 4.	B.M. Add. 18936-9; Tenbury, 354-8.
Miserere, No. 2. à 4.	B.M. Add. 18936-9; Add. 29246, fo. 48.
Precamur sancte Domine. à 4.	Tenbury, 354-8.
Sermone blando, No. 1. à 4.	Tenbury, 354-8.
Sermone blando, No. 2. à 4.	Tenbury, 354-8.
Te lucis. à 4.	Tenbury, 354-8.

The following are known only in lute tablature:

Christe qui lux.	B.M. Add. 29246, fo. 46^v.
Salvator mundi, No. 1.	B.M. Add. 29246, fo. 47^v.
Salvator mundi, No. 2.	B.M. Add. 29246, fo. 47^v.
Sermone blando, No. 1.	B.M. Add. 29246, fo. 15^v.
Sermone blando, No. 2.	B.M. Add. 29246, fo. 15^v.
Te lucis, No. 1.	B.M. Add. 29246, fo. 46^v.
Te lucis, No. 2.	B.M. Add. 29246, fo. 47^v.

CHAPTER XIV

KEYBOARD MUSIC

IF all knowledge of the vocal music produced in Tudor
England had perished, this country would still be able
to claim an important position in musical history, for the
reason that England was undoubtedly the birth-place of
keyboard music. The Elizabethans, both as composers and
performers, laid the foundation upon which the fabric of
all subsequent music for the clavichord, the harpsichord,
and the modern pianoforte was built. Prominent among
these founders are the names of Bull, Giles Farnaby, and
Orlando Gibbons; but the overshadowing figure was that
of Byrd.

The music to which this statement refers covers a period
from about 1560 to 1620; but even before this keyboard
music had been popular in England as nowhere else in
Europe.

Early in the sixteenth century a type of harpsichord had
been brought into very general use, and it came to be
known as the Virginal. The origin of this word in this
connexion has not been satisfactorily explained. Little music
seems to have been actually composed for the Virginal in
the first half of the century, and its use was limited to the
performance of dance tunes, popular folk-songs, and
arrangements of polyphonic vocal music.

Conspicuous among the early forerunners of the Elizabethan school of virginal composers was Hugh Aston.
Aston's Church music was of a very high order;[1] but more
interest has been attached to his instrumental compositions
by musical historians, who have acclaimed him as the
inventor of variation-form, as exploited in a piece called
My ladye Careys Dompe.[2] It is by no means certain that
this *Dompe* is by Aston, though it comes next to his *Horne-
pype* in the same manuscript. And as it has now been
plainly proved that Aston is not to be identified with Hugh

[1] See his collected works in *Tudor Church Music*, vol. x.
[2] B.M., Royal Appendix 58.

Ashton, Archdeacon of York and Canon of St. Stephen's, Westminster, who died in 1522,[1] the date of Aston's death remains unknown, and the *Dompe* may be of much later date than has been assumed. Hilda Andrews[2] has rightly described it as 'of so rudimentary a type that it does no more than foreshadow the advanced instrumental writing of the great school of Virginalists'.

Van den Borren suggests[3] that Cabezón, the blind Spanish organist and composer, who visited England in the train of Philip the Second in 1554, may have brought with him a more fully developed idea of variation-form. Cabezón and Tallis would certainly have met at Greenwich during this visit, and Byrd may have met Cabezón if he was also present at Greenwich as a pupil of Tallis at this time. For it was actually Byrd in whose hands variation-form was first brought to an advanced degree of interest and aesthetic excellence.

But Byrd's claim to greatness as a virginal composer rests upon a much higher achievement than this. It was he who by his supreme genius created something that was entirely new in the realm of keyboard music, both as regards form and style. Of this more will be said presently.

The English school of virginal composers, as just stated, dates roughly from 1560 to 1620, and it is noteworthy that it should have preceded that of the Madrigalists by some thirty years, although it is probable that few of the pieces which have survived are much earlier than 1580, even if some are actually dated before this. As with the string music, the craftsman no doubt played a considerable part in the development. The instruments underwent immense improvement in the second half of the century. It can scarcely be supposed that the finger-technique of such a virtuoso as Bull could have been evolved on the primitive instruments in use at the Court of King Henry the Eighth.

It is exceptionally fortunate that a wonderful corpus of the music of the English Virginal School of this great period

[1] *Tudor Church Music*, vol. x, Preface.

[2] *My Ladye Nevells Booke*, edited by Hilda Andrews, Historical Note, p. xxiii.

[3] C. Van den Borren, *Sources of Keyboard Music in England*, trans. by J. E. Matthew, p. 167.

survives to-day. No other European country has anything
that can remotely be compared with it. More than 600 pieces
are in existence, and nearly a quarter of these are by Byrd.

Among the contemporary sources of text *Parthenia* should
be mentioned first, as being the earliest known book of
engraved keyboard music. It was published in 1611, the
year in which Byrd's *Psalmes, Songs, and Sonnets* was
issued. So popular was it that during the following fifty
years it passed through six editions. As is well known, it
was devoted exclusively to the works of Byrd, Bull, and
Gibbons. It was followed by a kind of supplement entitled
Parthenia Inviolata. The only known copy of this latter
book is now in the Drexel collection in the New York
Public Library; but it includes nothing by Byrd.

Of much greater importance are the manuscript collections. Chief among these, at least in reference to Byrd,
is *My Ladye Nevells Booke*. It consists exclusively of Byrd's
compositions. This beautiful manuscript was written—it
might almost be said illuminated—by the famous John
Baldwin, lay-clerk of St. George's Chapel, Windsor. The
question of the identity of 'the Ladye' has been discussed
in a former chapter. It soon passed out of the family owner-
ship; but it was recovered by Lord Abergavenny from
Lord North in 1668 only to disappear again and to be found
later in the library of Charles Burney. After many further
vicissitudes it was bought by Lord Abergavenny about the
year 1830, and it still remains in its real home at Eridge
Castle. The text of this manuscript is of special value,
because it must have been seen by Byrd, and it is possible
that some corrections of the text are in his own hand. The
manuscript was finished in 1591.

In some respects the 'Fitzwilliam Virginal Book' is even
a greater treasure than the Nevell Book, for the reason
that it contains about 300 compositions, a large number of
which are by Byrd. The text of this manuscript is found
to be less accurate than that of the Nevell Book, when
pieces included in both collections are collated; yet there
are a few instances in which the Fitzwilliam text is to be
preferred. But even so, the collection is of immense importance, covering as it does the entire period, and including
the works of the lesser as well as the greater composers.

The book at one time was erroneously known as 'Queen Elizabeth's Virginal Book'. It is all written in one hand, thought to be that of Francis Tregian. Tregian was a member of a Cornish family, who, as a result of his activities in the Catholic interest, spent many years in the Fleet prison. He died there about the year 1619, and evidence points to his having written the manuscript in the Fleet. Members of this family have been mentioned in a former chapter in connection with the religious troubles.[1] In the eighteenth century the manuscript came into the hands of Lord Fitzwilliam, and so into its present home in the Museum at Cambridge which he founded.

Two valuable collections belonging to the Royal Library are now in the British Museum on permanent loan from his Majesty the King. One is William Forster's book, which is dated January 1623/4 under Forster's signature. Nearly half the pieces in this book are by Byrd. The other is Benjamin Cosyn's book; but this contains scarcely anything by Byrd.

Other collections of less importance are in the British Museum, including eight of the Additional MSS.[2] and one of the Egerton MSS.[3] The first of these eight is the Virginal Book of Elizabeth Rogers. Her identity is unknown. Four manuscripts at Christ Church, Oxford, include keyboard works of Byrd,[4] as also do two in the Bibliothèque du Conservatoire in Paris.[5] These two Paris books were formerly catalogued as Nos. 18547 and 18546. The first of these (Rés. 1122, or 18547) is in the hand of Thomas Tomkins, and consequently the text is of special value. In the Drexel Collection of Music in the New York Public Library there are two manuscripts containing works of Byrd; of these No. 5612 is much the more important; No. 5609 is of late date and largely transcribed from one of the Paris books. A manuscript at the Royal College of Music[6] completes the list of sources of text of Byrd's keyboard music, as far as is known.

---

[1] See page 43, and there spelt Tregion.
[2] Nos. 10337, 23623, 29996, 30485, 30486, 31392, 31403, and 36661.
[3] No. 2046.   [4] Nos. 371, 431, 1113, and 1175.
[5] Réservé 1122 and 1186.
[6] No. 2093.

The versatility of Byrd's genius is in some respects even more clearly revealed in his keyboard works than in his other compositions. This is not to suggest that in this department he approached the heights that he reached in his finest Church music. Keyboard music, as he left it, when considered in relation to the development of pianoforte and organ music during the following three and a half centuries, was still in its infancy, on the other hand polyphonic vocal music reached its zenith in a form that has not been surpassed since the sixteenth century. But whereas polyphonic vocal music was no novelty in Byrd's time, it is a fact, as stated by Hilda Andrews,[1] that 'keyboard music was virtually a new creation. Sprung full-grown from Byrd's infinite musical resource it was of a type hitherto unimagined'.

In this field of composition Byrd was a pioneer, but he was far more. Many of his works, it is true, are dull and uninspired, but the same thing may be said about those of other keyboard composers with great names. And the chief interest of some of his works may have relation to the historical rather than the artistic development of musical Art. But there are many that display artistic features of the highest quality, and not a few that make their appeal to musicians in our own time by their intrinsic beauty, regardless of any considerations of date.

Byrd's output of keyboard music was enormous. If Pavans and Galliards are counted separately the number of his works in this department alone approaches 150.

They may be grouped roughly under three headings. The first comprises what may be described as free compositions, or, as Thomas Morley expressed it in defining the Fantasy, 'that kind of musicke which is made without a dittie . . . and the composer is tide to nothing, but that he may adde or deminish and alter at his pleasure'.[2] This group includes Fantasies, Preludes, and Voluntaries. The second group consists of dance-forms of various kinds, such as Pavans, Galliards, Almans, Corantos, Lavoltas and Jigs as well as Marches. The third group includes Airs with variations based on song-tunes and dance-tunes, some of which were traditional melodies with names and some

[1] Op. cit., p. xxiii.
[2] Morley's *Plaine and Easie Introduction to Musicke*, 1597, p. 181.

original. There are also in this group compositions on ground basses and such structures as the hexachord.

Comment must necessarily be confined to a few individual pieces.

One of the finest of the Fantasies is that numbered 36 in the Nevell book and 103 in Fitzwilliam. It is certainly no 'antique', but a piece of living music characterized by a nobility of style that foreshadows the work of Bach. It opens quietly with a scale passage, treated in the fugal manner that became conventional a century or more later. Indeed, as the works of the English virginalists come to be examined it would appear that the conventions of 'real' and 'tonal' answers were already becoming established. This Fantasy is developed with progressive interest, a feature being the treatment of the opening subject in diminution. The later passages are especially brilliant, and the figuration anticipates the style of the eighteenth century. The following bars may be quoted:

Near the end is a broad sequential passage contrasting with a rapid passage;[1]

A few bars later this vigorous bass is repeated decorated

[1] The ornaments are omitted in all these examples with the exception of those on pp. 206, 208, 209 & 210.

with semiquaver phrases, ending with a final cadence of great strength:

The Fantasy found in the R.C.M. MS., 2093, p. 31, is identical with Byrd's three-part work for strings (B.M. Add. 29996 fo. 69). The British Museum MS. gives no more than half the text, but the string version seems to have been written first. Another example of a composition written alternatively as a keyboard piece or for strings, is 'A lesson of Voluntarie' (No. 29 in the Nevell book). It is more effective in the version for string quintet (B.M., Add. 17786–91) where it is called a Fantasy.

The Prelude in Fitzwilliam (No. 100) is stated in the MS. to belong to a Fantasy of fugal character (No. 52), thus foreshadowing the conventional association of Preludes and Fugues of Bach's day. Another of Byrd's Preludes (No. 151 in Fitzwilliam, without ascription) is called *A Parludam* and is ascribed to Byrd by Forster (fo. 194ᵛ). It is like a Toccata in character, with a semiquaver figure running throughout without a break.

Among the dance forms the Pavans and Galliards hold far the largest place. Of the Pavan Morley wrote[1]:

The next in gravity and goodnes unto this [the Fantasy] is called a pavane, a kind of staide musicke, ordained for grave dauncing, and most commonlie made of three straines, whereof everie straine is

[1] Op. cit., p. 181.

plaid or sung twice, a straine they make to contain 8. 12. or 16. semibreves as they list, yet fewer then eight I have not seene in any pavan. In this you must cast your musicke by foure. . . . After every pavan we usually set a galliard (that is, a kind of musicke made out of the other) causing it to go by measure which the learned cal *trochaicam rationem.*

A few of the Pavans have no Galliard attached to them, and there are also some independent Galliards; notably the first 'Mris Brownlo' Galliard. The first of the ten Pavans in the Nevell book (two of them with no Galliard) is found also in the Fitzwilliam book with a note: 'the first that ever hee made'. One of the most beautiful of Byrd's Pavans is that found in Forster's MS., p. 65ᵛ. The second strain ends in A major with a richly harmonized passage in a low register and the third strain opens with a very melodious phrase in C major repeated in G major and again in F major.

The Pavans and Galliards varied considerably in length. The example found in *Parthenia* (Nos. 6 and 7) with the title *The Earle of Salisbury*, is a very slight little composition and contrasts with the Ninth or *Passanezzo*, or *Passinge Mesures Pavan*, with its Galliard (Nos. 24 and 25 in the Nevell book). This Pavan consists of six sections of 32 bars each and the Galliard is on the same extended scale. It is

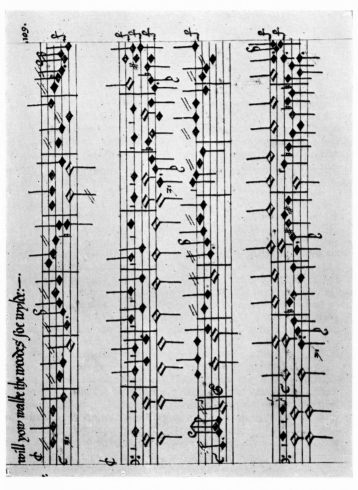

A page from 'My Ladye Nevells Booke' in the hand of John Baldwin (1591)

Reproduced by permission of the Marquess of Abergavenny, Miss Hilda Andrews, and Messrs. J. Curwen & Sons, Ltd.

one of Byrd's finest works. Another fine and very extended example is that entitled the *Quadran Pavan and Galliard.* The sixth of the Nevell Pavans has the title *Kinlough Goodd.* The meaning of this is obscure. It is spelt *Kinbrugh* in the printed edition of the Nevell book. There is a Pavan and Galliard by 'Mr Kinlough' in a British Museum MS.

The Corantos are pleasant short pieces; and there is a particularly attractive little Alman (No. 156 in the Fitzwilliam book). The upper line of the third and final strain may be quoted here together with its reprise:

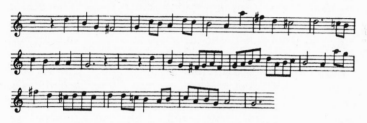

In length and importance *Munsers Almain,* and the *Variatio,* as a separate number, are in marked contrast to the little piece just quoted. They are fine examples of their kind. The Alman in Byrd's hands differed in form from the Allemande of a later period, when it had its established place as the opening number of the conventional 'Suite'.

There are a good number of pieces by Byrd which may in a general way be described as Themes with variations. They bear the names of the songs and dance-tunes on which they are constructed. Among these pieces *The Carman's Whistle, Sellingers Round,* and *O Mystris Myne* are well known. The title of this last had led to the association of it with Shakespeare's song in *Twelfth Night.* The two songs seem to have no relation to each other. In the first two lines the words 'roaming' and 'coming' are something of a misfit, because the perfect poise of the melody is disturbed if the minim is split into two syllables; but after that the metre of the words and the music are wholly at variance.

Other fine sets of themes and variations are *Jhon come kiss me now* and *All in a garden grine. Callino Casturame* is a beautiful melody, set with much restraint and simplicity in five variations. The melody is Irish, and the title is a corruption of *Colleen age asthore.* It is alluded to by Shakespeare

in *Henry V*, Act IV, Sc. 4 where it is spelt *Callino Castore me.*
Goe from my windoe is another lovely tune; the variations
are assigned to Byrd, probably correctly, both in the Forster
and CosynMSS., but the setting in the Fitzwilliam book (No.
9) is by Morley. *Bony swete Robin* is ascribed to Byrd in the
Drexel MS. 5612, but it is more probably the work of Bull,
as stated in B.M., Add. 23623. The setting in the Fitzwilliam Book (No. 128) by Farnaby is a different work.
The Huntes upp is No. 8 in the Nevell book; it appears
twice in the Fitzwilliam book, as No. 59 and No. 276. In
this second case it is entitled *Pescodd Time.* The No. 59
version includes an extra variation between the fifth and
sixth, and from this point the variations stand in a different
order.

The 'Ground' was another form in which the keyboard
composers liked to express themselves. Byrd's examples are
not among his more interesting pieces. The *second Grownde*
(Nevell, No. 30) is constructed on the same unusual bass
as that he employed in the five-part composition for strings
called a 'Prelude' and already commented on.[1]

The Bells is a composition of great ingenuity, designed
on a ground-bass of a single bar, repeated throughout the
piece with scarcely any change:

This phrase was also used by Vautor in his madrigal *Sweet
Suffolk Owl*[2] to represent 'the tolling of the bell'; and again
by Byrd in the burial number of *The Battell.* The opening bars of Byrd's work represent the ringing-up, beginning
with the tenor, or lowest, bell in accordance with the custom
that still obtains among bell-ringers. His fertility of invention is nowhere better exemplified than in this composition,
where he succeeds in sustaining the interest throughout
nine variations, confining his figuration almost entirely to
scale passages.

Closely akin to the Ground are the compositions framed
upon the notes of the hexachord. The most interesting of
these is found in the Paris MS. Rés. 1122, p. 1. A curious

[1] P. 190.   [2] *Songs of divers Ayres and Natures*, 1619, No. 12.

feature of this piece is that it is necessary for 'the playne
song Briefes to be played by a second person'. It is a composition of much interest and considerable beauty. It is
constructed upon five repetitions of the hexachord in breves
up and down from C to A. At the opening of the third
statement the rhythm changes from square measure to
triple. At that point the first four bars of the popular song
Will you walk the woods so wild are introduced. As the development proceeds, snatches of this tune are treated in
canon, and the effect becomes increasingly fascinating
because of the modulations involved by the progress of the
controlling hexachord. The following few bars will serve to
illustrate this:

A little later another popular tune is brought in and the two
tunes are interwoven with great ingenuity.

One more of the keyboard pieces must be mentioned. It
is quaintly entitled *Mr. Birds Battell*. This piece has little to
recommend it as music except for *The Earle of Oxford's
Marche*, called alternatively in the Nevell Book *The Marche
before the Battell*. As a descriptive piece of music dating
from the sixteenth century the Battell is unique. It consists
of a suite of pieces which follow thus in the Nevell Book:

The marche before the battell.	The flute and the droome.
The souldier's sommons.	The marche to the fighte.
The marche of footemen.	tantara tantara.
The marche of horsmen.	the battels be joyned.
The trumpets.	The Retreate.
The Irishe marche.	The Galliarde for the vic-
The bagpipe and the drone.	torie.

Additional numbers are found in manuscripts of later date than the Nevell Book. In Elizabeth Rogers's book *The buriing of the dead* and *The souldiers delight* follow *The Retreate*; and *The Morris* and *The souldiers dance* (very similar to *The souldiers delight*) are interpolated between *The marche to the fighte* and *The Retreate* both in the Paris and Drexel manuscripts. The Christ Church MS. 431 begins with *The souldiers sommons* and ends abruptly just before *The battels be joyned*.

Byrd appears less successful in his method of arranging pieces of concerted vocal music for the keyboard, such, for example, as Dowland's *Lachrymae* (Fitzwilliam, No. 121), or even his own exquisite *Lullaby* (Drexel 5612). The beauty and pathos of Dowland's lovely melody seem to be obscured by the somewhat conventional figuration with which it is overloaded. The original melody opens thus:

and it appears in the following form in Byrd's first variation:

Dowland's *If my complaints*, or *Pyper's Galliard* (Ch. Ch. MS. 431) is treated more simply and with happier results. This setting must not be confused with the anonymous setting in Forster (p. 222ᵛ) which is a different composition.

Recalling the statement that this music was 'of a type hitherto unimagined', certain characteristic features may be briefly touched upon.

(1) Figuration. It was Byrd's creative genius that first devised much of the figuration that became a commonplace a century and a half later in the keyboard music of

Bach. His seemingly unlimited power of inventing new phrases, and thus securing an immense range of variety, has been mentioned in former chapters in relation to his vocal music; but it is equally conspicuous in his keyboard works, and especially in the department of figuration. Examples of this may be seen in illustrations already quoted, but some further passages should be mentioned. A noteworthy feature of the *Ten variations* on an original theme, preserved in the Paris and Drexel collections, is the variety of figuration. The following is quoted from the upper stave of the sixth variation:

Another example comes from a fine composition called *A Medley* (Fitzwilliam, No. 173). Phrasing of this graceful passage has here been added to this illustration by the author.

The following three bars are from a Pavan in the Drexel collection. They have a distinct eighteenth-century flavour:

(2) Varied rhythm. This feature of Tudor music, so long overlooked and neglected in performance, has in these latter days come to be recognized and understood. In the realm of vocal music it often involves difficulties in performance, especially in complex instances when the rhythm is not coincident in all the voices. Nevertheless each voice is independent in such cases, and the difficulty can be approached by single brains. Complex rhythms of this kind in keyboard music must be regarded as offering an almost insuperable difficulty for the single performer, and it must cause some doubt as to whether certain passages could actually have been played strictly at their face value. Some examples may be quoted from Byrd's compositions. In the *Passamezzo* Pavan the following passage occurs in which the quaver value remains constant:

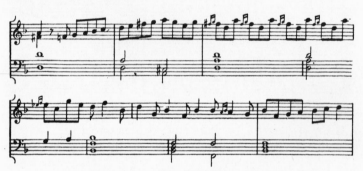

Here is a quotation from the Fancy called *Gloria tibi Trinitas* from one of the Paris manuscripts. The crotchet value here remains constant.

Such complex cases as these are fortunately not common.

The concluding bars of one of the variations in the *Hornpipe* (Forster, fo. 27b) are:

The bass of this last bar if phrased as in the manuscript produces an entirely different effect:

(3) Something must be said briefly of the ornaments, as indicated by either one stroke or two through the stem of a note. It is generally agreed that two strokes imply ♩♩, or ♩♩, preferably the former. The interpretation of the single stroke is more uncertain. It is regarded by many as implying ♩♩, but it is possible that it should be interpreted as a short appoggiatura ♩♩. For it is reasonable to suggest that if two strokes denote two grace-notes, one stroke stands for one. No effective contrast is produced if two grace-notes are indicated by both of these signs. That Byrd and his contemporaries regarded the two signs as having different interpretations is evident from the care with which they employed them in certain instances, notably in the opening passages of *A Hornpipe* (Forster, p. 27b), and again in *Ut mi re* (Fitzwilliam, 102).

These ornaments sometimes had accentual value and were apparently employed to indicate in triple measure whether a bar of six crotchets was to be phrased $\frac{3}{2}$ or $\frac{6}{4}$. This example from *Gipseis Round* will illustrate the point:

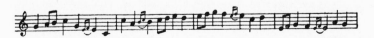

Another good example is found in the third section of
Qui passe.

In the seventh variation of *The Huntes upp* (or *Pescodd
Time*) the cross-rhythms are emphasized by ornaments.

In a general way too much importance must not be
ascribed to the exact position and textual value of the
ornaments. To eliminate them entirely in performance,
even on the pianoforte, would definitely affect the character
of the music just as it would in the works of Domenico
Scarlatti a generation later. The ornaments were an affecta-
tion of the time, and they seem often to have been employed
to excess. But there is evidence pointing to their being
largely a matter for the taste and discretion of performers.
In support of this last statement it will be sufficient to quote
three authoritative manuscripts of the opening bars of *The
Huntes upp* each of which differs in a striking manner as to
the insertion of ornaments:

In performance on the harpsichord the ornaments should
be played as in the early text. On a pianoforte they should
be sparingly observed.

Phrases such as ♦♦♦♦♦♦♦♦♦♦ which have rather a
terrifying effect upon the eye, whether expressed in terms
of semiquavers or demi-semiquavers, are in execution
equivalent to a shake with a turn as expressed in modern

notation ♦♦♦♦ and the phrases of six notes, usually

written ♦♦♦♦♦♦ are far simpler if interpreted as

. The notation as written out, for example in the manuscript of the first Galliard (Nevell 11), has exact the effect of a 'turn', as expressed in more modern notation .

(4) The composers of keyboard music did not bind themselves to the same strict principles of technique in relation to their progressions as those which were observed with such uniformity in vocal writing. Consecutive fifths and octaves are of frequent occurrence. Byrd's technique was no exception in this matter. The following are typical examples:

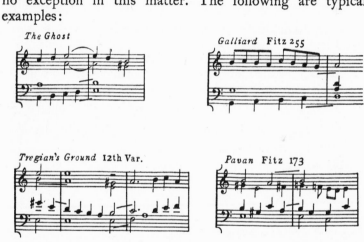

In the author's former book[1] allusion was made to a number of small pieces described as being made 'upon the Fa burden of (certain) playne Songs'. They are found in B.M., Add. MS. 29996, fo. 158–78, in a hand said to be that of Thomas Tomkins. They are in short score and are apparently designed for performance on a keyboard instrument. The author, after careful examination of the manuscript, can find no definite evidence that these pieces are by Byrd, and he regrets the error which was based upon information that at the time had the appearance of being authoritative.

[1] *William Byrd: A Short Account of his Life and Work*, pp. 111 and 117.

List of Keyboard Music

In order to facilitate reference, Fancies, Grounds, Misereres, Preludes, Voluntaries, Pavans, and Galliards, and other dance-forms are arranged and numbered. Pavans and Galliards are set out thus: (1) The set of ten numbered examples in the Nevell Book. (2) Those with titles arranged alphabetically. (3) Those without title arranged according to key, using the notes of the hexachord system, 'Gam ut through Fa ut'. This plan is adopted in accordance with certain notes made by Thomas Tomkins in the Paris MS. Rés. 1122, and the arrangement of the pieces in Drexel 5612. Tomkins's notes, which refer to the copying of the 'greate Booke of wch was my Brother Johns', are as follows:

and all Especiall good lessons in that key of A re to be placed together.

they being in a key of gamut to be suited and sorted together.

And what ever Fancies or selected Voluntaries of worthe to be placed in their owne native keyes not mingling or mangling them together wth others of a Contrary keys but put in theyre Right places.

In Drexel 5612 the pieces are grouped under 'Lessons in Gam ut', 'Lessons in A re', &c.

The other forms are here similarly arranged: (1) alphabetically according to title; (2) according to 'key'.

All in a garden grine.   Nevell, 32; Fitz. 104

Almans:
1. Monsieur's Alman.   Fitz. 61; Forster, fo. 124^v.
   Variatio (Mounsers Alman).   Nevell, 38 (Title, 'Munsers Almaine'); Fitz. 62; Forster,[1] fo. 184^v; B.M. Add. 30485, fo. 92^v (without title).
2. The Queenes Alman.   Fitz. 172.
3. Alman.   Fitz. 156; Forster, fo. 38^v.
4. Alman and Galliard.   Fitz. 163; 164.
5. Alman.   Fitz. 63.
6. Alman Galliard (a fragment).   Ch. Ch. 175, fo. 20^v (Title, 'Galliard').

[1] In Forster the Variatio does not follow the Alman but is found later in the book under the title of 'Mounsers Alman'.

As I went to Wallsingham, *see* Walsingham.

The Barelye Breake.	Nevell, 6.
Mr. Bird's Battell.	Nevell, 4; B.M. Add. 10337, fo 11ᵛ; Ch. Ch. 431 (incomplete); Paris, Rés. 1186, fo. 93ᵛ, Drexel, 5609, 1st version, p. 14, 2nd version, p. 56.
The Bells.	Fitz. 69.
Callino Casturame.	Fitz. 158; B.M. Add. 30485, fo. 96ᵛ.
The Carman's Whistle.	Nevell, 34; Fitz. 58; Forster, fo. 67 (Title, 'Grounde'); B.M. Add. 30485, fo. 65; Add. 30486, fo. 19; Add. 31403, fo. 25ᵛ (Title 'The Carter's Whissell').

Corantos:
1. The First French Coranto.	Fitz. 218; Forster, fo. 9ᵛ.
2. The Second French Coranto.	Fitz. 205; (anonymous) Forster, fo. 10ᵛ.
3. The Third French Coranto.	Forster, fo. 11ᵛ.
4. Coranto.	Fitz. 241; Drexel, 5612, p. 114 (Title, 'Mr. Birds Gigg').

Fancies, or Fantasies:
  In Gam ut.
1. Fancy.	Fitz. 8.
2. Fancy.	Fitz. 261; B.M. Add. 30485, fo. 85ᵛ; Ch. Ch. 1113, p. 157.
3. Fancy.	Paris, Rés. 1122, p. 16.

  In A re.
4. Fancy.	Fitz. 52;[1] Paris, Rés. 1122, p. 58.

  In C fa ut.
5. Fancy.	Nevell, 36; Fitz. 103.
6. Fancy, *see also* Fantasy à 3 for strings.	B.M. Add. 29996, fo. 69ᵛ (incomplete, Title, '3 parts of Mr. Birds'), R.C.M. 2093, p. 31.
7. Fancy.	Paris, Rés. 1122, p. 38 (Title, 'A Verse').

  In D sol re.
8. Fancy.	Nevell, 41; B.M. Add. 30485, fo. 103ᵛ.

[1] For the 'Praeludium to yᵉ Fancie' *see* Prelude No. 3.

9. Fancy.	B.M. Add. 30485, fo. 33ᵛ (Title, 'Mr. bird 2 partes').
10. Fancy (incomplete).	R.C.M. 2093, p. 25 (reversed.)

Fancy, *see* Voluntary, No. 2.

Fortune.	Fitz. 65; Forster, fo. 127ᵛ.
The Ghost.	Fitz. 162.
Giggs, *see* Jigs.	
Gipseis Round.	Fitz. 216.
Gloria tibi Trinitas.	Paris, Rés. 1122, p. 36 (Title, 'two pts. gloria tibi trinitas').
Goe from my windoe.	Forster, fo. 163ᵛ; Cosyn, fo. 83.

Grounds:
1. My Ladye Nevels Grounde.	Nevell, 1.
2. The Second Grounde.	Nevell, 30.
3. Hughe Ashtons Grownde.	Nevell, 35; Fitz. 60 (Title, 'Treg(ians) Ground'); Forster, fo. 196ᵛ; B.M. Add. 30485, fo. 61.
4. A Ground.	Forster, fo. 3ᵛ.
5. A Ground.	Forster, fo. 130ᵛ.
6. A Ground.	Forster, fo. 133.

A Ground, *see* Carman's Whistle.

Have with yow to Walsingame, *see* Walsingham.	
Horn-pipe.	Forster, fo. 27ᵛ.
The Huntes upp. (Pescodd Time).	Nevell, 8; Fitz. 59.
If my complaints (or Pyper's gal[liard]).¹	Ch. Ch. 431, fo. 18ᵛ.
In nomine, *see* Miserere, No. 2.	
In nominey Parsons, *see* list of pieces with alternative ascriptions	

Jigs:
1. A Galliard's Gygge.	Nevell, 7.
2. A Gigg.	Fitz. 181.
Mr. Birds Gigg, *see* Coranto, No. 4.	
Jhon come kisse me now.	Fitz. 10.
Kapassa, *see* Qui passe.	

---

¹ In Drexel 5612, p. 4, there are two short pieces entitled 'Captaine Piper's Pavion' and 'The Galliard'. The Galliard is a setting of 'If my complaints'. There is no evidence in that MS. as to authorship. The setting in Forster is anonymous; it is a different setting from that in Ch. Ch. 431, which alone is ascribed to Byrd.

Lavoltas:

1. La volta (T. Morley, set by   Fitz. 159.
      Byrd).
2. A Levalto.   Forster, fo. 12ᵛ; Fitz. 155.

A Lesson of Voluntarie, *see* Voluntaries.

Lord Willobies Welcome home.   Nevell, 33; Forster, fo. 13ᵛ;
                                 Fitz. 160 (Title, 'Rowland');
                                 B.M. Egerton, 2046, fo. 33ᵛ
                                 (lute tablature); Paris, Rés.
                                 1186, fo. 64ᵛ; Drexel, 5609,
                                 p. 146.

Lullaby (arr. from Carol, q.v.). B.M. Add. 30485, fo. 57ᵛ (in-
                                 complete); Drexel, 5612, p.
                                 194.

Malts come down.   Fitz. 150.

Marche before the Battell.   Nevell, 3; Fitz. 259 (Title, 'The
                                 Earle of Oxford's Marche').
                                 Drexel, 5609, p. 241.

Marche, The Earle of Oxford's, *see* Marche before the Battell.

The Maydens Song.   Nevell, 28; Fitz. 126.
A Medley.   Fitz. 173.

Misereres:

1. Miserere of 3 parts.   Fitz. 176; B.M. Add. 30485, fo.
                                 34ᵛ (Title, 'Upon a playn-
                                 songe').

2. Miserere of 4 parts.   Fitz. 177; B.M. Add. 30485, fo.
                                 35 (Title, 'In nomine').

3. Miserere.   Ch. Ch. 371, fo. 15.

O Mystris Myne.   Fitz. 66.
A Parludam, *see* Prelude, No. 2.

Pavans and Galliards:

1. The Firste Pavian.[1]   Nevell, 10; Fitz. 167; Drexel,
                                 5612, p. 132.

   The Galliarde to the Firste   Nevell, 11; Fitz. 168; Drexel,
      Pavian.   5612, p. 134.

2. The Seconde Pavian.   Nevell, 12; Fitz. 257 (Title,
                                 'Pavan Fant'); Forster, fo.
                                 59ᵛ; B.M. Add. 30485, fo. 6ᵛ.

---

[1] Note in the Fitzwilliam MS. 'the first that ever hee made'.

	The Galliarde to the Seconde Pavian.	Nevell, 13; Fitz. 258; Forster, fo. 122ᵛ; B.M. Add. 30485, fo. 7.
3.	The Third Pavian.	Nevell, 14; Fitz. 252; B.M. Add. 30485, fo. 4; Add. 31392, fo. 1 (incomplete); Drexel, 5612, p. 62.
	The Galliarde to the Third Pavian.	Nevell, 15; Fitz. 253; B.M. Add. 30485, fo. 5ᵛ; Add. 31392, fo. 2ᵛ; Drexel, 5612, p. 64.
4.	The Fourth Pavian.	Nevell, 16; B.M. Add. 30485, fo. 81ᵛ (anonymous).
	The Galliarde to the Fourth Pavian.	Nevell, 17; B.M. Add. 30485, fo. 82ᵛ (anonymous).
5.	The Fifte Pavian.	Nevell, 18; B.M. Add. 31392, fo. 3ᵛ; Drexel, 5612, p. 136.
	The Galliarde to the Fifte Pavian.	Nevell, 19; B.M. Add. 31392, fo. 5ᵛ; Drexel, 5612, p. 138.
6.	Pavana the Sixte: Kinlough Goodd.	Nevell, 20; B.M. Add. 30485, fo, 105ᵛ; Add. 31392, fo. 9ᵛ.
	The Galliarde to the Sixte Pavian.	Nevell, 21; B.M. Add. 30485, fo. 107; Add. 31392, fo. 11ᵛ.
7.	The Seventh Pavian.	Nevell, 22; Fitz. 275 (Title, 'Pavana Canon: Two parts in one').
8.	The Eighte Pavian.	Nevell, 23.
9.	The Nynthe Pavian.	Nevell, 24 (Title, 'The Passinge Mesures'); Fitz. 56 (Title, 'Passamezzo Pavana'); Forster, fo. 111 (Title, 'Passa measures pavan'); B.M. Add. 30486, fo. 7.
	The Galliarde to the Nynthe Pavian.	Nevell, 25; Fitz. 57 (Title, 'Galiard as Passamezzo'); Forster, 117ᵛ (Title, 'Passa measures gall(iard)'; B.M. Add. 30486, fo. 11.
10.	The Tennthe Pavian.	Nevell, 39 (Title, 'Mr. W. Peter'); Parthenia, 2 (Title, Pavana S. Wm. Petre'); Forster, fo. 157; B.M. Add. 30486, fo. 14; Drexel, 5612, p. 100 (Title, 'A Pavion Sr. Wil: Peter').

	The Galliarde to the Tennthe Pavian.	Nevell, 40; Parthenia, 3; Forster, fo. 160ᵛ; B.M. Add. 30486, fo. 16 (incomplete).
11.	Pavana-Bray.	Fitz. 91.
	Galiarda.	Fitz. 92.
12.	Galliard. Mris. Marye Brownlo.	Parthenia, 5.
13.	Galliard Secundo. Mris. Marye Brownlo.	Parthenia, 8.
14.	Pavana Delight and Galliarda (E. Johnson, set by Byrd).	Fitz. 278; Forster, fo. 139ᵛ (Title, 'Johnsons Delighte. pavin').
15.	Sr Jhon Grayes Galiard.	Fitz. 191.
16.	Galiard (J. Harding, set by Byrd).	Fitz. 122; Forster, fo 191 (anonymous).
17.	Pavana. Lachrymae (J. Dowland, set by Byrd).	Fitz. 121; Forster, fo. 167.
18.	Lady Montegles Paven.	Fitz. 294.

Pypers Galiard, *see* If my complaints.

19.	Pavan. The Earle of Salisbury.	Parthenia, 6; Drexel, 5612, p. 60.
	Galliard.	Parthenia, 7; Drexel, 5612, p. 61.

Pavana. Ph. Tr., *see* list of pieces with alternative ascriptions.
Galiarda, *see* list of pieces with alternative ascriptions.

20.	The Quadran Paven.	Fitz. 133; Forster, fo. 145ᵛ; B.M. Add. 30485, fo. 8.
	Galiard to the Quadran Paven.	Fitz. 134; Forster, fo. 152ᵛ; B.M. Add. 30485, fo. 11ᵛ.

In Gam ut.

21.	Pavana.	Fitz. 165.
	Galliarda.	Fitz. 166.
22.	Pavan.	B.M. Add. 30485, fo. 79ᵛ.
	Galliard.	B.M. Add. 30485, fo. 80ᵛ.
23.	Pavan.	B.M. Add. 30485, fo. 2; Drexel, 5612, p. 16.
	Galliard.	B.M. Add. 30485, fo. 3.
24.	Pavan.	Forster, fo. 65ᵛ.
25.	Galliard.	Forster, fo. 162ᵛ.
26.	Pavan (a fragment).	Forster, fo. 100 (without title).
27.	Galliard.	Forster, fo. 95ᵛ (without title, but called 'Pavan' on p. 36 of the Catalogue of the King's Music Library).

In A re.

28. Pavan.	Fitz. 173.
Galliard.	Fitz. 174; Drexel, 5609, p. 132 (anonymous).[1]
29. Pavan.	B.M. Add. 31392, fo. 6ᵛ.
Galliard.	B.M. Add. 31392, fo. 8ᵛ.
30. Pavan.	Drexel, 5612, p. 66.
Galliard.	Drexel, 5612, p. 68.

In B mi.

31. Pavan.	B.M. Add. 30485, fo. 107ᵛ (anonymous); Drexel, 5612, fo. 96.
Galliard.	B.M. Add. 30485, fo. 109; Drexel, 5612, p. 98.
32. Pavan.	B.M Add. 30485, fo. 78ᵛ.
Galliard.	B.M. Add. 30485, fo. 79.
33. Pavan.	Drexel, 5612, p. 140.
Galliard.	Drexel, 5612, p. 142.
34. Pavan.	Fitz. 256.

In D sol re.

35. Pavan.	Fitz. 254.
Galliard.	Fitz. 255.
36. Pavan and Galliard.	Forster, 96ᵛ (without title and the two sections run on as one piece).

In F fa ut.

Pavan, *see* list of pieces with alternative ascriptions.

Pescodd Time (The Huntes upp).   Fitz. 276.

Preludes:

1. Prelude.	Parthenia, 1.
2. Prelude.	Fitz. 151; Forster, fo. 194ᵛ (Title, 'A Parludam').
3. Prelude.	Fitz. 100 (Title, 'Praeludium to yᵉ Fancie'; *see* Fancy, No. 4).
4. Prelude.	Parthenia, 4; Fitz. 24 (anonymous).
Qui Passe.	Nevell, 2; Forster, fo. 34 (Title, 'Kapassa').

Rowland, *see* Lord Willobie's welcome home.

[1] This Galliard in the Drexel MS. follows a different Pavan and neither is ascribed to Byrd.

Sellingers Rownde.   Nevell, 37; Fitz. 64; Drexel,
                                  5609, p. 215 (a nineteenth-
                                  century transcription).

Three parts of Mr. Birds, *see* Fancy, No. 6.

A Toutch, *see* list of pieces with alternative ascriptions.

Two parts of Mr. birds, *see* Fancy, No. 9.

Upon a Plainsong, Mr Birds.   B.M. Add. 30485, fo. 32.

Upon the same Plainsong, 3 parts. B.M. Add. 30485, fo. 33 (with-
                                  out title).

Upon a Plainsong, *see* Miserere, No. 1.

Ut re mi fa sol la.   Nevell, 9; Fitz. 101.

Ut re mi fa sol la.   Paris, Rés. 1122, p. 1 ('the
                                  playnesong breifes to be played
                                  by a second person').

Ut mi re.   Fitz. 102.

Variations, Ten.   Paris, Rés. 1186, fo. 101ᵛ (with-
                                  out title); Drexel, 5609, p. 72
                                  (without title).

A Verse of two parts, *see* Fancy No. 7.

Victorie, *see* The Battell—The Galliarde for the Victorie.

Voluntaries:

  1. A Voluntarie: for my ladye Nevell, 26.
    nevell.

  2. A Lesson of Voluntarie.[1]   Nevell, 29; Paris, Rés. 1122, p.
                                  19 (Title, 'Mr. Birdes Fan-
                                  tasy: two pts. in one in the
                                  fourth above').

  3. A Voluntarie.   Nevell, 42.

Walsingham.   Nevell, 31 (Title, 'Have with
                                  yow to Walsingame'); Fitz.
                                  68; Forster, fo. 39ᵛ (Title, 'As
                                  I went to Wallsingham');
                                  B.M. Add. 30486, fo. 2.

Wilson's Wilde.[2]   Forster, fol 37ᵛ (only one note is
                                  written); Paris, Rés. 1186, fo.
                                  17 (anonymous); Drexel,
                                  5609, p. 103 (anonymous).

[1] This is an arrangement of the Fantasy a 5 for strings, B.M. Add. 17786 -
17791.   [2] This is a version of Wolsey's Wilde.

Will yow walke the woods soe wylde.	Nevell, 27; Fitz. 67 (Title, 'The woods so wilde'); Forster, fo. 61 (anonymous); B.M. Add. 30485, fo. 47; Add. 31403, fo. 23^{v}; Add. 36661, fo. 41^{v}; Paris, Rés. 1186, fo. 17 (first two variations); Drexel, 5609 p. 90 (first two variations).
Without title:	
see Pavan, No. 26.	Forster, fo. 100.
see Galliard, No. 27.	Forster, fo. 95^{v}.
see Pavan and Galliard, No. 37.	Forster, fo. 96^{v}.
see Upon the same Playnsong.	B.M. Add. 30485, fo. 33.
see Ten Variations.	Paris, Rés. 1186, fo. 101^{v}; Drexel, 5609, p. 72.
Wolsey's Wilde.	Fitz. 157.

Pieces with alternative ascriptions

Bony sweet Robin.	*Byrd:* Drexel, 5612, p. 192; *Bull:* B.M. Add. 23623, fo. 13^{v}.
Parsons In nominey	*Byrd:* Forster, fo. 137^{v}; *Parsons (? J or R)*: Fitz. 140.
Pavan Ph. Tr.	*Byrd:* Fitz. 93; *Morley:* Drexel, 5612, p. 216.
Galiarda.	*Byrd:* Fitz. 94; *Morley:* Drexel, 5612, p. 216.
Pavan F fa ut.	*Byrd:* Drexel, 5612, p. 220; *Morley:* Fitz. 169 (with Galliard).
A Toutch.	*Byrd:* B.M. Add. 31403, fo. 13; *Gibbons:* Paris, Rés. 1186, fo. 83 (Title, 'A Voluntarie'); *Gibbons:* Drexel, 5609, p. 155 (Title, 'A Voluntarie').

CHAPTER XV

SOME FEATURES OF BYRD'S VOCAL TECHNIQUE

TO discuss the individual style of any of the composers of the latter half of the sixteenth century, whether English or foreign, is a wellnigh impossible task. Within the narrow limits of the harmonic range, as it was understood before the opening of the seventeenth century, there was little scope for individuality of style. And the same thing is true with regard to the contrapuntal features of the music, as generally exploited by the composers of this period. Certain formulae came into use, and various easily wrought contrapuntal imitations became common property. Pupils were definitely taught, as may be seen in Morley's *Plaine and Easie Introduction to Practicall Musicke*,[1] how to construct a variety of final cadences that should serve as stock-in-trade for their compositions. Even in the writings of the best madrigalists certain formulae are apt to recur with disappointing frequency; and some of the madrigals of the lesser and later composers were reduced to little more than a series of formulae, when the thematic material available for originality of development was becoming exhausted.

Examples may be given:

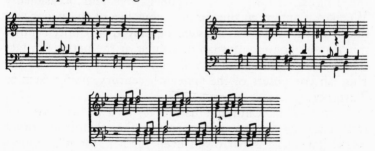

It is, of course, possible to press this point too far, and

[1] pp. 132–42.

things of this kind can even be said concerning the works of the greatest of the 'Classical' composers. It is true, also, that certain distinctive features of style and technique are to be found in the works of particular composers. For instance, among the English madrigalists Weelkes's name is associated with chromatic experiments; Farnaby's with complex rhythms; Ward's with massive discords and suspensions; Gibbons's with closely woven strands of counterpoint; Morley's with a gaiety of style and purity of technique; Wilbye's with a fine sense of colour and feeling for orchestration in his vocal score. Yet in point of fact there are few madrigals by any of these composers that even an expert could readily identify as regards their authorship if a number of their works were anonymously placed before him. And the Church music of the period would present an even greater difficulty in the matter of identifying the composers if their names were withheld.

Much of Byrd's madrigalian work, on the other hand, might possibly be recognized in such conditions, because, as has already been shown, his style is definitely different from that of all the other English madrigalists as regards construction. It is strange, however, that in his secular vocal work Byrd should have adhered so consistently to conventional practice in the matter of harmony because it is in very marked contrast with his usage in his Latin motets. *Come, woeful Orpheus* (*Psalmes, Songs, and Sonnets*, No. 19) is the only madrigal in which he employed chromatic chords. In one detail, however, he differed from all the English madrigalists, except Kirbye and occasionally Weelkes, namely, in the simultaneous use of the major and minor third. This was a usage employed in Church music much more commonly than in secular at the period; in fact this feature is found in the sacred work of almost all the English composers of the sixteenth century, going back to Taverner.

It was in his Church music that Byrd showed his real independence of conventional rules rather than in his other work. The field is narrowed even further, for it is almost exclusively to his Latin Church music, and not his English, that this statement applies. His English Services, Anthems, and Psalms are, on the whole, strictly orthodox in their harmonic features. It is also noteworthy that the three Masses provide very few examples of unusual harmony.

In turning to a detailed examination of Byrd's harmonic usage, as exhibited in his Latin music, it is necessary to revert to the dissonances, mentioned above, that result from the use of the major and minor third together. Byrd no doubt had these in his mind, as well as other kinds of discord which will be mentioned presently, when he issued a warning to his critics that they would discover unexpected features in his work which they might find difficult to explain away. This warning was addressed to the 'Benigne Reader' of his first printed publication in 1588, and it was clearly intended to refer to all his music, not merely to this volume of *Psalmes, Sonets, and songs*. He said: 'In the expressing of these songs . . . if ther happen to be any jarre or dissonãce, blame not the Printer, who (I doe assure thee) through his great paines and diligence doth heere deliver to thee a perfect and true Coppie.' There are, as will be seen from the examples quoted below, many 'jarres and dissonances' in Byrd's work which the more academic critics of his day would have been prone to explain as misprints, perhaps not daring to condemn them as errors, for Byrd's great reputation was already universally acknowledged.

The clash of the major and minor chords must always be regarded horizontally rather than perpendicularly; in other words, as a contrapuntal rather than a harmonic feature. It must also be understood that this particular form of dissonance, even to modern ears, is far less harsh in vocal music when sung with the intervals of the natural vocal scale, than it is when played on a modern keyboard instrument, tuned on the principles of equal temperament. And in performance the clash should never be emphasized or made prominent. One or other of the notes will always have the more important value in the contrapuntal, or horizontal, line of the phrase. For instance, in the following example from *Levemus corda* (*Cant. Sac.* ii. 16), the sharpened F between the two G's in the tenor line should be very lightly sung with a subconscious feeling that the suspended G and the succeeding G have a large value in the harmonic scheme, and that this note is only as it were momentarily bent back a semitone. Meanwhile, the alto voice enters on the F natural with confidence, conscious of its importance in introducing fresh thematic material. It may also be noticed that the F sharp comes on a very light syllable (provoca*vi*mus), and this will be found to be the case in a large proportion of these dissonances.

A rather harsher instance of this dissonance may be quoted from *Aspice, Domine, de sede* (*Cant. Sac.* i. 18–19).

Here the G sharp must be very lightly sung. The dissonance cannot be explained away by suggesting that the G natural is a misprint for E, for the imitations of this phrase are clearly defined.

One more example of this kind is from *Beati mundo corde* (*Gradualia* i. i. 32). In this instance the weight of the second syllable of *iustitiam* in the tenor voice quickly expends itself, even though the note is a dotted minim; and the crotchet is of small value against the C natural in the alto voice.

The clash or juxtaposition of such notes can be of great beauty, as for instance in the *Lullaby* (1588 set, No. 32).

A very large number of passages could be cited from the *Cantiones Sacrae* and the *Gradualia* to illustrate Byrd's independence of orthodoxy, as accepted in his day and later. His genius was far too great to be hampered by rules. There are, however, very few instances of consecutive fifths or octaves in his work. The following example from *Plorans plorabit* (*Gradualia*, i. i. 28) shows consecutive octaves between the soprano and tenor parts; and, on the same beat, fifths between the alto and bass are only avoided by dotting the G in the bass:

Fifths are narrowly avoided between the soprano and the tenor in this passage from *Alleluia. Ascendit Deus* (*Gradualia*, ii. 26) and there are numberless instances of the following kind:

There was no hesitation about writing consecutive octaves by contrary motion, as instanced in the final cadence of the first section of *Resurrexi* (*Gradualia*, ii. 20). The closeness with which the first alto part runs in octaves with the bass on the strong beats will be observed in a passage that occurs in *Vide, Domine, afflictionem* (*Cant. Sac.* i, 9–10). The crotchet A in the second bar is also difficult to explain. It may be a misprint for G, but Byrd's warning about misprints must be remembered.

The following examples show Byrd's use of consecutive fourths. The first is from *Recordare Domine* (*Cant. Sac.* ii. 17–18), and the second from the All Saints' Day *Gaudeamus omnes* (*Gradualia*, i. i. 29):

In this latter motet a curious kind of dissonance occurs where D in the tenor part comes in anticipation of the succeeding chord, but right out of the harmony into which it intrudes. A similar bit of writing, strangely enough at the very same words, appears in *Salve sancta Parens* (*Gradualia*, i. i. 6):

The lovely form of cadence in which the dominant seventh is introduced as a free passing note became a commonplace in later Tudor music. It is found occasionally in Tallis, as for instance in the motet *In ieiunio et fletu*, but it was Byrd who seems to have brought it into general use. The following example is from the anthem *Have mercy upon me* (1611 set, No. 25). In this example also there is an unusual bit of writing, both in the alto and tenor parts, the third rising on a crotchet to the fourth before falling a tone:

There is a beautiful cadence of this same kind in *Ecce Virgo concipiet* (*Gradualia*, i. i. 15), where in an exceptional way Byrd brings in B flat as a passing note against C sharp,

while F natural is sung by the tenor. The harmonic effect
of this is very rich and quite unlike conventional sixteenth-
century writing.

Several passages can be mentioned in which Byrd used the
dominant seventh freely without preparation. Two examples
are given here; one from the All Saints' Day *Gaudeamus
omnes* (*Gradualia*, I. i. 29) and one from *Lord, in thy rage*
(*Songs of sundrie natures*, No. 1):

The first inversion of the dominant seventh, with the
seventh taken freely, is found in *Beati mundo corde* (*Gradualia*, I. i. 32) and in *O sacrum convivium* (*Gradualia*, I. ii. 7),

and there are examples of the second inversion, for instance, in *Salve Regina* (*Gradualia*, I. ii. 12). Here the
chord is approached diatonically as a prepared discord.

A few bars earlier in this motet the chord of the diminished
seventh is used; and the discord on the first beat of the
next bar should be noticed.

Another chord used sometimes by Byrd is that of the added sixth on the subdominant. Three examples may be quoted; the first from *Felix namque* (*Gradualia*, 1. i. 19); the second from *Gaudeamus* (B.V.M.) (*Gradualia*, 1. i. 23), and the third from *Salve Regina* (*Gradualia*, 1. ii. 12):

The final cadence in *Vide, Domine, afflictionem* (*Cant. Sac.* i. 9–10) has already been mentioned in a former chapter. Byrd was here expressing the heart-broken and despairing appeal of the exiles, and he employed harmony that few of his contemporaries would have dreamt of, and such as was probably not used again before the nineteenth century. In the penultimate bar a chord somewhat similar to the Neapolitan sixth is introduced, and this is followed up in the final bar by the suspension of the minor sixth against the major third of the chord.

The first inversion of the chord of F in this next example, following the chord of A major, produces a special effect that gives colour to the words in a somewhat similar manner.

This quotation is from *Christus resurgens* (*Gradualia*, i. ii. 10):

The most unexpected of all Byrd's harmonic experiments was the use of the chord of the augmented sixth. Four instances of the employment of this chord are to be found in the *Cantiones Sacrae*, and yet another in the madrigal *Penelope ever was praised*, where it is recorded in two independent MSS. of good authority. The fact that there are at least five examples in Byrd's works is sufficient evidence that he used the chord deliberately. It was perhaps one of the features about which he warned 'the Benigne Reader'. The following example is from *Tristitia et anxietas* (*Cant. Sac.* i. 6–7):

One of the other examples occurs in *Civitas sancti tui* (*Cant. Sac.* i. 21), better known in its English version *Bow thine ear*; but all editors, dating back to Boyce and even Barnard, have regarded it as a misprint and ruled out the accidental.

A number of instances could be quoted of Byrd's unorthodox use of suspended discords. Thus he does not hesitate to employ the note on which the discord will resolve in another voice-part before the resolution is made. The following example is from *Tristitia et anxietas*:

The following examples of how Byrd sometimes resolved his discords call for some comment, as being different from

the ordinary practice of his day. The first is from *Domine,
exaudi* (*Cant. Sac.* ii. 10–11). The ornamental resolutions
in the second bar of this example are, of course, not uncommon; but the progression of the tenor part in the
previous bar is quite unusual. The second example is
from *Ab ortu solis* (*Gradualia*, ii. 13–14) and is similar in
idea; but the insertion of the B between D and G is in itself
a distinctive feature, rarely found elsewhere:

In the final cadence of *Beata viscera* (*Gradualia* i. i. 11)
three consecutive notes in the scale are brought into simultaneous use on the penultimate dominant chord.

There is a similar passage in *Tui sunt coeli* (*Gradualia*,
ii. 4); and in the following quotation from *Alleluia. Ave .
Maria* (*Gradualia*, i. i. 20) the F natural, next to G and A
above it, is approached with a skip:

A cadence of great beauty occurs in *Hodie beata Virgo*
(*Gradualia*, i. ii. 19). Four consecutive notes of the scale,
D, E, F, and G, are sung simultaneously, though not in
juxtaposition, on the first beat of the second full bar quoted
here:

A still more remarkable example is to be found in the passage quoted from the *Lullaby* on page 154, where A, B, C, and D are further complicated by C♮ and C♯.

Byrd did not hesitate to ignore the convention that passing notes must necessarily proceed diatonically from concord to concord; and sometimes these free passing notes clashed with each other in relation to the harmony. These harmonic clashes, which are by no means discordant, resulted from the necessity of retaining the shape of the melodic figures, especially when they occurred in sequential form. A good example of this point may be quoted from *Sacerdotes Domini* (*Gradualia*, I. ii. 3):

A similar instance occurs in *Exsurge, Domine* (*Cant. Sac.* ii. 19); and here, though the clash comes between the D and E, it is far from being unpleasant:

Thomas Tomkins, Byrd's great pupil, may have had these phrases in mind when at a later date he wrote his fine madrigal, *Music divine*,[1] in which the following rolling sequential phrase occurs:

A rather different instance of this usage in Byrd's work may be found in *Facti sumus opprobrium*, the fourth section of

[1] Tomkins, *Songs*, No. 24.

Deus, venerunt gentes (*Cant. Sac.* i. 11–14). Byrd could have written E instead of D in the tenor part to avoid the discord, as against C in the alto; but by doing so the exact imitation of the other voice parts would have been impaired and the strength of the phrase entirely ruined.

Byrd was not averse from letting a voice enter on a discord, as, for instance, in *Vidimus stellam* (*Gradualia*, ii. 12). This passage provides another example of the simultaneous use of four consecutive notes of the scale in juxtaposition: C, D, E, and F.

The skip of a sixth was discouraged by the old contrapuntists, but this is frequently found in Byrd's music. The skip of the seventh is less common; the example of this in *Domine, quis habitabit* has been referred to in a former chapter.[1] More striking is the example in the alto part of *Come to me, grief, for ever* (*Psalmes, Sonets, & songs*, No. 34):

There is a skip of a tenth in *Ave Regina* (*Gradualia*, i. ii. 14):

and more remarkable still is the skip of a minor ninth in *Exsurge, Domine* (*Cant. Sac.* ii. 19). It occurs in the tenor

[1] Chap. VII, p. 108.

part near the end of the motet, where Byrd repeats the opening words, and it gives tremendous force to the appeal:

ex - sur - ge, Do - mi - ne,   ex - sur - ge, Do - mi - ne,

Another curious feature is the use of the arpeggio, as found in *Ave maris stella* (*Gradualia*, I. iii. 4):

A very large proportion of the passages quoted in this chapter illustrate harmonic usage peculiar to Byrd at this period. Many more of a similar kind might be cited, but these are sufficient to demonstrate the remarkable originality of his work. Many of these harmonic effects were not reproduced by other composers for several generations, and it will be recognized that there is a ripeness and maturity in his music, even when it is considered on a harmonic basis alone, which sets it on a very high level. Added to this, his never-failing invention in designing contrapuntal figures enabled him to produce an immense output with scarcely a suggestion of a repeated phrase. And above all he was endowed marvellously with the divine gift of inspiration, which, to use his own expression, caused him 'in some inexplicable way' to think of musical phrases exactly suited to 'the life of the words'.

CHAPTER XVI

CONTEMPORARY APPRECIATION

BYRD was held in great veneration by all the English musicians of his own day, and, although there is little evidence to prove it, his fame must have spread also to the continent of Europe. It is known that he corresponded with Philip de Monte, and it cannot be doubted that other famous musicians outside England knew something of his work. Baldwin's poem[1] says of him, 'And farre to strange countries abroade his skill dothe shyne'.

Byrd must have stepped into fame in his own country very early in his career. He was little more than thirty years old when he and Tallis published jointly their set of *Cantiones Sacrae* in 1575. By that time he was already regarded as sharing with Tallis the leadership of English music. Exceptionally skilled, as he undoubtedly was, he may nevertheless be reckoned fortunate to have earned such fame while so young. Various reasons may be suggested for this success. As a pupil of Tallis his abilities would have been recognized from childhood. If he was a chorister of the Chapel Royal, as seems highly probable, he may have laid the foundations of his reputation as a boy soloist, not indeed in the Chapel itself, for solo singing had not yet been introduced as a feature of Church music; but there were opportunities in secular surroundings for a boy soloist to earn distinction, notably in connexion with the drama. It is more than likely that in early youth he wrote music that was performed at the services in the Chapel Royal, just as Purcell did a century later. As an executant he had already marked himself out in early manhood as one of the most brilliant performers of the day on the organ and the virginal.

However this may be, the prefatory matter of the *Cantiones Sacrae* provides abundant evidence that by that date he had become famous. A short set of Latin elegiacs is printed there, headed *De Anglorum musica*, in which the

[1] See p 238.

assurance is given that English music, patronized by such
a cultured Queen, and supported by such 'parents' as Tallis
and Byrd, need fear no comparison with that of any other
country.

The two lengthy sets of Latin elegiacs by Richard Mulcaster and Ferdinand Richardson, which follow, have been
mentioned in a former chapter. In both of them the vener-
able Tallis and his pupil Byrd are jointly praised for their
leadership in upholding the banner of English music,
and Byrd is given equal honour with Tallis. The significance
of this can only be fully understood when it is remembered
that Tallis had held a pre-eminent position for some forty
years. Tallis had,   fact, been held in high favour by King
Henry the Eighth even before the dissolution of Waltham
Abbey, to which he was attached, in 1540; and as his age
increased it is not surprising that he came to be venerated as
a 'father of music'. For this reason it was a remarkable
compliment to the younger man that he should be associated with Tallis as sharing his supremacy on equal terms.

Reference has been made in a former chapter to Father
Weston's description of a secret gathering of Jesuits in
1586 at which Byrd was present; and how Weston called
him 'the most celebrated musician and organist of the
English nation who was held in the highest estimation'.
This was a year after the death of Tallis, and two years
before he began his first series of important publications.
And it was only in 1588, when he had just issued his
Psalmes, Sonets, and songs, that Nicholas Yonge, in the
preface to his own *Musica Transalpina,* recorded his great
admiration for Byrd and his recent publication in the
following terms: 'There be some English songes lately
set forth by a great Maister of Musicke, which for skill
and sweetness may content the most curious.' There can
be no question that at this date Byrd's reputation in the
musical world was already on a very high level and was
universally accepted as such.

Contemporary opinion about Byrd and his work is reflected in a number of small comments which the scribes
who wrote the part-books so frequently added at the conclusion of motets or anthems. Robert Dow, the writer of
a fine set of part-books at Christ Church, Oxford, the date

of which is *circa* 1581–5, appended a rather more elaborate
note than usual at the end of one of Byrd's compositions.
Dow was evidently a scholar as well as a musical scribe,
and his note runs as follows:[1]

Cicero ad Atticum, lib. 4. Britannici belli exitus expectatur: etiam
illud iam cognitum est, neque argenti scrupulum esse ullum in ea
insula, neque ullam spem praedae, nisi ex mancipiis, ex quibus nullos
puto te literis aut musico eruditos expectare.
Unus Birdus omnes Anglos ab hoc convicio prorsus liberat.

Dow's quotation from Cicero was to the effect that little
was to be expected by way of gain as a result of the war
in Britain, which was shortly going to end; and that even
if the people were taken to Rome as slaves, they would be
found devoid either of literary or musical culture. Dow's
comment upon this is that things have changed: 'Hence-
forth Byrd by himself liberates all Englishmen from such
an accusation.' Dow may also have had in his mind a
reference to Byrd's undoubted literary gifts, quite apart
from his music, and that the double accusation was refuted
in him alone. His Latin dedications and addresses show
that he was no mean scholar, and those in his English
sets are obviously the work of a man of culture. Moreover,
Byrd was not content with poetry of trivial value for his
purposes as a composer. A mere glance at the poems of his
three English sets of madrigalian works will show how
fine was his literary taste.

Another of Dow's comments is in the form of an elegiac
couplet:

Birde, suos iactet si Musa Britanna clientes
Signiferum turmis te creet illa suis.

This may be translated: 'If the British muse should hold
a review of her followers, she would appoint you, master
Byrd, as standard-bearer of her squadrons.'

A contemporary song by an anonymous composer evidently refers to Byrd.[2]

A bird I have that sings so well,
None like to her their tunes can raise;
All other birds she doth excel,
And of birds all best worthy praise.

[1] Ch. Ch. MS. 985. [2] R.C.M. MS. 2049, rev. fo. 4.

Now this my bird of endless fame,
Whose music sweet, whose pleasant sound,
Whose worthy praise, whose worthy name
Doth from the earth to heaven rebound.

This song calls to mind George Gascoigne's skit on Philip Sparrow which Bartlet set to music.[1]

Of all the birds that I do know,
Philip, my sparrow, hath no peer.

The most famous musical scribe of this period was John Baldwin. He was appointed a lay-clerk of St. George's Chapel in Windsor Castle about the year 1575 and died in 1615. He has already been mentioned as the writer of the 'Ladye Nevell booke', in which he described Byrd as *homo memorabilis*. He also expressed his admiration for Byrd in a lengthy poem which he inserted at the conclusion of another famous manuscript, belonging to the Royal Music Library and now in the British Museum.[2] Baldwin must have had his hands full just at this time, because this manuscript is dated 25 July 1591 and the 'Ladye Nevell booke' was finished on 11 September of the same year.

The poem is doggerel, but the references to contemporary musicians other than Byrd lend sufficient interest to it to justify quoting it here almost in full:

Reede, here, behold, and see: all y^t musicions bee: anno 1591
  What is in closde heere in: declare I will begine: iulij 25.
A store housse of treasure: this booke maye be saiede:
  of songes most excelente: and the beste that is made:
collected and chosen: out of the best autours:

.   .   .   .

the autours for to name: I maye not here for gett:
  but will them now downe put: and all in order sett:
I will begine with white: shepper, tye and tallis:
  parsons, gyles, mundie th'oulde: one of the queenes pallis:
mundie yonge, th'oulde mans sonne: and like wysse others moe:
  there names would be to longe: therefore I let them goe:
yet must I speake of moe: even of straingers also:
  and first I must bringe in: alfonson ferabosco:

[1] Bartlet's *Booke of Ayres*, 1606, No. 10.
[2] Royal Music Lib., B.M. 24. D. 2.

a strainger borne hee was: in italie as I heere:
   Italians saie of hime: in skill hee had no peere:
luca merensio: with others manie moe:
   As philipp demonte: th' emperous man also:
and orlando by name: and eeke triquillion [*sic*]:
   cipriano rore: and also andreon:
All famus in there arte: there is of that no doute:
   there workes no lesse declare: in everie place aboute:
yet let not straingers bragg: nor they these soe commende:
   for they maye now geve place: and sett them selves be hynde:
an englishe man, by name: willm birde for his skill:
   wᶜ I should have sett first: for soe it was my will:
whose greate skill and knowledge: doth excelle all at this tyme:
   and farre to strange countries: abroade his skill dothe shyne:
Famus men be abroade: and skilfull in the arte:
   I doe confesse the same: and will not from it starte:
but in ewropp is none: like to our englishe man:
   wᶜ doth so farre exceede: as trulie I it scan:
as ye can not finde out: his equale in all thinges:
   throwghe out the world so wide: and so his fame now ringes:
with fingers and with penne: hee hathe not now his peere:
   for in this world so wide: is none can him come neere:
the rarest man hee is: in musicks worthye arte:
   that now on earthe dothe live: I speake it from my harte:
or heere to fore hathe bene: or after him shall come:
   none such I feare shall rise: that maye be calde his sonne:
O famus man of skill: and iudgemente great profounde:
   lett heaven and earth ringe out: thy worthye praise to sownde:
ney lett they skill it selfe: thy worthie fame recorde:
   to all posterie [*sic*]: thy due deserte afforde:
and lett them all which heere: of thy greate skill then saie:
   fare well fare well thou prince: of musicke now and aye:
Fare well I saie fare well: fare well and heere I end:
   farewell melodious birde: fare well sweete musicks f ende:
all these thinges doe I speake: not for rewarde or bribe:
   nor yet to flatter him: or sett him upp in pride:
nor for affeccion: or owght might move there towe:
   but even the truth reporte: and that make knowne to yowe:
Loe heere I end fare well: comittinge all to god:
   who kepe us in his grace: and shilde us from his rodd:
                           Finis: jo: baldwine:

Morley, Byrd's most famous pupil, dedicated his *Plaine
and Easie Introduction to Musicke* to his master, and printed
a lengthy address to him. This was in 1597, when Morley

himself had become famous and was in a position of great influence and importance among musicians. Doing homage to his master, he says:

There be two whose benefites to us can never be requited: God, and our parents, the one for that he gave us a reasonable soule, the other for that of the we have our beeing. To these the prince & (as *Cicero* tearmeth him) the God of the *Philosophers* added our maisters as those by whose directions the faculties of the reasonable soule be stirred up to enter into contemplation, & searching of more than earthly things: ... The consideration of this hath moved me to publish these labors of mine under your name both to signifie unto the world, my thankfull mind: & also to notifie unto your selfe in some sort the entire love and unfained affection which I beare unto you. And seeing we live in those days wherein envie raigneth; and that it is necessary for him who shall put to light any such thing as this is, to choose such a patron, as both with iudgement may correct it and with authority defend him from the rash censures of such as thinke they gaine great praise in condemning others: Accept (I pray you) of this booke both that you may exercise your deepe skill in censuring of what shall be amisse, as also defend what is in it truely spoken, as that which sometime proceeded from your selfe.

Referring to his master in the course of the book itself, Morley speaks of Byrd as a man 'never without reverence to be named of the musicians'.[1] Byrd was at this time no more than fifty-four years old, but Morley, fifteen years his junior, had but five or six more years to live. There was a bond of affection between Byrd and his pupil, just as there had been between his own master, Tallis, and himself. There is little doubt that he was referring to the premature death of Morley, and his grief for his loss, in the dedicatory address to Lord Petre printed in the second book of *Gradualia*.

Byrd had another famous pupil in Thomas Tomkins, a much younger man and the last of the Englishmen to carry on the great Elizabethan tradition. Tomkins published his book of madrigals in 1622 under the title of 'Songs', when Byrd was nearly eighty, and he dedicated one of these madrigals, *Too much I once lamented*, 'To my ancient & much reverenced Master, William Byrd'. Both these great pupils used the word 'reverence' in speaking of their master, whose personality and fame in his old age

[1] p. 115.

must have made him one of the most outstanding figures
in English life, even at that brilliant period.

In the second book of *Gradualia* there was printed an
epigram, signed by 'G Ga.', and addressed to 'Amicissimo
mihi, multis colendo, omnibus suspiciendo, D Gulielmo
Byrde Brittanicae Musicae Parenti'. Here again, in 1607
as in 1575, Byrd is styled 'Parent of British Music'; and
indeed, when his work is reviewed to-day in all its branches
and with a true sense of perspective in relation to the period
and conditions in which he lived and worked, it certainly
seems that the claim cannot be disputed. The identity of
'G Ga.' has not been established;[1] his verses are a little
obscure in their meaning, but they are evidently intended
to stress the devout religious feeling by which Byrd was
inspired in composing the *Gradualia*.

> Those which of olde were skil'd in *Augurie*,
> By Flight, by Song, by Colour did devine
> Of future haps, and labour'd to discrie
> What was above us, by each outward signe.
> But blind Antiquitie was led a-stray,
> Enforcing things of absurd consequence:
> Will you bee guided by a truer way?
> Loe heer's a *BYRDE* explaines the difference
> Twixt what hee shewes, and what they did inferre,
> And proves perspicuously that those did erre.
> They to the Divel sacrifis'd oppressed,
> By this your hearts are unto God addressed.

One more important contemporary reference should be
quoted. Henry Peacham, in *The Compleat Gentleman*, published in 1622, the last year of Byrd's life, discussed the
authors of his day who he considered should be imitated;
and turning to music he said:[2]

For Motetts and Musicke of pietie and devotion as well for the
honour of our Nation, as the merit of the man, I prefer above all
our *Phoenix* M. William Byrd, whom in that kind I know not
whether any may equall . . . and being of him selfe naturally disposed
to Gravitie and Pietie, his veine is not so much for light Madrigals
or Canzonets, yet his *Virginella* and some others in his first Set cannot
be mended by the best Italian of them all.

[1] Possibly George Gascoigne.
[2] *The Compleat Gentleman*, p. 100

A phoenix used to denote something unique. Peacham, in the punning manner of his time, meant that the composer was a unique Byrd, like that other unique bird the phoenix. He rightly recognized that Byrd's finest work was what he wrote for the Church and that this special excellence was due to his natural disposition to 'Gravitie and Pietie'. Peacham was also right in saying that 'his veine was not so much for light madrigals'; but Peacham's opinion, as expressed here, has been much misunderstood and misinterpreted, for he not only picked out *La Virginella*, but also 'some others', as being better than anything that the best of the Italians could do. And Peacham would have rightly classed many of Byrd's madrigalian works as 'songs of gravitie'. No one would suggest that *Come, woeful Orpheus* or *Why do I use my paper, ink and pen?* were 'light Madrigals', and Peacham's praise is not excluded from other pieces of the lighter sort, such as *While that the sun, Come, jolly swains*, or *This sweet and merry month of May*, which, in fact, could scarcely 'be mended by the best Italian of them all'. Byrd wrote some other admirable things in the lighter vein, for instance *Who made thee, Hob, forsake the plough?*; but he wrote very few.

And so we reach the close of this wonderful life. The actual end is recorded in few words, but these eloquently express the great veneration with which he was regarded. '1623. Wm Bird a Father of Musick died the 4 of July.' So reads the entry in the official 'cheque book' of the Chapel Royal.

Enough has been said to demonstrate how sincerely this great Englishman was venerated and loved in his own day. His pre-eminence as a composer was universally acknowledged. As a man he commanded affection and respect. And he was a man of deep and sincere religious conviction; this is made abundantly clear by a study of his Church-music, both Latin and English. His religious opinions also must have been definite, for he was consistent in his recusancy throughout the long period from his going to live at Harlington until his death at Stondon. How, then, is all this to be explained in reference to the many protracted and bitter lawsuits in which he was involved? It may have been largely due to misfortune and chance circumstances. In several instances he seems to have acquired leases, whether by grant or purchase, with doubtful titles, leading directly to litigation; and the lengthy disputes with Mrs. Shelley concerning Stondon Place were certainly not of his own seeking. Byrd must have had a legal mind and a taste for the Law. In his first set of *Psalmes, Sonets, and songs*, in 1588, he showed his fondness for legal ideas and phraseology. This was in early days before the disputes with the Shelleys; but Byrd had already at that date had ample experience of the law-courts. The second stanza of *Where Fancy fond for Pleasure pleads* (No. 15 of this set) may be quoted:

> My Eyes presume to judge this case
> > Whose judgement Reason doth disdain.
> But Beauty with her wanton face
> > Stands to defend, the case is plain;
> And at the bar of sweet Delight
> She pleads that Fancy must be right.

The next number in this set is Sidney's poem, *O you that hear this voice*, from *Astrophel and Stella*, in which the following verses occur:

> This side doth Beauty take,
> > For that doth Music speak,
> Fit orators to make
> > The strongest judgements weak.
> The Bar to plead their right
> Is only true delight.

> Thus doth the voice and face,
> > These gentle lawyers, wage,
> Like loving brothers, case
> > For father's heritage,
> That each, while each contends,
> Itself to other lends.

> .   .   .   .   .
> Music doth witness call
> > The ear his truth to try;
> Beauty brings to the hall
> > Eye-witness of the eye.

What pleasure have great princes (No. 19) is another poem with legal allusions. The fourth stanza runs:

> For lawyers and their pleading
> They esteem it not a straw;
> They think that honest meaning
> Is of itself a law;
> Where conscience judgeth plainly
> They spend no money vainly.

It is probable that Byrd was endowed with a strong sense of justice, tempered, perhaps, with a certain degree of obstinacy, which led him to the law-courts, rather than compromise with an adversary, when he felt that right was on his side.

Byrd, as just stated, was one of the great personalities in England in the days of Shakespeare, Burleigh, Raleigh, Drake, and a host of other famous men. It does indeed seem strange that in so short a time after his death he and his music passed completely into oblivion. Taste in all the arts underwent rapid changes during the seventeenth century. Byrd was not alone among the great Elizabethans whose music fell into neglect, as being out of date and dull, when Charles II was restored to the throne, and when the musical taste of the Court was dominated by the contemporary French school. The deplorable decay of English musical taste which spread throughout this country after the death of Purcell and Blow, precluded all possibility of reviving Elizabethan music until the dawn of the twentieth century. Now, at long last, Tudor music is even becoming fashionable, and once more 'Byrd's name is mentioned' with the 'reverence' which Morley demanded as his due.

Byrd, indeed, is again recognized as standing supreme in English music. It may even be right to place him at the head of the sixteenth-century composers of all countries. This is not to say that he actually excelled such contemporaries as Palestrina, Lassus, or Victoria as a composer of polyphonic music for the Church, even if some might be found who would endorse Peacham's opinion that in this branch of composition also Byrd was at least their equal. But Byrd is outstanding because of his amazing variety of achievement. He excelled in every branch of composition known in his day and led the way into certain fields not previously explored, whereas most of the great musicians of the sixteenth century confined their outlook mainly to a single branch of composition. For example, Palestrina did little outside his glorious church music except a few serious madrigals, and these are of no outstanding distinction. And some of the greatest madrigalists, like Luca Marenzio and John Wilbye, did little apart from their madrigals. Byrd's wonderful versatility enables him to invite comparison with all the specialists of his time. Like Palestrina, he wrote magnificently for the Latin rites of the Church. For the English rites of the Church his work stands above that of all others, more especially as regards the setting of the Canticles. In this department he was a pioneer, and yet he brought his art to such a degree of perfection that it is safe to say that his 'Great' service has never been surpassed in this department of composition. As a madrigalist he attempted little in the lighter vein, and if he is surpassed in this vein by such fine madrigalists as Wilbye, Weelkes, Morley, and certain of the Italians, yet these composers can set little in the vein of 'gravitie and pietie' beside Byrd's work of that type; and it is this type which so largely predominates in his three large madrigalian sets. Gibbons was almost alone, with his magnificent *What is our life?* and several other numbers, in following Byrd's lead in the direction of the 'grave' type of madrigal.

As a contrapuntist he was at least equal if not superior to any of his contemporaries in constructing ingenious and complex canons and other contrapuntal devices; and, unlike some of his contemporaries, he had the wisdom to use this skill with such restraint that it rarely obtrudes itself or mars the artistic quality of his music.

As a song-writer he was a pioneer; and, as such, he holds a position of the highest importance in the history of song. Preferring the viols to the lute as the medium for instrumental accompaniment to the voice, he contributed something entirely new to the Art of Music in this department. Some fifty of his songs with viol accompaniment have survived. Most of these represent pioneer work, but *My little sweet darling* is a gem of the first water. Byrd may be claimed as the originator of the art-song.

Byrd's position in the history of keyboard music has already been fully discussed. In this department of composition also he was a pioneer, and yet more than a pioneer, for it is probable that he carried the principles of form and technique as far as was possible on the instruments manufactured in his day. As a composer for the keyboard he certainly excelled all his contemporaries.

And, lastly, Byrd was one of the *virtuoso* performers of his day, both on the virginal and the organ. In brilliant finger-work he may perhaps have been surpassed by Bull; yet Bull seems to have had some of the faults of the modern virtuoso, occasionally sacrificing musicianship to display. Byrd combined musicianship and exceptional technique with the control of an artist of the first rank. He takes a high place among the world's musicians.

The time has not yet arrived when it can be said that his work is as widely known and appreciated as it should be. Few musicians as yet know, or have even heard of, a tithe of his compositions. Material for studying his music in all its branches is now for the first time available, and it may be prophesied with confidence that the days are not far distant when he will be acknowledged as the greatest composer before the period of Handel and Bach. It used to be said that the peaks of musical development are represented by three B's: Bach, Beethoven, and Brahms. Representing the peak of pre-Bach development there stands a fourth B. His name is Byrd.

APPENDIX A

THE WILL OF WILLIAM BYRD

Copied from a photograph of the original will in Somerset House.

In the name of the most glorious and undevided Trinitye Father
sonne holy Goste three distinct persons and one eternall God Amen |
I William Byrd of Stondon Place in the pish of Stondon in the
Countye of Essex gentleman doe now in the 80th yeare of myne age
but through ye goodnes of God beeinge of good health and pfect
memory make & ordayne this for my last will & Testament: First:
I give & beequeth my soule to God Almyghtye my Creattor &
redemer and preserver: humblye cravinge his grace and mercye for
ye forgivenes of all my Synnes and offences: past psent and to come.
And y^t I may live and dye a true and pfect .member of his holy
Catholycke Church wthout wch I beeleve theire is noe Salvation for
mee my body to bee honnestly buryed in that pish and place wheire
it shall please God to take mee out of this lyve wch I humbly desire
yf soe it shall please God maye bee in the pish of Stondon wheire my
dwellynge is: And then to bee buryed neare unto the place where
my wife lyest buryed. or eles wher as God & the tyme shall pmytt
& Suffer. And wheire I have beene longe desireous to setle my
poore estate in the Fearme of Stondon place accordinge to an awarde
latlye made beetweene Catheren Byrde my daughter in law & mee
bee a very good Frend to hus both. wch award wee both give our
cristian pmisses to pforme. but havinge beene letted & hyndred
theirein: by the undutifull obstinancie of one whome I am unwilling
to name: do nowe ordayne & dispose of the same as Followeth.
First the whole Fearme to remayne to my selfe & my assignes duringe
my lyfe: and after my desscease: I give the same to my daughter in
law m^{ris} Catheren Byrd for her life: upon the condicõns folowinge
vidz: to paye Twenty eight pounds fiftene shillinges & foure pence
yearly to m^r Anthony Lutor or his assignes for the fee fearme rent
And to pay to m^{ris} Dawtrey of dedinghurst 15^s shillings yearly for
the quitrent of malepdus freehould: Allsoe to paye unto my sonne
Thomas Byrde Twenty pounds yearly duringe his life: And to my
daughter Rachell Ten pounds a yeare duringe her life And the same
peaments to beegine at the next usiall Feasts of peament after the day
of my death: And after the disscease of my sayde daughterinlaw m^{ris}
Catheren Byrde & of the aforsayde lyffes: I give and beequeth the
whole Fearme of stondon place to Thomas Byrde my granchild:

sonne of Christofer Byrd my eldest sonne by the sayde Catheren; and to his heyres lawfully beegotten for ever: And for wante of such heires of the sayde Thomas Byrde sonne of ye sayde Christofer: I give the same Fearme of Stondon place to Thomas Byrde my sonne to his heires lawfully beegotten: And for want of such heires: I give the Inheritance of the sayde Fearme to the foure sonnes of my daughter mary Hawksworth wiffe of Henrie Hawksworth gentleman as the are in age & Seniority vidz: First to william Hawksworth & his heires lawfully beegotten and for want of such heires to Henrie Hawksworth his seconde brother his heires lawfully beegotten & For want of such heires to George Hawksworth and his heires lawfully beegotten & for wante of such heires to Iohn Hawksworth the fourth sonne of ye sayd mary Hawksworth my daughter: And to his heires lawfully beegotten And for want of such heires of ye foure sonnes of mary Hawksworth my daughter & her husband To william hooke sonne unto Rachell Hooke my daughter and to his heires lawfully bee-gotten and for want of such heires: To the right heires of mee the sayde william Byrde for ever: It I give and beequeth to my daughter-inlaw m^{ris} Catheren Byrde & her sonne Thomas Byrde all my goods moveables and unmoveables at stondon place And alsoe all the woodes and Tymber trees wheiresoever the are groinge in & upon ye sayde Farme: upon this condic͠on only to see mee honestly buryed and my debts truly discharged to wch end & porposse: I doe make & ordayne Catheren Byrde my sayde daughterinlaw & Thomas Byrde her sonne whole executors of this my last will & Testament. It I give & bequeth unto my sonne Thomas Byrd all my goods in my lodginge In the Earle of wosters howse in the straund: And wheire I purchassed a ppetuall annytye or rent charge of 20^{li} a yeare of Sr Francis Fortescue knight unto 200^{li} bee payde in wch annyty I have given to Elizabeth Burdet my eldest doughter for her lyfe: I doe now declare how it shall bee dispossed of after my sayde daughters desscease first yf my sayde sonne Thomas Byrde concurr wth this my last will & Testament & except of his Annyty accordinge to ye same: Then I give the one halfe of y^t Annyty beeinge Ten pounds a yeare ore one hundreth pound yf it bee payde in: to the sayde Thomas Byrd his heires execu-tors and assignes And the other halfe of y^t annyty I give & beequeth to michaell walton wth marriage of his wiffe Catheren hooke my gran-childe for her mariage portion Allwayes pvided y^t yf my sonne Thomas Byrd do seeke by lawe or other wayes to disturb or troble my executors & not agree to ye same: Then I doe heireby declare That my will & intention is: That the sayde Thomas Byrde my sonne shall have noe parte of the sayde Annyty: but I doe heireby give y^t part of ye annyty That I had given to my sonne Thomas Byrd: to Thomas Byrd my granchild to hym and his heires for ever And havinge now by the leave of god Finished this my last will accordinge to the trew meaninge of the sayde awarde & our christian pmisses: I doe now by this my last will & Testament utterly revocke & annill all former grants writtings & wills as far as in mee lyeth whatsoever is contrary to this my last will & Testament: In wittnes wheirof I the sayd william Byrd have set my hand & seale the Fiftenth day of November in the yeares of ye reigene of our Sowagine lord James by the grace of God Kinge of England France & Ireland the Twenteth and of Scotland Fiftie six defender of the fayth re 1622:

By me Wyllm Byrde

Sealed & delivered in the psence of
  Hen^y Hawksworth.

[Proved by Thomas Byrd and Catherine Byrd 30 October 1623.]

APPENDIX B

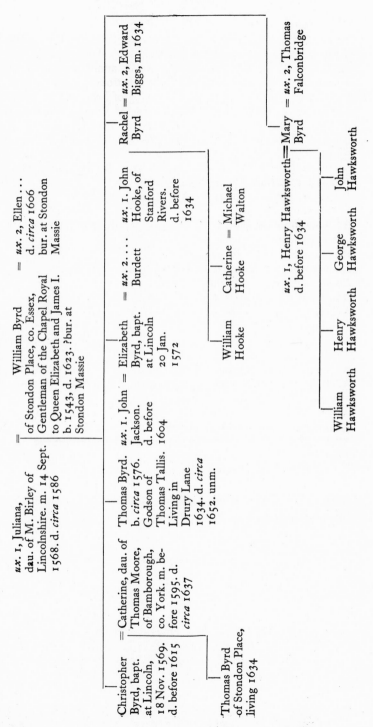

BYRD'S MOTETS

arranged alphabetically with reference to source

Ab ortu solis. à 4.	Grad. II. 13-14.
Venite, comedite.	
Ad Dominum cum tribularer. à 8.	MS.
Heu mihi, Domine.	
Ad punctum in modico. à 5.	MS.
In momento indignationis.	
Ad te igitur, *see* Infelix ego.	
Adducentur in laetitia, *see* Diffusa est gratia.	
Adducentur regi, *see* Diffusa est gratia.	
Adoramus te, Christe. à 5.	Grad. I. i. 26.
Adorna thalamum tuum. à 3.	Grad. I. iii. 11.
Subsistit Virgo.	
Afflicti pro peccatis. à 6.	Cant. Sac. II. 27-8.
Et eruas nos a malis.	
Alleluia. Ascendit Deus. à 5.	Grad. II. 26.
Alleluia. Ave Maria. à 5.	Grad. I. i. 20.
Virga Jesse floruit.	
Alleluia. Cognoverunt discipuli. à 4.	Grad. II. 16.
Alleluia. Confitemini Domino. à 3.	MS.
Alleluia. Emitte spiritum tuum. à 5.	Grad. II. 32.
Alleluia. Quae lucescit. à 3.	Grad. I. iii. 6.
Vespere autem Sabbathi.	
Alma Redemptoris. à 4.	Grad. I. ii. 13.
Angelus Domini descendit. à 3.	Grad. I. iii. 8.
Aperis tu manum, *see* Oculi omnium.	
Apparebit in finem. à 5.	Cant. Sac. II. 12.
Ascendit Deus. à 5.	Grad. II. 28.
Ascendit Deus, *see* Alleluia. Ascendit Deus.	
Aspice, Domine, de sede. à 5.	Cant. Sac. I. 18-19.
Respice, Domine.	
Aspice, Domine, quia facta. à 6.	Cant. Sac. (1575), 10.
Assumpta est Maria. à 5.	Grad. I. i. 24.
Assumpta est Maria, *see* Gaudeamus omnes (B.V.M.).	
Attollite portas. à 6.	Cant. Sac. (1575), 11.
Audi, filia, *see* Diffusa est gratia.	
Audivi vocem. à 5.	MS.

Ave Maria. à 5.   Grad. I. i. 14.
Ave Maria, *see* Alleluia. Ave Maria.
Ave Maria, *see* Beata Virgo, cuius viscera.
Ave Maris. stella. à 3.   Grad. I. iii. 4.
  Sumens illud.
  Solve vincla reis.
  Monstra te esse Matrem.
  Virgo singularis.
  Vitam presta.
  Sit laus Deo.
Ave Regina. à 4.   Grad. I. ii. 14.
Ave verum Corpus. à 4.   Grad. I. ii. 5.

Beata coeli nuncio, *see* Quem terra, pontus.
Beata es, Virgo Maria. à 5.   Grad. I. i. 10
Beata Mater, *see* Quem terra, pontus
Beata Virgo cuius viscera. à 4.   Grad. II. 9.
  Ave Maria.
Beata viscera.   Grad. I. I. 11
Beati mundo corde. à 5.   Grad. I. i. 32.
Benedicta et venerabilis. à 5.   Grad. I. i. 7.
Benedictio et claritas, *see* O quam gloriosum.
Benedixisti, Domine, *see* Rorate coeli.
Benigne fac, Domine. à 5.   MS.

Cantate Domino. à 5.   Cant. Sac II. 29.
Cantate Domino, *see* Puer datus, puer natus.
Caro mea vere est cibus, *see* Oculi omnium.
Christe, qui lux. à 5.   MS.
  Precamur, sancte Domine.
Christe Redemptor. à 4.   MS. (instrumental).
Christe Redemptor (another setting). à 4.   MS. (instrumental).
Christus resurgens. à 4.   Grad. I. ii. 10.
  Dicant nunc Judaei.
Cibavit eos. à 4.   Grad. I. ii. 1.
  Exultate Deo.
  Gloria Patri.
Circumdederunt me. à 5.   Cant. Sac. II. 15.
Circumspice Jerusalem. à 6.   MS.
  Ecce enim veniunt.
Civitas sancti tui, *see* Ne irascaris.
Confirma hoc, Deus. à 5.   Grad. II. 34.
Confitemini Domino, *see* Alleluia. Confitemini.
Cogitavit Dominus, *see* De lamentatione.

Cognoverunt discipuli, *see* Alleluia. Cognoverunt.

Constitues eos principes. à 6.   Grad. II. 39.
   Pro patribus tuis

Contumelias et terrores, *see* Tribulatio proxima est.

Cui luna, *see* Quem terra, pontus.

Cunctis diebus. à 6.   Cant. Sac. II.30

Da mihi auxilium. à 6.   Cant. Sac. (1575) 23

Da tuis fidelibus, *see* Veni sancte Spiritus, et emitte.

De lamentatione Jeremiae prophetae. à 5.   MS.
   Heth. Cogitavit Dominus.
   Teth. Defixae sunt in terra.
   Jod. Sederunt in terra.
      Jerusalem convertere.

Decantabat populus. à 5.   MS.

Dedit fragilibus, *see* Noctis recolitur.

Defecit in dolore.   Cant Sac. I. 1-2.
   Sed tu, Domine, refugium.

Defixae sunt in terra, *see* De lamentatione.

Deo gratias. à 4.   Grad. I. ii. 20.

Deo Patri sit gloria, *see* O lux beata Trinitas.

Descendit de coelis. à 6.   Cant. Sac. II. 21–2.
   Et exivit per auream portam.

Deus in adiutorium. à 6.   MS.
   Avertantur retrorsum.
   Exultent et laetentur.
   Ego vero egenus.

Deus iudicium, *see* Ecce advenit.

Deus, venerunt gentes. à 5.   Cant. Sac. I. 11-14
   Posuerunt morticinia.
   Effuderunt sanguinem.
   Facti sumus opprobrium.

Dic nobis, Maria, *see* Victimae Paschali.

Dic regi, *see* Plorans plorabit.

Dicant nunc Judaei, *see* Christus resurgens.

Dies mei transierunt, *see* Libera me, Domine, et pone.

Dies sanctificatus. à 4.   Grad. II. 3.

Diffusa est gratia.   Grad I. i. 22.
   Propter veritatem.
   Audi, filia.
   Vultum tuum.
   Adducentur regi.
   Adducentur in laetitia.

Diliges Dominum. à 8.   Cant. Sac. (1575), 25.

Diverte a malo, *see* Quis est homo?

Domine, ante te omne desiderium. à 6.   MS.
Domine Deus omnipotens. à 5.   MS.
 Ideo misericors.
Domine, exaudi orationem meam. ? à 5.   MS.
Domine, exaudi orationes. à 5.   Cant. Sac. ii. 10-11.
 Et non intres in iudicium.
Domine, non sum dignus. à 6.   Cant. Sac. ii. 23.
Domine, praestolamur. à 5.   Cant. Sac. i. 3-4.
Domine, probasti me, *see* Nunc scio vere.
Domine, probasti me, *see* Resurrexi et adhuc.
Domine, quis habitabit ? à 9.   MS.
Domine, salva nos. à 6.   Cant. Sac. ii. 31.
Domine, secundum actum meum. à 6.   Cant. Sac. (1575), 24
 Ideo deprecor.
Domine, secundum multitudinem. à 5.   Cant. Sac. i. 27.
Domine, tu iurasti. à 5.   Cant. Sac. i. 15.
Dominus in Sina. à 5.   Grad. ii. 27.

Ecce advenit. à 4.   Grad. ii. 10.
 Deus iudicium.
 Gloria Patri.
Ecce enim veniunt, *see* Circumspice, Jerusalem.
Ecce quam bonum. à 4.   Grad. i. ii. 9.
 Quod descendit.
Ecce Virgo concipiet. à 5.   Grad. i. i. 15.
Effuderunt sanguinem, *see* Deus, venerunt gentes.
Ego sum panis vivus. à 4.   Grad. ii. 17.
Ego vero egenus, *see* Deus in adiutorium.
Emendemus in melius. à 5.   Cant. Sac. (1575), 1.
Emitte spiritum tuum, *see* Alleluia. Emitte spiritum.
Eia ergo, *see* Salve Regina.
Eripe me, *see* Ne perdas cum impiis.
Eructavit cor meum, *see* Salve sancta Parens.
Et eruas nos, *see* Afflicti pro peccatis.
Et exivit per auream portam, *see* Descendit de coelis.
Et Jesu benedictum, *see* Salve Regina.
Et non intres, *see* Domine, exaudi.
Exsurgat Deus, *see* Spiritus Domini.
Exsurge, Domine. à 5.   Cant. Sac. ii. 19.
Exultate Deo, *see* Cibavit eos.
Exultate, iusti, *see* Gaudeamus. (Omn. Sanct.)
Exultent et laetentur, *see* Deus in adiutorium.

Fac cum servo. à 5.   Cant. Sac. ii. 5.
Facti sumus opprobrium, *see* Deus, venerunt gentes

Factus est repente. à 5.   Grad. II. 35.
Felix es, sacra Virgo. à 5.   Grad. I. i. 9.
Felix namque es.   Grad. I. i. 19.

Gaude Maria. à 5.   Grad. I. i. 21.
Gaudeamus omnes. (B.V.M.) à. 5.   Grad. I. i. 23.
   Assumpta est Maria.
Gaudeamus omnes. (Omn. Sanct.) à 5   Grad. I. i. 29.
   Exultate iusti.
   Gloria Patri.
Gloria Deo, *see* Petrus beatus.
Gloria Patri qui creavit. à 6.   Cant. Sac. (1575), 32.
Gloria Patri, *see* Cibavit eos.
Gloria Patri, *see* Ecce advenit.
Gloria Patri, *see* Gaudeamus. (Omn. Sanct.)
Gloria Patri, *see* Nunc scio vere.
Gloria Patri, *see* Puer natus est nobis.
Gloria Patri, *see* Resurrexi et adhuc.
Gloria Patri, *see* Rorate coeli.
Gloria Patri, *see* Suscepimus Deus.
Gloria tibi, Domine, *see* Memento, salutis auctor.
Gloria tibi, Domine, *see* O gloriosa Domina.
Gloria tibi, Domine, *see* Quem terra, pontus.

Haec dicit Dominus. à 5.   Cant. Sac. II. 13-14.
   Haec dicit Dominus.
Haec dies. à 6.   Cant. Sac. II. 32.
Haec dies. à 5.   Grad. II. 21.
Haec dies. à 3.   Grad. I. iii. 7.
Heu mihi, Domine, *see* Ad Dominum cum tribularer.
Hodie beata Virgo. à 4.   Grad. I. ii. 19.
Hodie Christus natus est. à 4.   Grad. II. 6.
Hodie Simon Petrus. à 6.   Grad. II. 42.
Hunc arguta, *see* Laudibus in sanctis.

Ideo deprecor, *see* Domine, secundum actum meum.
Ideo misericors, *see* Domine Deus omnipotens.
In manus tuas, Domine. à 4.   Grad. I. ii. 15.
In momento indignationis, *see* Ad punctum in modico.
In resurrexione tua. à 5.   Cant. Sac. I. 17.
Infelix ego omnium. à 6   Cant. Sac. II. 24-6.
   Quid igitur faciam?
   Ad te igitur.
Inferni claustra penetrans, *see* Jesu nostra redemptio.

Inquirentes autem, *see* Timete Dominum.
Ipsa te cogat pietas, *see* Jesu nostra redemptio.

Jerusalem, convertere, *see* De lamentatione.
Jesu nostra redemptio. à 4.   Grad. i. ii. 19.
  Quae te vicit clementia.
  Inferni claustra penetrans.
  Ipsa te cogat pietas.
  Tu esto nostrum gaudium.
Justorum animae. à 5.   Grad. i. i. 31.

Laetania. à 4.   Grad. i. ii. 16.
Laetentur coeli. à 5.   Cant. Sac. i. 28-9.
  Orietur in diebus.
Laudate Dominum. à 6.   Grad. ii. 45.
Laudate, pueri, Dominum. à 6.   Cant. Sac. (1575), 17
Laudibus in sanctis. à 5.   Cant. Sac. ii. 1-2.
  Magnificum Domini.
  Hunc arguta.
Levemus corda nostra. à 5.   Cant. Sac. ii. 16.
Libera me, Domine, de morte. à 5.   Cant. Sac. (1575), 33
Libera me, Domine, et pone. à 5.   Cant. Sac. (1575), 5.
Lingua mea, *see* Speciosus forma.
Lumen ad revelationem, *see* Nunc dimittis.

Magnificum Domini, *see* Laudibus in sanctis.
Magnus Dominus, *see* Suscepimus, Deus.
Mane nobiscum, *see* Post dies octo.
Maria, Mater gratia, *see* Memento salutis auctor.
Memento, Domine. à 5.   Cant. Sac. i. 8.
Memento, homo, quod cinis es. à 6.   Cant. Sac. (1575), 18.
Memento, salutis auctor. à 3.   Grad. i. iii. 3.
  Maria, Mater gratia.
  Gloria tibi, Domine.
Memor esto fili, *see* Omni tempore benedic.
Miserere mei, Deus. à 5.   Cant. Sac. ii. 20.
Miserere mihi, Domine. à 6.   Cant. Sac. (1575), 29.
Miserere. à 4.   MS.
Miserere (another setting). à 4.   MS.
Miserere (another setting). à 4   MS.
Miserere (round). à 3.   MS.
Miserere (round), another setting. à 3.   MS.
Miserere (Canons).   MS.

Ne irascaris. à 5.   Cant. Sac. I. 20-21.
   Civitas sancti tui.
Ne perdas cum impiis. à 5.   MS.
   Eripe me.
Nobis datus, nobis natus. à 4.   Grad. I. ii. 8.
   Verbum caro.
   Tantum ergo.
Noctis recolitur. à 5.   MS.
   Dedit fragilibus.
   Panis angelicus.
Non nobis Domine.   Playford's *Musick and*
                                     Mirth (1651).
Non vos relinquam orphanos. à 5.   Grad. II. 37.
Nos enim pro peccatis, *see* Tribulationes civitatis.
Notum fecit Dominus, *see* Viderunt omnes fines.
Nunc dimittis. à 5.   Grad. I. i. 4.
   Quia viderunt.
   Lumen ad revelationem.
Nunc scio vere. à 6.   Grad. II. 38.
   Domine, probasti me.
   Gloria Patri.

O admirabile commercium. à 4.   Grad. II. 7.
O Domine, adiuva me. à 5.   Cant. Sac. I. 5.
O gloriosa Domina. à 3.   Grad. I. iii. 2.
   Quod Eva tristis.
   Tu regis alti ianua.
   Gloria tibi, Domine.
O lux beata Trinitas. à 6.   Cant. Sac. (1575), 12.
   Te mane laudem carmine.
   Deo Patri sit gloria.
O lux beatissima, *see* Veni sancte Spiritus, et emitte.
O magnum misterium. à 4.   Grad. II. 8.
O quam gloriosum. à 5.   Cant. Sac. I. 22-3.
   Benedictio et claritas.
O quam suavis est. à 4.   Grad. II. 18.
O Rex gloriae. à 5.   Grad. II. 30.
O sacrum convivium. à 4.   Grad. I. ii. 7.
O salutaris hostia. à 6.   MS.
O salutaris hostia. à 4.   Grad. I. ii. 6.
Oculi omnium. à 4.   Grad. I. ii. 2.
   Aperis tu manum.
   Caro mea vere est cibus.
Omnes gentes plaudite, *see* Viri Galilei.

Omni tempore benedic. à 5.   MS.
    Memor esto fili.
Optimam partem elegit. à 5.   Grad. i. i. 25.
Ora pro nobis, *see* Regina coeli.
Orietur in diebus, *see* Laetentur coeli

Panis angelicus, *see* Noctis recolitur
Pascha nostrum. à 5.   Grad. ii. 24.
Peccantem me quotidie. à 5.   Cant. Sac. (1575), 6.
Peccavi super numerum. à 5.   MS.
Per immensa saecula, *see* Petrus beatus.
Petrus beatus. à 5.   MS.
    Quodcunque vinculis.
    Per immensa saecula.
    Gloria Deo.
Pietas omnium virtutum (round). à 3.   MS.
Plorans plorabit. à 5.   Grad. i. i. 28.
    Dic regi.
Post dies octo. à 3.   Grad. i. iii. 9.
    Mane nobiscum.
Post partum. à 5.   Grad. i. i. 18.
Posuerunt morticinia, *see* Deus, venerunt gentes.
Precamur, sancte Domine. à 4.   MS.
Precamur, sancte Domine (another setting).
    à 4.   MS.
Precamur, sancte Domine, *see* Christe qui lux.
Pro patribus tuis. à 6.   Grad. ii. 39.
Propter veritatem, *see* Diffusa est gratia.
Psallite Domino. à 5.   Grad. ii. 29.
Puer natus est nobis. à 4.   Grad. ii. i.
    Cantate Domino.
    Gloria Patri.

Quae lucescit, *see* Alleluia. Quae lucescit.
Quae te vicit clementia, *see* Jesu nostra redemptio.
Quem terra, pontus. à 3.   Grad. i. iii. 1.
    Cui luna.
    Beata Mater.
    Beata coeli nuncio.
    Gloria tibi, Domine.
Quia quem meruisti, *see* Regina coeli.
Quia viderunt, *see* Nunc dimittis.
Quid igitur faciam? *see* Infelix ego.
Quis ascendit? *see* Tollite portas.

Quis est homo? à 5.   Cant. Sac. ii. 3-4.
   Diverte a malo.
Quod descendit, *see* Ecce quam bonum.
Quod Eva tristis, *see* O gloriosa Domina.
Quodcunque ligaveris. à 6.   Grad. ii. 44.
Quodcunque vinculis, *see* Petrus beatus.
Quomodo cantabimus? à 8.   MS.
   Si non proposuero.
Quoniam amaritudine, *see* Vide, Domine, quoniam tribulor.
Quotiescunque manducabitis. à 4.   Grad. i. ii. 4.

Recordare, Domine. à 5.   Cant. Sac. ii. 17-18.
   Requiescat, Domine.
Reges Tharsis. à 5.   MS.
Reges Tharsis. à 4.   Grad. ii. 11.
Regina coeli. à 3.   Grad. i. iii. 5.
   Quia quem meruisti.
   Resurrexit.
   Ora pro nobis.
Respice, Domine, *see* Aspice, Domine, de sede.
Responsum accepit Simeon. à 5.   Grad. i. i. 5.
Resurrexi, et adhuc. à 5.   Grad. ii. 20.
   Domine, probasti me.
   Gloria Patri.
Requiescat, Domine, *see* Recordare, Domine.
Rorate, coeli. à 5.   Grad. i. i 12.
   Benedixisti, Domine
   Gloria Patri.

Sacerdotes Domini. à 4.   Grad. i. ii. 3.
Salvator mundi. à 3.   MS.
Salve, Regina. à 5.   Cant. Sac. ii. 6-7.
   Et Jesum benedictum.
Salve, Regina. à 4.   Grad. i. ii. 12.
   Eia ergo.
Salve, sancta Parens. à 5.   Grad. i. i. 6.
   Eructavit cor meum.
   Gloria Patri.
Salve, sola Dei Genetrix. à 4.   Grad. i. ii. 17.
Sanctus. à 3.   MS.
Sed tu, Domine refugium, *see* Defecit in dolore.
Sed tu, Domine qui non, *see* Tristitia et anxietas.
Sed veni, Domine, *see* Vide, Domine, afflictionem.
Sederunt in terra, *see* De lamentatione.

Senex puerum portabat. à 5.	Grad. i. i. 3.
Senex puerum portabat. à 4.	Grad. i. ii. 18.
Sermone blando. à 4.	MS.
Sermone blando (another setting). à 4.	MS.
Si non proposuero, *see* Quomodo cantabimus?	
Sicut audivimus. à 5.	Grad. i. i. 2.
Siderum rector. à 5.	Cant. Sac. (1575), 19.
Similes illis fiant. à 4.	MS.
Sit laus Deo, *see* Ave Maris stella.	
Solve iubente Deo. à 6.	Grad. ii. 40.
Solve vincla, *see* Ave Maris stella.	
Speciosus forma. à 5.	Grad. i. i. 17.
Lingua mea.	
Spiritus Domini. à 5.	Grad. ii. 31.
Exsurgat Deus.	
Sponsus amat sponsam.? à 5.	MS.
Subsistit Virgo, *see* Adorna thalamum.	
Sumens illud, *see* Ave Maris stella.	
Surge illuminare. à 4.	Grad. ii. 15.
Suscepimus, Deus. à 5.	Grad. i. i. 1.
Magnus Dominus.	
Gloria Patri.	
Tantum ergo, *see* Nobis datus, nobis natus.	
Te deprecor supplico. à 6.	Cant. Sac. (1575), 31.
Te lucis ante terminum. à 4.	MS.
Te mane laudem, *see* O lux beata Trinitas.	
Terra tremuit. à 5.	Grad. ii. 23.
Timete Dominum. à 5.	Grad. i. i. 30.
Inquirentes autem.	
Timor et hebetudo, *see* Tribulationes civitatum.	
Tollite portas. à 5.	Grad. i. i. 13.
Quis ascendit?	
Tribue, Domine. à 6.	Cant. Sac. (1575), 30.
Tribulatio proxima. à 5.	Cant. Sac. ii. 8-9.
Contumelias et terrores.	
Tribulationes civitatum. à 5.	Cant. Sac. i. 24-6.
Timor et hebetudo.	
Nos enim pro peccatis.	
Tristitia et anxietas. à 5.	Cant. Sac. i. 6-7.
Sed tu, Domine, qui non.	
Tu es Pastor ovium. à 6.	Grad. ii. 43.
Tu es Petrus. à 6.	Grad. ii. 41.
Tu esto nostrum gaudium, *see* Jesu nostra redemptio.	

Tu regis alti ianua, *see* O gloriosa Domina.

Tui sunt coeli. à 4.   Grad. ii. 4.

Turbarum voces. à 3.   Grad. i. iii. 10.

Unam petii a Domino. à 5.   Grad. i .i. 27.
   Ut videam voluntatem.

Veni, Domine, *see* Domine, praestolamur.

Veni, sancte Spiritus, et emitte. à 5.   Grad. ii. 36.
   O lux beatissima.
   Da tuis fidelibus.

Veni, sancte Spiritus, reple. à 5.   Grad. ii. 33.

Venite, comedite, *see* Ab ortu solis.

Venite, exultemus Domino. à 6.   Grad. ii. 46.

Verbum caro, *see* Nobis datus, nobis natus.

Vespere autem Sabbathi, *see* Alleluia. Quae lucescit.

Victimae Paschali. à 5.   Grad. ii. 22.
   Dic nobis, Maria.

Vide, Domine, afflictionem. à 5.   Cant. Sac. i. 9-10.
   Sed veni, Domine.

Vide, Domine, quoniam tribulor. à 5.   MS.
   Quoniam amaritudine.

Viderunt omnes fines. à 4.   Grad. ii. 2.
   Notum fecit Dominus.

Viderunt omnes fines. à 4.   Grad ii. 5.

Vidimus stellam. à 4.   Grad. ii. 12.

Vigilate, nescitis enim. à. 5.   Cant. Sac. i. 16.

Virga Jesse floruit, *see* Alleluia. Ave Maria.

Virgo Dei Genetrix. à 5.   Grad. i. i. 8.

Virgo singularis, *see* Ave Maris stella.

Viri Galilei. à 5.   Grad. ii. 25.
   Omnes gentes plaudite.

Visita, quaesumus. à 4.   Grad. i. ii. 11.

Vitam praesta, *see* Ave Maris stella.

Vultum tuum. à 5.   Grad. i. i. 16.

Vultum tuum, *see* Diffusa est gratia.

GENERAL INDEX

INDEX OF MUSICAL ILLUSTRATIONS

Set in Great Britain by
Latimer Trend and Co. Ltd
and reprinted lithographically by
Jarrold and Sons Ltd
Norwich